I0150630

Arthur Paone stands in front of the Wall in Bethlehem. April, 2007.

ISRAEL,

OUR

FRANKENSTEIN

ARTHUR J. PAONE

BELMAR PUBLICATIONS

The Author:

Arthur J. Paone was born and raised in Brooklyn, NY, and received his law degree from Cornell Law School in 1964.

Also by Arthur J. Paone:

> *Liberating Korea?* (2003)
> *So Sue Me!* (2004) (pseud. Meier & Cellini)
> *Hillary in Gilo* (2007)

For

Gus The Great

CONTENTS

INTRODUCTION

America created this Frankenstein and the monster is now, with foolhardy arrogance, rushing to its destruction. Israel's destruction, of course, would entail a lot of collateral damage. That is what concerns me.

Yet its creator cannot stop it.

Israel proceeds with its rack and ruin activities mindless of their effect on U.S. interests. As a respected American commentator recently observed:

> "It is time Israel realized that it has obligations to the United States, as well as the United States to Israel, and that it become far more careful about the extent to which it test the limits of the U.S. patience and exploits the support of American Jews."

Yet Israel mocks our President and pulls the strings on our Congress—most of whose members have long ago been either purchased with pro-Israel American money or been intimidated into robot-like support. It confidently calls upon its Fifth-Columnists whenever it needs to manipulate the American Government into submission. At its signal there appear the usual absurd full-page ads in the *Wall Street Journal*, the *New York Times* and the *Washington Post,* paid for by its agents—the likes of Abe Foxman and Ronald Lauder—not so much to influence public opinion or the Congress, which they already control, but to strut about and show off how they can afford to just throw their money out the window—or perhaps they are payoffs to those newspapers.

All the while, mindless, malignant American billionaires, such as the Las Vegas gambling magnate, Sheldon Adelson, and California bingo hustler Irving Moskowitz, continue to provoke unrest and chaos in Palestine with their funding of controversial and aggressive Jewish colonies in East Jerusalem and the West Bank. Their loyalties are first and last with Israel and they could care less about what is important to the U.S., much less the rest of the world.

I think, however, there is one group that trumps all of these, which could bring our Frankenstein down in a minute. That is the vast majority of Jews in the U.S., the kind of people that I know, who have no love lost for the Occupation or the oppression of the Palestinians or for the nuclear threat that Israel brandishes over the world. These are the American Jews who are loyal first to America. But instinct and history have kept them silent so far—Israel is, after all, the homeland of the Jewish nation; the refuge of the Holocaust survivors. But the time for comfortable myths and delusions is over. Frankenstein has become dangerous to us all. He must be restrained—and now.

The task for the American Jews will not be easy or without pain. Some years ago, perhaps just a disapproving glance from them might have sobered up the people running that nation, but today the game is almost up and only radical surgery can possibly save us. Recently it took the combined forces of the Jewish-American Senators and Members of Congress plus the biggest American Jewish groups that raised money for Israel to derail a Conversion Bill in Israel that would have put the status of Conservative and Reform Jews in some jeopardy. To change fundamental Israeli policies would take even more effort and resources. But I believe it can be done.

Not part of the "family"

I will try to show these Jewish-Americans that this Frankenstein is not a member of their "family"; that the Israelis of today do not share any of our values, much less our core values, nor is Israel the kind of democracy that we are familiar with.

Living in New York City as I do, one learns early on that Israel is an important topic in this town. People talk as if it were a suburb of NYC. You also learn either to praise Israel, or keep your mouth shut unless you want a vicious argument on your hands. Emotions on this subject run high at the very beginning of any discussion, if any is tolerated, and it only gets worse. When Israel does something that my friends would severely criticize if done by some other country, like the oppressive Occupation or the totally out of proportion bombardment of Gaza last year, and indeed the inhumane blockade of Gaza itself, we are told that we must have sympathy and understanding for Israel's special security situation. It is a small country, they say, which could be overrun in hours if it were not mighty militarily and forever alert; it must always keep its neighbors in trembling fear with its threat of brutal deterrence; it is surrounded by enemies who want to drive it into the sea, etc.

These concerns may have had some validity many years ago, but they are not persuasive now that Israel is the regional superpower in the Middle East, dwarfing militarily all of the states in the area—combined. But more than that, any argument justifying evil would work both ways. Suicide bombers could point to the lands of their ancestors that were stolen from them; hundreds of thousands of their parents and grandparents driven from their homes; millions of people living under the brutal

iii

yoke of the Occupation etc. Two wrongs, however, do not make a right.

On the subject of Israel our politicians all seem to be reading from the same book of instructions; their references to Israel seem always to fall into one of several well-worn myths that have been so often repeated that any deviation from them sounds sacrilegious: "shared values"; "like family"; "the only democracy in the Middle East."

It was sometime in early 2002, with headlines of a massive Israeli incursion into the Occupied Territories accompanied by much killing and destruction, that I began to seek out some foreign online newspapers for more in-depth information. There I read about Israeli snipers shooting three- and six-year-olds between the eyes to enforce curfews that they had imposed. Something was terribly wrong.

The foreign press

My usual reading, the *New York Times*, seemed inadequate. My first discovery that there was much more to the subject than what the *Times* was reporting was through the online British papers, the *Guardian Unlimited* and the *Independent*. They gave me more details of what was going on, and seemed much more balanced and objective. I later learned that the Israeli Press, which I had not as yet begun to read, would have been of no help in trying to find out what was happening during that invasion. There is little dissent or objectivity among the Israeli public when their soldiers are shooting, no matter who they are shooting at. And whatever may have passed through the sieve of patriotic self-censorship would not in any event have passed the very real Military Censor. Later, however, I found much of the information I was looking for in daily reading of the online English versions of Israel's left-leaning *Haaretz Daily* and its right-leaning *Jerusalem Post.*

What I had been hearing about Israel and the Occupied Territories in the American Media and from our politicians bore little relationship to the activities of Israel as portrayed in the foreign press, including its own. Since then, I have read much more, and I have visited Israel, the West Bank, and Gaza.

The myths about Israel, however, are not confined to New York City. Reading speeches delivered at conferences of the American Israel Public Affairs Committee (AIPAC) over the years is like reading the same speech over and over again—only the name of the speaker has changed.

The mantra

Back in 2005 it was then Senator Hillary Clinton's turn, gushing even beyond the usual slogans:

> "[O]ur future here in this country is intertwined with the future of Israel. . . . I want to start by focusing on [the] deep and lasting bond between the United States and Israel.
> "Now, these are bonds that are **more than shared interests**. There are bonds **forged in a common struggle** for human rights, for democracy, for freedom. . . .
> "[T]hey are **rooted in fundamental beliefs** and values about the dignity and rights of men and women to live in freedom, free from fear, free from oppression. . . .
>
> "Israel is not only . . . a friend and ally for us, it is a **beacon of what democracy** can and should mean."
> [Emphasis added.]

Anyone at all familiar with Israel's discrimination against the Arabs among its own citizens in Israel, not to mention its oppression of the millions during its 40-plus years harsh military occupation of East Jerusalem, the West Bank, and the Gaza Strip, can only gasp at the absurdity of these comments—*"struggling for human rights . . . . free from oppression . . . . a beacon of . . . democracy."*

Yet this is the alternate-reality language routinely used, not just by pro-Israel organizations and their spokesmen, but by almost every one of our politicians whenever they mention Israel, like not leaving home without it.

On just one day, for example, April 21, 2010, in the U.S. House of Representatives, one could hear the endless drone of AIPAC's mantra about our "shared values" repeatedly spilling out of the mouths of our seemingly brainwashed representatives in embarrassingly identical slop:

Congressman Ted Deutch (D-FL):

> *"The relationship between the United States and Israel is unbreakable. The relationship is one between two peoples, our common values, the history we have, our commitment to freedom . . . . "*

Congressman Rush Holt (D-NJ):

> *"Our* [Israel and the US] *nations' special relationship extends beyond friendship. It is built on the common values of equality and opportunity for all and our shared commitment to freedom, justice, and peace. Israel is more than just an ally; Israel is an inspiration."*

Congressman Mike Honda (D-CA):

> "I rise to celebrate the 62nd anniversary of a great democracy and our close friend and important ally, Israel. The United States and Israel share a unique and unbreakable bond. This bond is based upon friendship, common values, and a strong interest in a peaceful future for the Middle East. . . . As the sole democracy in the region, Israel is . . . ."

Congressman Niki Tsongas (D-MA):

> "The strong bonds that exist between Israel and the United States are based on our shared ideals -- democracy, opportunity, freedom, and peace . . . ."

Congressman Harry Mitchell (D-AZ):

> "Israel is not just a vitally important ally to the United States, it is a beacon of democracy . . . ."

Congressman Howard Berman (D-CA):

> "The U.S.-Israeli friendship is based on shared democratic values, progress, and our hope for peace between nations. . . ."

These slogans seem to be contagious and no official, no matter how supreme, is immune.

President Barack Obama, as every President since 1948, regularly observes the ritual, as in a White House speech on May 27, 2010:

> "[I]t's our common values that lead us to stand with allies and friends, including the state of Israel . . . . [O]ur bond with Israel is unbreakable. (Applause.) It is the bond of two

peoples that share a commitment to a common set of ideals: opportunity, democracy and freedom."

God! Who writes this stuff? Don't they at least own a Thesaurus?

A new language: "IsraelSpeak"

In any attempt to analyze Israeli society or its institutions, one must be mindful of the peculiar alternate-reality language that Israelis and their blind supporters have developed since 1948. It is not English, Yiddish or Hebrew, or any combination of these. Rather, it is a language born of the circumstances in which Jewish fighters found themselves in 1948.

At that time they represented the survivors of the Holocaust— the German attempt to eradicate all Jews from the world. They were the victims, and many of their descendants have tried desperately to maintain that status.

But they also represented the Zionists who had strove for decades, first to establish homes in Palestine and then to organize and fight the British and the Arabs to establish their own state. But the dream of the Zionists ran somewhat short— about 150,000 human beings short. They were able to chase most, about 750,000 natives out of Palestine, people who apparently had borrowed the Chosen People's land for some 1,300 years. But try as they might, they were constrained by many circumstances from eliminating or removing those 150,000 stragglers—mostly farmers and herders. (See, e.g., Ilan Pappe's *The Ethnic Cleansing of Palestine*.)

One of those constraining circumstances was that in 1948 there were nations who, having had just destroyed, at the cost of tens of millions of their own citizens' lives, the monstrous regime of Nazism, were proclaiming a New Order. This new world order would be based on such themes as freedom from tyranny, self-determination for populations, equality of citizens, the existence of basic and inalienable human rights, etc.

This was a tough task for the Jews setting up a Homeland to handle—while the world was looking over their shoulders they would try to reconcile these lofty ideals with the ugly task of removing tens of thousands of people already populating Palestine who seemed not to have heard that God had irretrievably bequeathed their ancestors' land to a little tribe many centuries earlier.

There were some close moments where language and reality almost met. Like the time that Jewish terrorists assassinated Count Folke Bernadotte, the first official mediator in the UN's history. A terrible mistake and tragedy, they said, performed by a renegade group that was soon disbanded. There were so many who wanted to believe, and they chose readily to believe this. The make-believe nature of this explanation, however, was later evidenced, if more were needed, by the fact that the leader of this supposedly disgraced terror unit subsequently became a Prime Minister of Israel while the actual murderer of Count Bernadotte became that Prime Minister's personal bodyguard.

The Declaration of Independence

A glorious War for Independence—took place simultaneously with the relentless dispossession of the natives. A unique language to reconcile such a lofty goal with the savage process of exterminating a people was needed. The contradictory process begged for a special way of talking to be developed, and it was—beginning with the Declaration of Independence itself—a carefully worded document intended in part to sooth the consciences of world leaders, who were just standing by while hundreds of thousands of people were being forced from their homes. Perhaps it can be called "IsraelSpeak"—something that only Israelis speak and apparently only Americans, thanks to the tutelage of the Israeli Lobby, understand.

In what could only be described as speaking from both sides of his mouth, and probably chuckling at the same time, David Ben-Gurion, on May 14, 1948, solemnly extended the hands of the newly self-proclaimed Israelites:

> *"**We appeal** -- in the very midst of the **onslaught launched** against us now for months -- **to the Arab inhabitants** of the State of Israel to preserve peace and participate in the up building of the States on the basis of full and equal citizenship and due representation . . . ."* [Emphasis added.]

What "**Arab inhabitants?**" He was chasing them all out at that very moment.

What "**onslaught launched?**" The armies of the Arab states had not yet entered Palestine. Had the Palestinian farmers and city dwellers simply launched themselves by the hundreds of thousands onto the dusty roads to take a Sunday walk to the West Bank, Gaza, Lebanon, Syria, and Jordan with just the clothes on their backs? In quiet moments the delegates gathered in Tel Aviv's Museum that day, and if they had listened carefully, they would have been able to hear the echoes of their footsteps—men, women and children.

While Ben-Gurion was reading those words out loud for the benefit of the foreign leaders, he was almost certainly thinking that soon there would not be a single Arab left to accept this "appeal," or so was his scheme. According to Ilan Pappe's *The Ethnic Cleansing of Palestine*, which cites Ben-Gurion's diaries and the archives of the Hagana, the umbrella Jewish military organization, from December 1947 the Jewish fighter-terrorists, under Ben-Gurion's direction, had already been invading Arab villages, towns, and cities and expelling the Arabs—two hundred Arab villages had already been destroyed, scores of towns emptied and 250,000 Arab inhabitants were on the road.

In March of 1948 the Jewish leadership under Ben-Gurion had formally ratified this ethnic cleansing process by officially adopting "Plan D," which called for the systematic and total expulsion of the Arabs, friend or foe alike. By the May 14 Jewish ceremony, dozens of villages and neighborhoods had already been evacuated by force, beginning with the defenseless villages of Deir Ayub and Beit Affa near Ramla in December 1947 and the killings and expulsions in the Arab neighborhood of Haifa. The terror process had included selective massacres of entire villages. By May 14 tens of thousands of dispossessed Arab families were on the roads, their villages and towns either destroyed or immediately occupied by Jews to ensure that the Arabs could not return.

Pappe wonders in disbelief when commenting on the scene of 50,000 men, woman, and children being forced to march to the West Bank without food or water from Ramla, al-Lydd and surrounding villages, on the orders of the Commander Yitzhak Rabin who was acting on Ben-Gurion's instructions to "Drive them out."

> *"Again, the inevitable question presents itself:*
> *three years after the Holocaust, what went through the*

minds of those Jews who watched these wretched people pass by?"

Ben-Gurion's "appeal" to the soon-to-be phantom Arab inhabitants to live in peace and equality may mark the auspicious birth of "IsraelSpeak."

Ignoring America's interests

Things have not changed one iota since that day in May of 1948. Now it's the unarmed civilians on the Gaza Freedom Flotilla's *Mavi Marmara* who have launched themselves into the bullets of the masked Israeli commandos dropping out of the sky in the middle of the night.

The discourse in the U.S. on Palestine has been dominated by this "IsraelSpeak"—doubletalk, myths, mantras and slogans, having very little to do with reality and all in favor of Israel.

While a little headway has been made recently to penetrate this IsraelSpeak (by two books in particular: *The Israel Lobby* by John Mearsheimer and Stephen Walt together with their spirited follow-up activities; and President Jimmy Carter's *Peace, Not Apartheid*, and the formation of a new organization, the DC lobby group known as "J Street"), it still is the primary language used in the "debate."

Thus, whenever there is some kind of dispute between the U.S. Government and that of Israel, it is our government that is cautioned by politicians and pro-Israeli groups—again, all reading it seems from the same prepared script of mantras, slogans and clichés.

Take, for example, a recent flap between Israel and the U.S. In a series of public statements over several months beginning in December of 2009, our Government had been trying to make Israel understand that some of its policies were working against important American interests. We have tens of thousands of men and women in uniform fighting in Iraq, Afghanistan and Pakistan. Aside from all the other valid or invalid reasons given for our troops being there, one unquestioned vital national interest being protected is the supply of oil to the U.S. In addition, we are engaged in a fierce global battle with anti-American extremism, presently in the form of Al-Qaeda, whose danger was manifested in its 9/11 assault on innocent American civilians.

Yet all of these vital interests are being undermined by our failure to craft a peaceful solution for the Israeli-Palestinian conflict. Due to America's involvement in the creation of Israel in 1948 and its steadfast financial, diplomatic, military and moral support since then, the world views Israel as an American protégé, if not surrogate. Thus, our Arab allies get almost as outraged against America as they do against Israel every time Israel intrudes into Arab East Jerusalem with house demolitions and Jewish settlements right up against Islam's second-most sacred religious site, the Dome of the Rock. It seems that each time we are in the process of talking to our Arab allies about ways to destroy Al-Qaeda, some Israeli action—be it the brutal bombardment of Gaza in December of 2009 or the eviction of Palestinians from their homes in East Jerusalem, disrupts the American talks with the Arabs.

In November of 2009 Israel's Prime Minister, Benjamin Netanyahu, confirmed that permits for the construction of 900 additional apartments in the Jerusalem-Bethlehem settlement of Gilo had been approved. The land on which Gilo is situated had been acquired by Israel in the 1967 war. It had been part of the municipality of Beit Jala, a suburb of Bethlehem. The Palestinian landowners were chased out and a new Jewish-only community was created. Since the creation of Gilo, the Israeli barrier-wall has been constructed and at this point the Wall runs between Gilo-Jerusalem on one side and Bethlehem and the remnants of Beit Jala on the other. Each new apartment built in Gilo, then, provokes anger from the Palestinians, particularly the exiled population of Beit Jala, now housed on the other side of the Wall. The announcement of the 900 additional apartments, then, was another provocation.

President Obama on November 18, 2009, certainly at the urging of his National Security advisors, after the customary ritualistic formula about America's commitment to Israel's security, stated with respect to these new apartments in Gilo:

> *"I think that additional settlement building does not contribute to Israel's security. I think it makes it harder for them to make peace with their neighbors. I think it embitters the Palestinians in a way that could end up being very dangerous."*

Israel's response at the time was to ignore the American President's gentle warning.

The Administration tried again in March 2010, this time through the highly respected General David Petraeus, the head of the U.S. Central Command (CENTOM). In a prepared statement for delivery at a Senate Committee hearing, the General had these comments on the effect of the Israeli-Palestinian conflict on

American interests in the Middle East and Near East, CENTOM's Area of Responsibility ("AOR"), including Iraq, Afghanistan, and Pakistan:

> "[T]here are a number of cross-cutting issues that serve as major drivers of instability, inter-state tensions, and conflict. These factors can serve as root causes of instability or as obstacles to security."

At the very top of the General's list of these "root causes of instability" was the following:

> **"Insufficient progress toward a comprehensive Middle East peace.** The enduring hostilities between Israel and some of its neighbors present distinct challenges to our ability to advance our interests in the AOR. . . . The conflict foments anti-American sentiment, due to a perception of U.S. favoritism for Israel. Arab anger over the Palestinian question limits the strength and depth of U.S. partnerships with governments and peoples in the AOR and weakens the legitimacy of moderate regimes in the Arab world." [Emphasis added.]

Indeed the General also had much to say about the problem of militant Islamist movements, but it was his comments about how the failure to solve the Israeli-Palestinian conflict has hindered our ability to advance our interests that caught the attention of the Middle East watchers. It was viewed as another message to Israel that its intransigence was contrary to the interests of the U.S. — now being raised in public for the first time by a high official of the U.S. military establishment.

To the barricades! – 1

Immediately, the usual elements in the Israel Lobby tried to batter down and smother the public emergence of this truth before it grew legs. Some tried to accomplish this in subtle ways, some in dismissive terms, and some by simply ignoring the General's point. But always to be counted on, over-the-top Abraham Foxman of the Jewish Anti-Defamation League, spent an enormous amount of his organization's money to put full-page ads in the *New York Times* and the *Wall Street Journal*. In the ads he contended that the General had "simply erred in linking" America's challenges in the area to the Israeli-Arab conflict. *"This linkage is dangerous and counterproductive."* Now, according to the newly-minted military and strategic analyst, Abe Foxman, the General's ideas, hardly original and actually obvious to most observers, were "**dangerous**."

A week earlier Vice President Joe Biden, on a visit to Israel to push along another "peace process" plan, was dumbfounded to learn that on the same day as his arrival, the Israeli government announced the approval of another 1600 apartments in one of the Jewish colonies in Arab East Jerusalem—the perfect provocation. A stunned Biden denounced the approval as undermining the peace efforts. (Though the very next day we find him nonsensically repeating the usual mantras—"no space" between Israel and the U.S. on security matters, etc.) The Secretary of State, Clinton, followed with her own words of disapproval as did President Obama. It was widely reported that Obama had been angered by the blatant affront to the U.S.

To the barricades! – 2

Then, from everywhere, came the pro-Israeli, dual-loyalist advocates. Representative Anthony Weiner was quoted as saying: *"Israel is a sovereign nation and an ally, not a punching bag. Enough already."*

Congressman Steve Israel: *This administration, to the extent that it has disagreements with Israel on policy matters, should find a way to do so in private."*

Senator Joe Lieberman ("Mr. Israel" in the U.S. Senate):

> *"Let's cut the family fighting, the family feud. It is unnecessary, and it is destructive of our shared national interests. . . . It is time to lower our voices, get over the family feud between the U.S. and Israel. "*

The Israeli-American lobby, AIPAC, quickly drafted letters to the Secretary of State, Hillary Clinton, to be signed by members of the House of Representatives and the Senate. Dutifully, 76 Senators and 333 Members of the House personally penned their signatures to the AIPAC's assault on Obama. The letters were replete with the usual myths, slogans and mantras. The March 26, 2010 House-letter stated in part:

> *"Israel continues to be the one true democracy in the Middle East that brings stability to a region where it is in short supply,"* [Contra To Gen. Petraeus' statement that it was bringing instability.]
> *"We recognize that our government and the Government of Israel will not always agree on particular issues in the peace process. But such differences are best resolved amicably. . . "*

"The United States and Israel are close allies whose people share a deep and abiding friendship based on a shared commitment to core values including democracy, human rights and freedom of the press and religion."

"Our view is that such differences are best resolved quietly. . . ."

Since then Obama, Clinton, and Petraeus have been spending a lot of time explaining, and then re-explaining, how vital Israel is as an ally, how Israel itself is really not the problem in the Middle East and that there is "no space" between the security interests of the U.S. and those of Israel, etc. Obama even rushed over emissaries to Foxman's Anti-Defamation convention to sprout some of the usual slogans. Joint military exercises continued; approval of more loan guarantees went goes on— nothing changed and it seemed that the great disagreement just petered out.

A different kind of event a couple of months later though, seems to confirm that this Administration, like many before it, continues to act like the dog being waged by its tail. After Israeli commandos in international waters killed nine civilians on a ship headed for Gaza with humanitarian aid, the international community was furious and demanded an independent inquiry. Israel instead insisted that it would, as usual, investigate itself. When it came to forming the investigative body, however, the Israelis very publicly entered into a prolonged consultation with the American Government. Netanyahu handled it personally on one side and Vice President Joe Biden ("What's the big deal?") for the other, according to reports openly leaked out of the Israeli cabinet. The resulting lame panel announced by Israel

xviii

which now bore the fluorescent American stamp of approval, however, was met mostly with derision, both inside and outside of Israel. A singular act of self-immolation by the U.S.—having seemingly been uninvolved in the bloody slaughter itself—the Americans nevertheless gratuitously embraced the sulfurous leper and kissed it on its mouth.

The retreat seems to be permanent. A subsequent meeting in July between Obama and Netanyahu in which Obama embarrassingly disgorged the usual Israel-American brotherhood slogans was characterized by a *Washington Post* columnist as the raising of a "white flag" of surrender over the White House, and as "Finally, Presidential Empathy" by a *Jerusalem Post* writer.

The vast majority of Jewish-Americans that I am counting on to stop our Frankenstein do not have an easy task or much time.

Heading to Armageddon

Edward Said in the 90s foresaw a Palestine between the river Jordan and the Mediterranean with Jews and Palestinians living under Palestinian rule. John Mearsheimer in a speech at The Palestine Center on April 29, 2010 also saw a future with a Palestinian-governed state between the Mediterranean and the Jordan—but only after a long process which included a harsh Israeli apartheid regime which the world, and most Jews, would have turned against.

I wish it were that simple: mere time, much pain for the Palestinians during the apartheid regime, world denunciation and isolation—then demography would take its natural course and determine the outcome.

Unfortunately, this forecast does not consider the most likely event—violent intervention by the coalition of fundamentally ignorant Haredi, other ultra-orthodox sects, and the Settlers who will control the Army and Israel's nuclear arsenal some time soon. These fanatical and fatalist groups, who will not have to fight a civil war because those Jews opposing them would have already left the pariah state of Israel, would rather blow themselves and everyone else up rather than lose control of the land that God had given them when He chose them as His people.

The down stretch to that Armageddon is already in full view.

"This irresponsible, heedless, unlawful attitude that defies any human virtue . . ." is how Turkey's Prime Minister Recep Tayyip Erdogan described the June, 2010, Israeli commando-raid on the humanitarian flotilla trying to get supplies into Gaza.

"Irresponsible, heedless, unlawful . . ." could also describe the news in Israeli papers released by the government that it intends to send nuclear-armed submarines into Iran's waters for maneuvers. Was this a threat from a nation of seven million to annihilate a nation of 70 million?

This book examines the accuracy of the words put into the mouths of the 333 Members of the House by AIPAC mentioned above :

"The United States and Israel . . . [share a] commitment to core values including democracy, human rights and freedom of the press and religion."

Notes: Page 198.

IS THE COMPARISON FAIR?

In this study, I have attempted an analysis of Israeli and American societies to determine if there really are "shared values" between them, and whether "Democracy" means the same thing when that term is used to describe Israel's governance as opposed to that in the U.S. I have selected some of the most obvious characteristics of our American society today and then, sought to find them in Israel's society.

Some might note that the very attempt of comparing U.S. and Israeli societies may be unfair to Israel and even pointless—as they say, comparing apples and oranges.

There are several obvious facts that would seem to mitigate against a meaningful comparison.

The size difference

On the one hand, Israel has just seven to seven-and-a-half million people (depending on whether you count the Jewish population in the Occupied Territories, that is, East Jerusalem, the West Bank, Golan Heights, and the Gaza Strip); it is only 67-years-old; it emerged after a violent conflict with its neighbors with whom it still is mostly hostile; it is a tiny nation where half the population has to go into shelters whenever it decides to invade or bomb one of its neighbors.

On the other side, the United States is the world's only superpower, has a population of over three hundred and ten million; is 220-years-old; is safe and secure within its borders on North America, protected on the East by the Atlantic Ocean and on the West by the Pacific Ocean and can wage two or three wars across the globe without most of its citizens even noticing.

The paranoia

The cosmic dissimilarity between the American society and the Israeli society can perhaps be glimpsed by the comments of Moshe Arens, a former Defense Minister, in an April 23, 2010 opinion-piece of his, published in *Haaretz*. At the time a trial was going on charging a former female soldier with treason for leaking dozens of embarrassing, secret, Army documents to a *Haaretz* reporter. The reporter based several articles on those documents and after receiving approval from the Israeli military censors, published them. Arens nevertheless, severely criticizes *Haaretz* for publishing those articles. In the process he gives his view of Israel's society:

> *"Israel is a nation at war, surrounded by enemies . . . . Most Israelis are mobilized in one way or another in the defense of the country . . . . This is Israel's secret weapon. . . . Much of our security depends on keeping secret the information we receive connected to military strategy and tactics, weapon systems and operational plans. . . .*
>
> *"**Most Israelis are privy to some state secrets** because of their military service, their work in the defense industry or contact in some other way with matters that are best kept from our enemies. And they are prepared to protect these secrets."* [Emphasis added.]

By any stretch of the imagination, could anyone say that an American would feel the same way—every American clutching to state secrets, keeping them from our enemies? If what Arens says is true, that almost every Israeli harbors secrets which he or she forever vigilantly strives to keep from "the enemy," what would the effect of this have on the psychological condition of Israeli society? Could a nation subjugated to what sounds like paranoia possibly be counted on to make reasonable decisions, particularly in matters of war and peace? Could such people share our "values?"

Incidentally, Moshe Arens should know a thing or two about stealing secrets.

 Born in Lithuania in 1925, he emigrated with his family to the U.S. in 1939; went to a high school in NYC and served in the U.S. Army Corps of Engineers. Then, he got a B.S. degree from the Massachusetts Institute of Technology but later went to Israel during the outbreak of the 1948 war. In Israel, he joined the most extreme of the paramilitary groups, the Irgun, which as a terrorist group had been fighting both the British and the Arabs to establish an independent Jewish state.

The Irgun, under Menachem Begin, during and after the war was notorious for chasing the Arabs from their homes, emptying entire cities and villages of their Arab inhabitants in what later became the State of Israel. In one particular incident, in April of 1948, (it is not known if Arens was with them at this time or with the gang involved in this raid) the Irgun massacred dozens of Palestinian civilians in a village called Deir Yassin and forced the survivors to flee. This was one of a number of atrocities perpetrated by Jewish fighters; a terror process intended to force the evacuation of Palestinians towns and villages for eventual occupation by the Jews.

After the war, Arens settled in Israel. But then, he returned to the U.S. by himself and without his family, and got a Masters degree in aeronautical engineering from another major institution, the California Institute of Technology. Afterwards he worked in the American aviation industry. Finally in 1957 he returned to Israel. In Israel he made good use of all of the knowledge he had gained of American aeronautical technology. While he taught

Israeli students what he had learned of American aviation knowhow at the quasi-government Israel Institute of Technology, he also put that knowledge to immediate use while working at the Israel Aircraft Industries. Not surprisingly thereafter, he won fame in Israel for designing airplanes and developing missiles.

This procedure, which at first smells of espionage by an Israeli dual-citizen has nevertheless, become such a pattern that it is now not seen as unusual. Israelis attending U.S. Universities or participating in Pentagon programs then, return to Israel and pass on to the military establishment everything they have learned.

But an episode in May 2010 in New York has highlighted again this type of espionage. An individual, born in Pakistan emigrated to the U.S. He was educated in U.S. institutions, eventually became a naturalized American citizen and worked for a U.S. company. For whatever reasons he decided to harm the people he had been living with and constructed a bomb, thankfully incompetently, that he placed in NYC's Times Square, hoping it would blow off and kill a lot of people.

In the discussion after this event, both Republicans and Democrats suggested that there was a basic hole in the intelligence system in dealing with a particular phenomenon. *"Increasingly, the dilemma is the well-education man who moves through the education system of our country somewhat promisingly,"* said Senator Richard G. Lugar

"I've always felt that this was the future in America for what we have to watch for in terrorism," said Senator John D. Rockefeller.

Moshe Arens, then, and his followers now, have established the most deadly threats to Americans in our homeland.

Different immigrants
Different dreams

There are numerous other obvious dissimilarities between the two countries. The United States was populated over a 200-year period by waves of immigrants from all over the world under an open immigration system for much of that time, with peoples of dramatically different religions, cultures and races, seeking freedom from poverty or tyranny.

In contrast, Israel has been populated since 1948, after most of the native population had been violently removed over a swift two- or three-year span of time, by immigrants who identified themselves primarily as Jewish and who wanted to start, not just a new life, but a new life in a Jewish State—with billboards for Kosher foods; with no buses or business activities on the Sabbath; with only Jews as neighbors—a new life in a JEWISH state.

One of the largest groups of immigrants is from the New York City area. Some of them make up the most extreme elements among the settlers in the West Bank. Meir Kahane, the radical rabbi who became a member of the Israeli legislature and who preached the forceful removal of Arabs from the West Bank and Gaza to create the "greater Israel," was born in Brooklyn. So was one of his followers, Baruch Goldstein, who in 1994 massacred 29 unarmed Arab men praying in the Ibrahim Mosque in Hebron. The occasion is celebrated every year by Kahane's followers in the West Bank.

These immigrants, deliberately turned their backs on American values and its pluralism, and encouraged by generous financial incentives from the State of Israel, went to Israel to find something which they knew would be very different from America. One recent immigrant from New York, for example, gushed, in an article in *Haaretz* (April 16, 2010), how she "shuddered" at the sight of an American city on a recent return visit to the U.S. to see her grandfather in a Miami Beach-assisted living facility. Her immigration to Israel, she wrote, made her understand better what it was to be a Jew.

> *"What I discovered was that, for a Jew, living in Israel means allowing yourself to feel comfortable in your own skin. By its definition, Israel nationalism, or Zionism, means identifying with (and, if necessary, defending) the Land of Israel as the historical birthplace and spiritual, religious, and cultural soul of the Jewish people as well as the sovereign, Jewish national homeland."*

This is not the same experience one has living in Seattle, Chicago, San Francisco, Des Moines, Charlotte, Austin, or anywhere else in the U.S., except perhaps in one or two small towns in upstate New York that are almost totally populated by Hasidic Jews.

Aside from the differences in the types and motives of immigrants, they make up a vastly larger proportion of the State of Israel, than that of the U.S.

Immigrants make up 12.5% of the total American population; but between 40 and 50% of the Jewish population in Israel. Israel's official figures for immigrants are that they constitute about 30% of the total population. However, this 30% figure takes in the entire population, including the 20% of the total that is Arab. Under Israel's Law of Return, non-Jews, including Arabs of course, are not allowed to immigrate to Israel. So it is safe to say that all the Arabs living in what is now Israel were born there, and probably their ancestors were as well for innumerable generations. All the immigrants in Israel, then, are Jewish and constitute 40 to 50% of the Jewish or governing population.

Immigration is so crucial to Israel that the most recent wave, from the Soviet Union, has dramatically changed at least the face of Israel's society. Thanks to the Law of Return, the foreign Jews coming off the planes become instant citizens with the right to vote. As a consequence there already are prominent ministers in the government who were born and raised abroad. For example, the Foreign Minister and Deputy Prime Minister, in the inner circle of the Cabinet, Avigdor Lieberman, is a former bouncer from Kishinev, the capital of Moldova, formerly part of the Soviet Union; the Vice-Prime Minister and Minister for the Development of the Negev and Galilee, Silvan Shalom, was born in Tunisia; the Minister of Industry, Trade & Labor, Binyamin Ben-Eliezer, was born in Basra, Iraq; Yuli-Yoel Edelstein, the Minister of Information, was born in Chernivisi, the Soviet Union; the Minister of Tourism, Stas Misezhnikov, was born in Moscow; and Yossi Peled, born in Belgium, is a Minister without portfolio.

On top of that, the refugees from the Soviet Union quickly developed a far-right nationalistic political movement and have made convenient marriages with the right-wing religious parties. This powerful alliance practically dominates today's Israeli government. This sudden coalition of the far-right has frightened some Israelis because, without the protection of a written constitution or Bill of Rights similar to that in the U.S., they could have their most fundamental rights and privileges drastically changed by a simple majority in their legislature.

There is, therefore, simply nothing similar between the U.S. and Israel, and there could not possibly be, given these facts. It would be like trying to find similarities between an eagle and a ferret.

Nevertheless the supporters of Israel in the U.S. keep repeating the mantra that the U.S. and Israel share the same values and that it is the only democracy in the Middle East and that their citizens are like family to us. Therefore, that is why the U.S. must support Israel, no matter what Israel does. The perpetuation of this myth has, therefore, compelled this analysis, as silly as it would appear to be to an outside observer.

This exercise, however, is not entirely academic. Israel in large measure has been a creature of the United States, beginning with the infatuated Harry Truman 's dramatic announcement of recognition for the self-declared nation in 1948. Even today many say that it could not survive, certainly not in the robust and prosperous way it has done, without the continued financial, military and diplomatic support of the one great superpower remaining in the world. This extraordinary support is often said to rest on the perception of those "shared values" and that Israel is the only democracy in the Middle East. Any examination which calls into question this myth therefore, may have immediate and radical consequences.

TODAY'S AMERICA, NOT YESTERDAY'S

This analysis—comparing U.S. society and Israeli society for the purpose of determining whether we have any shared values, assumes that we are looking at our societies as they exist today. When we read about people saying that "America" or the "U.S." is "such and such . . .," we of course understand them to mean the America of 2010, not 1810. Similarly when politicians in the U.S. and in Israel speak of our "shared values," it is about what our societies are today, not yesterday.

Things were different back then.

In 1810, a person like Barak Obama would most likely have been in chains on some cotton plantation in the South.

And only white men who owned property could vote.

Then there were the Indians—they had the land, and the white men wanted it.

The long process of coercing the Native Indians off their lands and into reservations was just beginning in 1810. Joseph J. Ellis in his *American Creation* describes the fruitless efforts of President George Washington and his Secretary of War, Henry Knox, to fashion a federal plan for coexistence with the native Indians based on treaties, as equals, rather than on the principles of conquest. But it was already too late, as the original settlers from Europe and then, the colonial governments had established an inexorable pattern, treaties made with solemn promises to respect secured borders which were then immediately broken. As Ellis explains, at one point Washington had a Commission created to seek a treaty with the Creek Nation which claimed an area including parts of Georgia, Florida and what would become Alabama and Mississippi. The most prominent chief of the Creeks was one Alexander McGillivray, son of a Scottish loyalist who had had his estate confiscated and had gone back to Scotland and a half-French and half-Creek mother. McGillivray looked with deep skepticism at the offers made by the Commission because of his own experience with the state governments of South Carolina and Georgia. It is painful even now to read what McGillivray had to say about the white man and his promises:

> *"We have received friendly talks and replies, it is true, but while they are addressing us by the flattering appellations of Friends and Brothers, they are stripping us of our natural rights by depriving us of that inheritance which belongs to our ancestors and hath descended from them to us Since the beginning of time."*

It is said that Thomas Jefferson for his part envisioned the Indians eventually moving from east of the Mississippi onto some of the vast country that he had acquired with the Louisiana Purchase. He felt it was demographically inevitable. The "eventual" however, soon turned into the more immediately-effective military tactics of General Andrew Jackson. Jackson continued his entire life in a passionate quest to push the Indians further into the West and onto reservations—he believed that the white man in his Manifest Destiny quest needed their property, would put it to much better use and, in any event, it was impossible for civilized people to live with Indians. As President he enthusiastically signed the "Indian Removal Act" in 1830.

The process ended, for the Indians, at Wounded Knee in 1890 under President Benjamin Harrison. Ironically, while the final ragged band of Sioux resisters was being slaughtered in South Dakota to end one chapter of American history, Jacob Riis was publishing his "How the Other Half Lives" about the misery of immigrants from Europe living in the tenements of New York, beginning another chapter.

The stirring words in the Declaration of Independence of July 4, 1776 have inspired many peoples seeking freedom and universal equality:

> *"We hold these truths to be self-evident: That all men are created equal; that they are endowed by their Creator with certain unalienable rights; that among these are life, liberty, and the pursuit of happiness . . . ."*

The "facts on the ground," however, as some Israelis are fond of saying in another context, were quite different when it got to actual governing.

In 1810, according to the U.S. Constitution, only "free persons" were fully counted for the purpose of establishing how many representatives each state would have in Congress.

> *"Representatives and direct taxes shall be apportioned among the several States which may be included within this Union, according to their respective numbers, which shall be determined by adding the whole number of free persons, including those bound to service for a term of years, and excluding Indians not taxed,*

three-fifths of all other persons. . . ." (Article I, Section 3.)

The writers of the Constitution, which was the result of long and fierce debates, went out of their way to avoid offending either the slave-owners in the South or the slave-traders in the North, or presumably themselves, as they knew that this unique and historical document would travel the world, so they never mentioned in the Constitution the word "slave," even then, an odious term. Slavery and slave-trading had long been abolished in Europe and was condemned universally—though still practiced widely around the world. So instead of "slaves," they used the words: "other persons."

The "three-fifths" language was not meant as a gratuitous insult to the slaves, as if they amounted to only a fraction of a white person. Instead, it represented a practical political compromise between the Northerners, who argued that slaves should not be counted at all for representation in Congress because they were only property of the slave-owners, and the Southerners, who, though outnumbered by their slaves, wanted nevertheless to count their numbers so as to increase the South's representation in the new Congress. For the delegates it was not a philosophical measurement of a slave as a person at all, since everybody understood that a slave was just chattel or property. Their mathematical language was simply expressing a convenient political compromise as to power.

The delegates, in the next instance in the Constitution where they had to refer to the slaves in the new nation, utilized the phrase "person held to service." Thus, they agreed that:

"No person held to service or labour in one state, under the laws thereof, escaping into another, shall, in consequence of any law or regulation therein, be discharged from such service or labour, but shall be delivered up on claim of the party to whom such service or labour may be due." (Article IV, Section 2, Subsection 2.)

President George Washington in 1793, signed the "Act Respecting Fugitives from Justice," later popularly called the Fugitive Slave Law. The Act was passed by Congress to give legal effect to the Article IV subsection quoted above.

Thereafter, when one of his own slaves, Olney Judge, escaped while the President was residing in Philadelphia, he declined to use the Act to retrieve her. Using the Act would have meant that he would have had to go public because the Act provided for a procedure requiring an application to a judge of some sort in the location where the slave had been apprehended. Presumably Washington did not want his legacy soiled by the unseemly scene of the Father of Our Country chasing down a young lady. Though Ms. Judge, in interviews to the abolitionist press in the 1840s, described how Washington had employed others on two occasions to try secretly to abduct her in New Hampshire where she had been living.

So we need to keep in mind that we are comparing Israel to the America of Barak Obama's time, not to that of George Washington's. If the Israelis were given a couple of centuries to refurbish their reputation, then, the comparisons made in this book between America and Israel may be different. But we are not there, and that is not here and now.

Notes: Page 201.

1

"DEMOCRACY" --
For those who are
Jewish

> *"The United States and Israel . . . [share a]*
> *commitment to core values including democracy, human*
> *rights and freedom of the press and religion."*

(From a March 26, 2010 AIPAC-drafted letter to Secretary of State, Hillary Clinton, signed by 333 Members of the U.S. House of Representatives.)

The definition of "democracy" in the Merriam-Webster online dictionary is as follows:

> *a : government by the people; especially:*
> *rule of the majority b : a government in which the*
> *supreme power is vested in the people and exercised by*
> *them directly or indirectly through a system of*
> *representation usually involving periodically held free*
> *elections.*

Without a doubt under this definition Israel qualifies as a democracy—rule by the majority expressed in free elections.

In that case we can end this chapter, can't we?

But wait! Both Attila the Hun and Mother Teresa came within the dictionary definition of "human being." Did that mean they were the same type of people? Likewise Genghis Khan, Jack the Ripper and Osama Bin Laden as well as St. Francis of Assisi, Albert Einstein, and Lucille Ball are all encompassed within the same definition.

Simply put, to use a dictionary term as "Democracy" then, to describe the government of Israel is not enough. To say it is a democracy, which it is, but not to go on and explain what kind of a democracy actually exists in Israel would be a primary example of IsraelSpeak. This was the way in which the term was used in the AIPAC letter quoted above and all its manifold offshoots.

The Knesset

Israel has a single chamber or unicameral legislative body called the Knesset. It is composed of 120 members who are elected every four years unless elections are called sooner because the Government (the Prime Minister and his Cabinet Ministers) has lost the confidence of a majority in the Knesset. Knesset members, MKs, are elected on a national basis from party lists on a proportional basis. In the February, 2009 election which brought into office the Government of Benjamin Netanyahu, there were 33 parties with hundreds of candidates vying for the 120 seats. The election resulted in 12 of these 33 party lists getting some of their candidates elected, ranging from 28 seats for Kadima (Tzipi Livni), 27 seats for Likud (Netanyahu), 15 seats for Yisrael Beiteinu (Avigdor Lieberman), 13 for Labor (Ehud Barak), 11 for Shas (Eli Yishai) and then 3, 4 or 5 seats for each of the other 12 parties that won seats.

Two of the 33 party lists were Arab: the United Arab List-Ta'al and the Balad party list. A third party list was a mixed Arab-Jewish list, Hadash. In the election, ten Arabs and one Jew were elected from these three lists. They received 9.18% of the total vote.

At first sight this bewildering array of parties seems to evidence a healthy and vigorous democracy. But again, one must ask, what kind of democracy?

A foretaste of the nature of this democracy came just before the elections. Nearly all of the non-Arab parties joined together as members of the country's Central Elections Committee in a proceeding which disqualified two of the three Arab parties: the Balad and the United Arab List-Ta'al, on the grounds that they refused to recognize Israel as the Jewish homeland and that they advocated an armed conflict against Israel. This was just after the Israeli bombardment of Gaza codenamed by Israel as Cast Lead. Members of the Arab parties had vociferously criticized that war, calling it a slaughter of a defenseless population and totally out of proportion to any imagined provocation—the same thing that most of the world was saying. But for the Jewish parties in this heightened period of patriotism, this criticism amounted to terrorism and the avocation of Israel's destruction. The Central Election Committee threw the parties out of the election.

Avigdor Lieberman, whose party had brought the challenges to the Committee, praised the ejection and stated:

> *"Now that it has been decided that the Balad terrorist organization will not be able to run, the first battle is over. . . .The next battle is making Balad illegal*

because it is a terrorist organization whose objective is harming the State of Israel."

In previous elections the Central Election Committee had similarly disqualified Arab parties on the same grounds, but the High Court overruled the Committee each time and allowed the parties to run in that election. The same thing happened in 2009.

No one was surprised by this series of events. It all seemed to be a pantomime. The charges against the Arab parties were outlandish and in addition, no law supported such disqualification. But it was election time, emotions from Cast Lead were running high and the politicians were playing to the electorate. The Supreme Court's ruling, the only imaginable way it could have ruled without itself appearing ridiculous, suffused the incident with the false aura of respect for the law.

But the episode reflected one of the fundamental characteristics of Israeli democracy—the tyranny of the majority.

The meaningless right to vote

Let all the Arabs in Israel vote. Let them send representatives to the Knesset. Let them prance around in the Knesset and say anything they want to—after all, isn't this a wonderful democracy? Just so long as they always remain in the minority—like the 2009 Knesset: 10 Arabs and 110 Jews. In a pinch—and there is always a pinch, those minute-by-minute "existential" threats to Israel—nearly all the Jews could be counted on to vote one way. Those democratically elected Arab MKs may make noise, but they will forever be just like toy soldiers in the windows of department stores; or like limp mice being battered around in sport by the cat.

4

No Arab party has ever even been asked to join an Israeli Government, much less brought into one—they have been permanently marginalized. No Arab has ever held a significant Cabinet or Ministerial post—Arabs simply have no real part in making decisions in their government. A recent survey of the Knesset workforce commissioned by a Knesset Parliamentary Committee of Inquiry found that only six of the 439 people working for the Knesset were Arabs, none at any significant level of authority. Arab MK Ahmed Tibi concluded from this report that:

> "[t]he absence of Arabs in these positions means that Arabs are not included in the ministries' decision-making processes. This creates a sense of alienation . . . ."

However, a Likud MK, Yariv Levin, the chairman of the Knesset House Committee, in a typical comment heard in the Knesset about Arabs, had this to say concerning the disclosure:

> "The report . . . is delusional and ignores the fundamental fact that a significant portion of Israel's Arabs are disloyal to the state. These are people who do not contribute to the state, and even try to undermine it."

The Arab members of the Knesset would learn again in a few months time that their status as elected representatives of the people afforded them little protection against abuse by the majority.

5

No fundamental laws

There is no Constitution or Bill of Rights in Israel like there is in the U.S., a Supreme Law of the land that neither a Congress, by just passing a law, nor a President, by issuing an Executive Order, could contravene. Israel's so-called Basic Laws can be changed by a vote in the Knesset. In contrast, changes to the fundamental principles of the American Government and the rights of its citizens as enshrined in the Constitution and the Bill of Rights can be changed only by a process which the country's founders hoped would guarantee that it could not be done at the whim of a momentary majority.

Article V of the U.S. Constitution provides that amendments to the Constitution can be proposed only by a two-thirds vote in both Houses of Congress or by two-thirds of the State Legislatures. Then, such proposed amendments will have to be approved by three-fourths of the State legislatures, or if Congress so determines, by three-fourths of conventions held in the States. According to the *Wikipedia* article on Amendments online on May 25, 2010:

> *"Over 10,000 constitutional amendments have been introduced in Congress since 1789; during the last several decades, between 100 and 200 have been offered in a typical congressional year. Most of these ideas never leave Congressional committee, and far fewer get proposed by the Congress for ratification."*

In the U.S., then, our basic rights are to a large degree insulated against any tyranny of the majority, whether momentary or prolonged. Changes would be effected only if the vast majority

6

of Americans wanted such changes and only after a good period of time has passed for reflection.

In Israel, however, it could be here today and gone tomorrow. For example, what one would assume to be a fundamental right that of marrying whom one wished, was severely restricted instantly by an edict issued by the Cabinet which did not even wait to obtain a vote by the Knesset (see below). Every other right held by an Israeli citizen can just as easily be overruled by a simple majority vote in the Knesset. This is the definition of a "tyranny of the majority."

There is no supreme law in Israel to which one can appeal if a majority of the Knesset passes a law detrimental to a minority. The law of the land at any given moment is whatever a majority in the Knesset says it is. In any event, even if there is such a supreme law which a simple majority in the Knesset cannot abrogate, the Judicial branch of the Israeli Government does not have even a shadow of the authority and power that the U.S. Supreme Court has acquired as a check and balance to the other branches. For example, the Israeli Supreme Court's orders may or may not be followed, depending on the mood or inclination of any given Government or any General. Furthermore, the judges of the Supreme Court know that the Knesset, by a majority vote, can reverse any of their decisions and even eviscerate their Court at any moment it wishes. By a simple majority vote the Knesset can add 50 judges to the Supreme Court, or provide that the Supreme Court no longer retain any jurisdiction over anything concerning the freedom of the press, or the military, or the Occupation. Consequently the judges on that Court from the beginning have behaved accordingly, and been accommodating.

7

James Madison wrote a substantial part of what has been called the *Federalist Papers*, letters and pamphlets intended to educate his fellow citizens on the proposed U.S. Constitution and to encourage its ratification by the States.

Fundamental laws in America

On November 22, 1787 in one of his letters, later termed the Federalist No. 10, he acknowledged that complaints had been heard from various parts of the Confederate States at that time that *"measure are too often decided, not according to the rules of justice and the rights of the minor party, but by the superior force of an interested and overbearing majority."*

Madison expressed concern that a simple government of the people ("popular government")

> *"enables it* [the majority] *to sacrifice to its ruling passion or interest both the public good and the rights of other citizens. To secure the public good and private rights against the danger of such a faction, and at the same time to preserve the spirit and the form of popular government, is then the great object to which our inquiries are directed."*

In his letter to the People of the State of New York published on February 6, 1788, and later called the *Federalist No. 51*, he dealt with the need for checks and balances in a government to prevent one faction from persecuting another faction. In part he wrote:

> *"Justice is the end of government. It is the end of civil society. It ever has been and ever will be pursued until it be obtained, or until liberty be lost in the pursuit. In a society under the forms of which the strong faction*

8

can readily unite and oppress the weaker, anarchy may as truly be said to reign as in a state of nature, where the weaker individual is not secured against the violence of the stronger. . . ."

It would seem from the daily news in Israel and the Occupied Territories, where the weak seem to have no protection against the strong, that, as Madison said: *"anarchy may . . . be said to reign."* The majority faction, the Jews, have no checks; they have proceeded to run over the minority, the Arabs. Thus, as Madison would have seen it, the purpose of government and of civil society, justice, cannot be found in Israel.

The material differences

In what way does this majority faction, the Jews, "oppress the weaker," the Arabs? How does this "tyranny of the majority" take its form?

The result of this tyranny can be observed at various levels, two of them are: the material consequences and the political or legal consequences.

A collection of legal and administrative procedures, in addition to the lack of influence of the Arabs in governance, such as the setting of the budgets, the discretionary disbursement of funds, the unequal enforcement of even those laws that are themselves equal, have led to a wide disparity in the material status of the Arabs and the Jews in Israel. Numerous reports and statistics confirm this disparity.

Even very simple things like the designation and protection of "holy places" by the government and the ensuing financial support for their maintenance is lopsided and in favor of the

Jews. In a land that is sacred to the Jews, Christians and Muslims, Israel has only been able to find and designate 137 **Jewish** holy sites. The term "Holy Places" was used in various United Nations Reports and Resolutions from 1947 and thereafter. It generally referred to the sites in Palestine as being sacred to three religions: Christianity, Islam, and Judaism.

Israel's Ministry of Foreign Affairs has on its website the "Protection of Holy Places Law, 1967." The law provides:

> *"The Holy Places shall be protected from desecration and any other violation and from anything likely to violate the freedom of access of the members of the different religions to the places sacred to them or their feelings with regard to those places."*

That law made the Minister of Religious Affairs responsible for implementing the law and instructed him to *"make regulations as to any matter relating to such implementation."*

However, in the 2009 annual report that the U.S. State Department formulated on religious freedom in countries of the world, it had this to say about Israel's implementation of this law.

> *"The 1967 Protection of Holy Sites Law applies to holy sites of all religious groups within the country and in all of Jerusalem, but the Government implements regulations only for Jewish sites. Non-Jewish holy sites do not enjoy legal protection under it because the Government does not recognize them as official holy sites. At the end of 2008, there were 137 designated holy sites, all of which were Jewish. Furthermore, the Government has drafter regulations to identify, protect, and fund only Jewish holy sites. While well-known sites have de facto*

10

*protection as a result of their international importance,
many Muslim and Christian sites are neglected,
inaccessible, or threatened by property developers and
municipality."*

The Legal Center for Arab Minority Rights, Adalah, sued the government, demanding that Muslim and Christian sites be designated as sacred places so as to protect them from developer and municipal encroachments; that money be appropriated for their maintenance; and regulations be promulgated for their protection. After some years in the courts, the Supreme Court ordered the Minister of Religious Affairs to explain why no sites other than the Jewish ones had been designated.

The U.S. State Department's 2009 report continues:

> *"Following a 2007 order by the High Court to explain its unequal implementation of the 1967 Protection of Holy Sites Law, the Government responded in March 2008 that specific regulations were not necessary for the protection of any holy sites. The Government did not explain why it therefore promulgated regulations for Jewish sites but not for non-Jewish sites."*

Meron Benvenisti has written a book about the neglected Muslim sites, *Sacred Landscapes*. He describes not only the neglect of the sites, but also the Israeli government's hostility to Muslim groups or individuals who attempt to utilize the sites or maintain them.

The "Museum of Tolerance"

When I was in Palestine in 2007, there was a lot of controversy about one particular site sacred to Muslims, the thousand-plus

11

Mamilla Jerusalem Cemetery, burial place of thousands of Saladin 's warriors and Muslim elite, judges, and the like. This had been the largest Muslim cemetery in Palestine at the time the State of Israel was founded. The site however fell on the Jewish side of the 1949 Armistice line, the Green Line. Under Jewish control it did not just go into disrepair and neglect, but the Israeli Government prohibited Muslim organizations from maintaining the cemetery. Then, it began confiscating portions of the cemetery, declaring them public lands, removing many of bodies and constructing buildings and parks on them. By 2007 when I visited, there was about a quarter of the cemetery left. It was certainly a sad scene. To add insult to injury the Israelis had constructed an expensive looking walkway through the derelict cemetery together with a garishly-painted keepers' collage— apparently as part of a Disney-like tour for tourists.

The controversy involved, almost incongruously, the decision by the municipality of Jerusalem to give a portion of the remaining cemetery to an American group from Los Angeles, the Simon Wiesenthal Center. The Center proposed to build an outlandishly Gehry-designed set of buildings that to me looked like a huge vacuum floating in the sky to house a "Museum of Tolerance." The Muslim community of course went into an uproar and complained to the courts.

After some years the Supreme Court ruled that the municipality giving that particular portion of the cemetery to the Americans to build their Museum was proper because since 1948, the State had been confiscating portions of the cemetery and putting it to different uses.

12

"During all those years no one raised any claim, on even one occasion, that the planning procedures violated the sanctity of the site."

This is surely IsraelSpeak at its best, spoken by the highest court in the land. The confiscations were done mostly before 1966 when the Arabs in Israel were under martial law. Demonstrating against a government action would have brought bullets and long prison terms for the demonstrators. In any event, one group has come up with photos and letters indicating that some of the prominent Arab families of Jerusalem had protested to the government about the confiscations.

I note in today's online edition of *The Jewish Week,* August 7, 2010, a comment by the executive director of what appears to be another franchisee of Simon Wiesenthal Center's "Museum of Tolerance," this one in Manhattan. Rabbi May's interview with *Crain's New York Business* is quoted in the *Jewish Week* article. In speaking for the Wiesenthal Center, Rabbi May wanted to make clear, that he was not necessarily speaking for the Museum of Tolerance, since: *"We do not want to politicize the museum."* He was announcing for the Wiesenthal Center their position in opposition to the proposed construction of a mosque and community center in downtown Manhattan, near Ground Zero, the site of the World Trade Center tragedy. According to *Crain* Rabbi May said:

"Religious freedom does not mean being insensitive . . . or an idiot . . . Religion is supposed to be beautiful. Why create pain in the name of religion?"

Ingrained discrimination

There is a discussion of the discrimination against Arabs that is ingrained in Israeli society, a "core" value, in Bernard Avishai's 2008 book called *The Hebrew Republic*. Avishai is a political economist who was born in Montreal, Quebec, to Ben Shaicovitch, the president of Canada's Zionist Men's Association during the 1950's. He has lived in Israel and the U.S. and is a Contributing Editor at the *Harvard Business Review*.

> *"Israeli Arabs' second-class citizenship does not simply mean getting less official status than they would like from the majority. The Israeli government devotes about 8 percent of its infrastructural investments to Arab town, less than half per capital of what it invests in the Jewish sector. It is the same with the health ministry's budget. The Arab school system has been underfunded for many years and at all levels. . . ."*

> *"Roads and bridges are no better. They are notorious in Arab towns . . . which have grown without proper zoning, plumbing, or electricity. Ilan Katz . . . told me that his own town of Zichron Yaacov has been getting as much as thirty times more land and municipal support per capita than the neighboring [Arab] town of Faradis. Another nearby town, Ein Hod, is in even worse shape: 'The Arab town of Ein Hod, much of which was displaced by what has become the lovely artists colony at Ein Hod, was declared a municipality in 1994 [after nearly 40 years]. They are still waiting for roads, sewers, and electricity. Drive there; suddenly you hit a dirt road."*

In 2007 I visited the two Ein Hods. The reality of an Arab village that had been depopulated by Jewish fighters in 1948 and then converted into a cute Jewish Artist's colony was mindboggling. Part of the remains of a mosque had been garishly painted and served as an outdoor cafe. Almost just across the road, and onto a dirt road as noted in Avishai's book, were some of the former Arab inhabitants of Ein Hod and their descendants. After escaping from their village under fire and then re-grouping in the woods a hundred or so yards away, they were not allowed by the Israeli Army to return to their town when the firing stopped. They became internal refugees and what the Jewish state now called many other thousands of Arabs, in an early IsraelSpeak, "present absentees."

Such "absentees" under new Israeli laws lost their land to the State which in turn transferred them to Jewish-only settlement organizations, like the Jewish National Fund. So the dispossessed residents of Ein Hod continued to live in the woods and eventually constructed, solely on their own, with no water or electrical lines from what became the state of Israel, the handsome community which I saw in 2007. They had been petitioning the Government of Israel for decades to be recognized as a town in the hope that they would then be hooked up to the system of utilities and roads, but their requests were ignored. Finally they were granted formal recognition in 1994, but obviously this did not amount to much benefit.

The unkempt streets of Arab or East Jerusalem and the piles of garbage I saw when I was there were in stark contrast to the conditions in West Jerusalem—again, the same municipal government and the same taxes, but grossly disparate treatment. Likewise were the conditions I observed in Nazareth with its Arab population as compared to those in the new Jewish settlements of Upper Nazareth.

15

More figures about this discrimination can be found in the reports of the Association for Civil Rights in Israel. While the Jews and the Arabs are taxed alike, the government disbursements to the "Arab Sector" usually amount to less than 50% of those to the "Jewish Sector." The very term "Sector" is alien to an American's ear but is the norm in Israel—a society divided into racial and religious sectors.

Much of the disproportionate funding and support for Jews over Arabs in Israel can be traced to the very nature of the state of Israel. Agencies that had been set up by world Zionists, the Jewish Agency, the World Zionist Organization and the Jewish National Fund, to manage immigration to Palestine in the early twentieth century and to sustain the immigrants in Palestine continued to be in existence even after the founding of the State of Israel and have now become fundamental elements of its infrastructure. These quasi-government organizations by their nature are intended to *"serve only the Jewish sector and are responsible for immigration and settlement, education, social welfare and the purchase and development of land in Israel,"* (Boyle and Sheen, eds., *Freedom of Religion and Belief: A World Report.* 113). As this Report noted, then:

> *"Discrimination against non-Jews, therefore, for historical reasons is systemic and structural and these inequalities have had a cumulative effect. The unequal allocation of budgets and resources by government bodies to Jewish and non-Jewish localities affects the housing, education and services available in those localities.*
>
> *"Funding to local Arab councils is 25-30 per cent of that given to Jewish councils. In the mixed Jewish-Arab cities of Haifa, Acre and Jaffa, for example, government-owned houses occupied by Arabs are in*

16

disrepair through government neglect, while those of Jewish residents are properly maintained. Public housing projects in Jewish areas for outnumber those in Arab areas."

The Or Commission

After Ariel Sharon as Likud Party leader performed his infamous sacrilege by marching onto the holy site of the Al Aqsa Mosque with several thousand armed police, soldiers and other security forces, setting off a Palestinian uprising that ultimately resulted in the deaths of almost five thousand Arabs and a thousand Jews, the Israeli Government did what it often does after a major occurrence, it appointed a commission to study the matter. The commission was called the Or Commission after its chairman, Supreme Court Justice Theodore Or. Among its findings or recommendations issued in 2003 was the following:

> *"24. The Arab sector: The committee determined that this is the most sensitive and important domestic issue facing Israel today. . . . The committee determined that the issue has been neglected for many years, and demanded that immediate, medium-term, and long-term action be taken. The committee determined that action must be focused on giving true equality to the country's Arab citizens. . . .*

> *"The state must work to wipe out the stain of discrimination against its Arab citizens, in its various forms and expressions. In this context, the state must imitate, develop, and operate programs emphasizing budgets that will close gaps in education, housing,*

17

industrial development, employment, and services. . . . ."

A sensible-sounding recommendation which made headlines and was duly distributed to all the world organizations that were demanding answers for what had happened. Then, like so many other carefully-crafted and high-sounding reports— nothing happened. Ultimately, it was more IsraelSpeak.

Yet surprisingly, even seasoned observers seemed to have hoped that something real would be done this time. At least that is what I surmise from the tone of disappointment in the report by the Association for Civil Rights (ACRI) eight years after the events at the Al Aqsa Mosque and five years after the Or Report:

> *"In October 2000, 13 people - all except one Arab citizens of Israel - were shot dead by Israeli security forces during demonstrations in the country's North. As a result of a public campaign led by human rights organizations . . ., the government decided to appoint an inquiry commission. . . .*

> *"The Commission, headed by Justice Theodore Or, published the most voluminous, comprehensive, and momentous report to date on the plight of Arab citizens of Israel. It stated that "achieving equality for the Arab citizens of Israel should be a prime objective of the government...*

> *"Since the publication of the Or Commission report, little has been done to improve the standing of the Arab community in Israel. Consecutive governments have adhered to policies of discrimination and neglect and have absolved themselves of their obligations toward Arab citizens. In the absence of fair and enforced state policies, inequality continues to grow between Israel's Jewish and Arab citizens.*

18

"Below, we list a few areas in which discrimination and neglect have increased in the past 8 years." [The list consisted of the usual suspects—you see the full report at http://www.acri.org.il/eng/Story.aspx?id=556.]

The ACRI conclusion of course is from a group sympathetic to the plight of the Arab citizens of Israel. But that certainly could not be said of the American Jewish Committee. Yet a study of Israeli-Arab matters funded by it and written in 2008 by Professor Elie Rekhess, a senior research fellow at the Dayan Center for Middle Eastern Studies in Tel Aviv, made almost the same point:

> *"The definition of Israel as a Jewish state, with its pronounced privileges for the Jewish majority, created inherent discrimination against Israeli Arab citizens. Socioeconomic gaps between Jews and Arabs widened over the years. Although a series of Israeli governments in the early 1990's declared their commitment to improving Jewish-Arab equality, their declarations remained no more than political slogans and were not backed by significant action."*

Notes: Page 201.

2

"DEMOCRACY" --
Without Equality

Core Values:

Equality (U.S.) and Inequality (Israel)

Equality is a core American value. In the United States every citizen has equal rights and privileges and is treated the same under every law. This is a fundamental value protected by the Constitution.

The Frenchman, Alexis De Tocqueville traveled the U.S. in the early years of this nation's existence, and tried to analyze what made America so different from the countries that he knew.

> *"The more I advanced in the study of American society, the more I perceived that the equality of conditions is the fundamental fact from which all others seem to be derived. . . . "*

It may have taken a Revolution, a bloody Civil War and then a hundred additional years of struggle, to realize those words in the American Declaration of Independence: ***"We hold these truths to be self-evident, that all men are created equal . . . ,"*** but at this point the equality of every citizen before the law is ingrained in the American way of life and thoroughly cherished.

In Israel, the case is just the opposite.

At the core of the Israeli state is the value of inequality—and just as cherished: one group, the Jews, is by law, custom and practice privileged. Almost every Jewish citizen in Israel—right, left or center politically—accepts that, as do the Jews in the Diaspora.

Only Jews were allowed as members of the People's Council which issued the Israeli Declaration of Statehood/Independence on May 14, 1948 in which they *". . . hereby declare the establishment of a Jewish State. . . . The State of Israel will be open to the immigration of Jews . . . ."* Israel has abided by that declaration, and gone even further. Not only is it open to Jews, but it is closed to everyone else.

It is not a question of what is right and what is wrong for this is not what I am examining. The question is whether the nature and character of the State of Israel bears any resemblance to that of America, that is, whether the AIPAC mantra of "shared core values" has any validity.

The laws

There are many laws in Israel that treat one group, the Jews, differently, and better, than all the other groups of Israelis. Israeli citizens who refuse to acknowledge the superior status of the Jews are considered by much of Israel to be disloyal and tantamount to traitors, undermining the State. Every person who wants to serve in the national legislature must publicly accept this concept.

21

Just as Jefferson's statement that "all men are created equal" was not realized for over 160 years in the U.S., so too, the promise of equality for all its citizens, Jews and Arabs alike, set forth in Israel's Declaration, has not been realized during the first 62 years of its existence.

> *"The State of Israel . . . will uphold the full social and political equality of all its citizens, without distinction of race, creed or sex. . . . We appeal . . . to the Arab inhabitants . . . to . . . participate in the up-building of the State on the basis of full and equal citizenship and due representation in all its provisional and permanent institutions."*

It cannot be said that the Arab inhabitants ostensibly appealed to by Ben-Gurion either accepted or rejected this "appeal," as they were for the most part at the very moment being chased out of their homes and onto the roads into exile. Even if they had a choice, would anyone expect them to choose to turn over the land of their ancestors to these immigrants? Who would surrender his house to strangers for the promise that he would have a nice room in it, with equal access to the bathroom?

The Government of Israel nevertheless took no chances and made sure that those Arabs who by chance did remain had **no** rights at all, placing most areas where Arabs lived under martial law for the next 20 years. The website for Adalah, the Legal Center for Arab Minority Rights in Israel, explains what this meant:

> *"Military rule placed tight controls on all aspects of life for the Palestinian minority. These measures of control included severe restrictions on movement, prohibitions on political organization,*

limitations on job opportunities, and censorship of
publications. For example, in 1956, the Israeli army killed
49 Palestinian farmers in Kufr Kasem for "violating" the
curfew imposed on their village. Unaware that a curfew
had been ordered, the farmers were returning home from
working their agricultural lands when they were killed. . .
. Up to 1965, attempts by the Palestinian community in
Israel to form political parties to run for the Knesset, such
as the El Ard (The Land) Movement, were forcibly
stopped and their associations outlawed.

It would seem from a daily reading of the online English editions of the *Haaretz Daily* and *The Jerusalem Post* that in many respects things have not got much better for the Arab citizens of Israel since the lifting of military rule. The promise of equality has not been kept. As seen above, the promise of participation in the government and representation in all governing bodies has not been kept—Israeli Arabs take no meaningful part in their governance.

During the one week of May 19–26, 2010, for example, one newspaper article described a bill being proposed by Foreign Minister Avigdor Lieberman's party, which would take citizenship away from anyone who refused to serve in the Israeli Defense Forces (IDF) or do a term of national service. Of course the Arabs who lived under the military rule enforced by the IDF were not allowed to, and would not want to become part of the IDF. That remains true today as one of the main functions of the IDF has been to rule over the Arabs in the Occupied Territories.

Another proposed bill noted in the newspapers that week required that any person seeking a national identity card, and Israeli citizens over 16 have to compulsorily carry one, had to make a declaration of loyalty "to the state of Israel as a Jewish, Zionist and democratic state"—an oath of cultural and political inferiority that any Arab would find most difficult to take. Without this identification card a person would be considered a trespasser or "infiltrator" and subject to criminal prosecution or exile—to a place they had never lived in, like Gaza or the West Bank.

Commenting on another bill in the Knesset which would strip one of one's citizenship if convicted on charges of terrorism or espionage, a columnist wrote:

> "But the bill itself is not the problem. . . . The problem is a viewpoint that considers a community, by its mere existence, ethnic origin, language and links with what are described as enemy states as the target for this legislation. . . .
>
> "It is a dynamic process, and . . . it is getting worse.
>
> "The culture of isolation does not really need laws like the one being promoted by Yisrael Beiteinu and people with racists outlooks in other parties. This is because these laws, which enjoy a nod from a public, do not create anything new. They only express the reality that has been in place for many years."

Another story described a High Court ruling which allowed the continued isolation of a tiny Palestinian village. It seems that barrier or wall built by Israel disconnected the 2,000 residents of a Palestinian village, Sheikh Sa'ed, located on the south-eastern edge of Jerusalem's city limits, from its neighboring villages and from Jerusalem, on which it was dependent for all its services, like schools, hospitals, shopping, and employment. Now vehicles are not allowed to enter or exit, only pedestrians—and that too through a military checkpoint where the rules for passage frequently and capriciously change and are enforced with bureaucratic cruelty by young Jewish soldiers.

The Law of Return

Perhaps at the heart of the State of Israel is the concept that it is a nation to which all the Jews of the world belong, with some living in Israel and the others in the Diaspora. Flowing from this is the concept that any person who is Jewish, and can prove it, if living anywhere in the world, may immigrate to Israel where he or she automatically becomes a citizen. This is contained in one of the 14 Basic Laws, the 1950 Law of Return:

> "1. *Every Jew has the right to come to this country as an oleh.*
> "2. *(a) Aliyah shall be by oleh's visa.*
> *(b) An oleh's visa shall be granted to every Jew who has expressed his desire to settle in Israel."*

David Ben-Gurion in introducing the Law of Return and the Citizenship Law stressed that Israel was unique in that *"its gates are open to every Jew wherever he may be."* Israel was a Jewish state not because the majority was Jewish, he said, but because *"it is a state for Jews everywhere. . . ."* Ben-Gurion assured the world that this was not the granting of any special privilege to Jews over the non-Jewish citizens of Israel, as the *"State of Israel is based on the full equality of the rights and duties of all its citizens."* The reason this open door policy which was available only to Jews was not that a special privilege was being given to Jews.

> "[I]t is not the state which grants the diaspora Jews the right to return. This right preceded the State of Israel, and it was this right which built the State of Israel."

25

Now you see it, and now you don't. IsraelSpeak had an early start.

In 1970 after some controversy as to who was a Jew, the law was amended to adopt the religious, as opposed to the ethnic, definition:

> "4B. For the purposes of this Law, "Jew" means a person who was born of a Jewish mother or has become converted to Judaism and who is not a member of another religion."

A Jew who has been given a certificate of oleh under the Law of Return is entitled to the Right to Citizenship under the Citizenship or Nationality Law if he or she so desires. There are agencies in the government which are charged with encouraging Jews living abroad to immigrate to Israel. In addition, the government pays private organizations to recruit immigrants abroad. Travel and other expenses are paid for; special financial support is provided to the immigrants and absorption is eased with housing, jobs and education programs.

Photos of new immigrants making aliyah are routine in Israeli newspapers. The *Jerusalem Post* on April 17, 2010, for example, had a photo of dozens of people brandishing their new identity cards in front of them for the cameras:

> "A festive welcome was given to 210 new olim during a Jewish Agency gathering at the Ramada Renaissance Hotel in Jerusalem, immediately after their arrival in the country. . . . Ofer Dahan, director of the Programs Marketing Division for the Jewish Agency, praised the speed at which the new olim became Israeli citizens. They all receive their identify cards within 24 hours of landing. Dahan explained that with a 'welcome

26

*from the Jewish Agency you get everything covered -- a
certificate, health [coverage], banking [set up], cell
phones, work proposals' and housing."*

Family "Reunification"

There had been one exception to this exclusive Jewish
immigration, and that was when an Israeli-Arab married
someone abroad. The Palestinians remaining in Israel after the
1948 War and their descendants of course continued to have
cultural, family and historical ties to the Diaspora Palestinians
and it was natural that people met across the borders, liked each
other and then decided to marry. Though the Israelis made it
arduous and lengthy, it was possible for the spouse eventually to
obtain the status of a permanent resident in Israel and finally
citizenship.

But not anymore.

In 2002 the Israeli Cabinet decided that this "backdoor" entry
should be slammed shut. The closure, it was thought, could be
justified on the grounds that letting in more Arabs posed a
"security" risk, though members of the Cabinet freely
acknowledged that the real reason was simply to prevent the
entry of more Arabs into Israel—the newly perceived
"demographic threat." Israel's then-Prime Minister, Ariel
Sharon, is quoted as saying during a discussion of the new order
at a special Cabinet meeting: *"There is no need to hide behind
security arguments. There is a need for the existence of a Jewish State."*

The Cabinet's Decision #1813 of May 12, 2002 froze all
applications for family unifications. Of course since Jewish
spouses had an absolute right to immigrate to Israel and obtain

citizenship, the freeze in effect applied only to Arab citizens. The Knesset thereafter enacted a "temporary" order that banned Palestinians from the Occupied Territories, who married citizens of Israel from obtaining any legal status in Israel. But this temporary status was similar to the temporary taking of Palestinian land in the West Bank for Israel's military purposes. The temporary confiscation would be endlessly renewed while the land morphed from being used ostensibly by the military to a Jewish settlement. Thus the "*temporary*" ban on foreign spouses was renewed and even expanded. Now, in addition to the Occupied Territories, this covers spouses from Syria, Lebanon, Iraq, and Iran as well as "*to anyone living in an area in which operations that constitute a threat to the State of Israel are being carried out. . . .*"

If the Israelis do decide that an Israeli citizen who marries someone in the prohibited area can be granted an exemption and allowed to reside in Israel, that person must first take a specially designed "loyalty oath." The oath proclaims allegiance to the "*Jewish* democratic state." Proponents of the pledge claimed that this oath would screen suicide bombers. As if someone intent on ending his or her life for an ideal, however delusional, would hesitate to give a false oath. Rather, it is more of the same. The Jews demanding that the Arabs cry "uncle" before releasing their grip.

Given the severe restrictions on movements across Israel's borders and between Israel and the Occupied Territories, the result has been either the separation of thousands or of forcing them to live together like fugitives who could any day be arrested and jailed—for the simple reason that they tried to keep their families together.

28

The British journalist and author, Jonathan Cook, who has gone native in Nazareth, tells the story of a couple he knew, Morad, an Israeli lawyer, and Abir, a teacher in the West Bank, who came back from their honeymoon and found that the law had been changed while they were away. It was now illegal for them to live together. *"As they crossed over the border from Jordan, they were forced to part: Morad to his apartment in Be'ersheva, and Abir to her parents' home in the West Bank city of Bethlehem."*

The regulations were challenged in court but the Supreme Court ruled that they were perfectly OK under Israeli laws.

Human Rights Watch (HRW) issued a statement criticizing the Court's decision. HRW called the law discriminatory under international law and that neither the security nor demographic reasons given for it justified the unequal treatment of thousands of families. Such international criticism, as usual, was met with a shrug in Israel.

In the U.S., religion of course, plays no role in our immigration or naturalization laws or in procedures for the unifications of families, that is, arranging for the residence status of a foreign spouse. Such a concept is entirely alien to America, utterly repugnant.

Notes: Page 203.

3

FREEDOM OF RELIGION

Freedom of Religion: United States

Unlike the principle of equality in America, which took over 150 years to evolve into something that resembled what we have today, the issue of what role religion should or should not play in government was quickly fixed in stone at the very beginning. The Civil War over African slavery was yet to happen, but the wars over religion had already occurred. The Delegates in Philadelphia in 1787 were well-versed in their history and they also had the experiences from their own colonies under their belts. So the one thing they were absolutely certain about was that religion would have no part in the new government they were creating, and that the government in turn would have no part in the conscience of its citizens.

> *"If there is any fixed star in our constitutional constellation, it is that no official, high or petty, can prescribe what shall be orthodox in politics, nationalism, religion, or other matters of opinion, or force citizens to confess by word or act their faith therein."*
> Justice Jackson, <u>West Virginia State Board of Education v. Barnette</u>, 319 U.S. 624, 642 (1943).

Though most of these Christian men, all Protestants of various denominations except for two Roman Catholics, were conventionally religious, they also knew that politics and religion had been historically a toxic mix. Unlike most documents of its kind, therefore, this Constitution made no mention of God or of the Divine. It was a compact among and between men; the authority to govern was derived from the people, not from any mystic source, and was limited to specified and known powers as granted by the people.

In the minds of the Framers

The certitude of the Framers on this subject was derived not only from their knowledge of the religious wars and persecutions in Europe from where these descendants of the English, Scots, Dutch, German, Irish and French had come, but also their personal experiences of the struggle for freedom of religion in their own respective colonies, some more successful than others. In addition, many were also students of the Enlightenment philosophers, particularly John Locke, who had developed theories on the separation of the church and state. Those theories were now to be put to the test in the American experiment.

Two years earlier James Madison, in opposing a bill in the Virginia Legislature to levy a general assessment for the support of teachers of religion, wrote:

> "[W]e hold it for a fundamental and undeniable truth, 'that religion or the duty which we owe to our Creator and the manner of discharging it, can be directed only by reason and conviction, not by force or violence.' The Religion then of every man must be left to the conviction and conscience of every man; and it is the right

of every man to exercise it as these may dictate. This right is in its nature an unalienable right. ., ..

. . . .

"What influence in fact have ecclesiastical establishments had on Civil Society? In some instances they have been seen to erect a spiritual tyranny on the ruins of the Civil authority; in many instances they have been seen upholding the thrones of political tyranny: in no instance have they been seen the guardians of the liberties of the people. Rulers who wished to subvert the public liberty, may have found an established Clergy convenient auxiliaries. . . .

. . . .

"[The Bill] will destroy that moderation and harmony which the forbearance of our laws to intermeddle with Religion has produced among its several sects. Torrents of blood have been spilt in the old world, by vain attempts of the secular arm, to extinguish Religious discord, by proscribing all difference in Religious opinion. Time has at length revealed the true remedy. . . . The American Theatre has exhibited proofs that equal and complete liberty, if it does not wholly eradicate it, sufficiently destroys its malignant influence on the health and prosperity of the State. . . ."

James Madison. Memorial and Remonstrance Against Religious Assessments. 1785.

James Madison and his Remonstrance, or protest, would be frequently quoted by United States Supreme Court Justices in the coming years whenever they treated the subject of freedom of religion. His experience in Virginia was duplicated in other colonies by many of the other Framers.

Religious persecution

Most of the Delegates at the Constitutional Convention were educated enough to recite at least parts of the history of the religious wars in Europe—a period of bloody excesses and fanaticism over dogma that spanned a period from approximately 1520 to 1710. Perhaps they were less schooled, except for the legends, about the Crusades during the previous 500 years where a succession of Popes, with religious exhortations and promises of Paradise, had sent untold numbers of Europeans on the long and perilous journey to "recover" the Holy Land. Jerusalem was indeed cleansed by the first wave of this horde, with every man, women and child put to the sword—Muslim, Jew and for all they knew, Christian, as well, in a sea of blood (a deed which Saladin chose not to reciprocate after retaking Jerusalem).

The Crusaders, however, were able only to interrupt the thousand-year Muslim governance of Jerusalem for only about 100 years. The last of the great Crusades stopped well short of Palestine, to besiege and then loot and settle in the Christian city of Constantinople. Notwithstanding all of this, the Pope was still able, sometimes with the connivances of princes or kings, to send out thousands of the faithful on violent crusades against fellow Christians in Europe who had deviated from orthodox religion, or possessed land coveted by the Pope or an allied prince—so the Christian Crusaders went out to kill, and incidentally take the property of, such heretics as the Cathars in the Albigensian wars. The Pope's treasury for these expeditions was limitless as he could produce, as if by magic, endless indulgences to these crusades for the forgiveness of their sins and guarantee them entrance into the eternal pleasures of

Paradise. The language of the holy wars of the Crusades was remarkably similar to that of Islam's holy wars, or Jihad.

But perhaps more fresh in the minds of the Philadelphia Delegates, though some of them in their speeches did make references to events in ancient Greece and Rome, were the confrontations between the Catholic Holy Roman Emperor Charles V and the followers of Martin Luther; the chasing of the Calvinists, Anabaptists and other non-Lutheran Protestants out of Germany after Charles and the Lutheran Princes had made their peace or Henry VIII's beheading or burning at the stake ministers, monks, and common people as well for supposed deviations from the orthodoxy of the Church of England. No country or religious sect was sparred. Tens of thousands were killed in the name of God.

For thirty years Catholic and Huguenot armies ravaged each other, the people and the landscape of France, with some observers counting eighteen massacres of Protestants and five massacres of Catholics, plus endless assassinations. Thomas Cramer, Archbishop, was burned at the stake in part for his work on the Common Book of Prayer, a frequent source of friction and violence among the faithful. Stories of burnings and torture overseen by the Inquisition were part of every European's understanding of religion.

The result of every one of these efforts to impose unity and to suppress dissent was to create more disunity and dissent so that the map of Europe was littered with opposing and multiplying religious sects.

Persecution of the non-orthodox continued even after the massacres ended and armies no longer battled over religion, the forms of persecution less violent, but still including imprisonment or exile, certainly exclusion from public office. Puritans fled to America to escape being forced into conformity with the Church of England. No sooner settled in New England, however, before they set up their own established church to which they demanded obeisance.

The newly arrived colonists in Virginia established the Church of England as the official religion and taxed all inhabitants to support the churches and their clergy.

Maryland was founded under a Charter obtained by the Catholic Lord Baltimore as a refuge for persecuted Catholics. The Catholics however always formed a minority in numbers and were soon themselves not allowed openly to practice their faith.

In short, most of the immigrants brought over with them the principle of an established church, to which all were to adhere, under pain of some penalty.

But dissenters were dissenters. By the time of the American Revolution there were such a multitude of denominations or sects that people seemed to have lost track of who they were chasing. Public religious persecutions were rare, though Catholics and Jews were in most places still barely tolerated. Most characteristic of this phenomenon were the "middle colonies," New York, New Jersey, Pennsylvania and Delaware. One scholar estimated that there was no dominant sect in the Middle Colonies and that there were congregations of Presbyterians, German-Lutherans, German-Reformed, Quakers, Dutch-Reformed, Anglicans, Mennonites, Moravians, Catholics, Baptists and English-Methodists. Visitors from Europe were astounded at this diversity, as well as by the fact that the larger population seemed to have to adhere to no denomination at all.

In Europe, America had already developed the reputation as being free from religious orthodoxy.

James Madison would point to these Middle Colonies, where there had been no established church, and observe that *"certainly the religious conditions of those Colonies will well bear a comparison with that where establishment existed."*

The Constitution: No religious test

The one instance where the Delegates did expressly mention religion in the proposed Constitution was when they provided that there would be no religious test for an office holder. That same section has a more oblique reference to religion in that it provided for either an "oath" or "affirmation" of office, where an oath would be taken before God while an affirmation would not.

> *"The Senators and Representatives before mentioned, and the Members of the several State Legislatures, and all executive and judicial Officers, both of the United States and of the several States, shall be bound by Oath or Affirmation, to support this Constitution; but no religious Test shall ever be required as a Qualification to any Office or public Trust under the United States."*
> U.S. CONST. art. VI, § 3.

Though not debated, this oath/affirmation provision as well as the "no test" clause was a significant deviation from most of the existing state Constitutions which required an oath and also property and religious tests. Yet among these Delegates, the principles set forth in this Section 3 were almost as if their underlying principles were assumptions held by all.

The records we have of the debates at the Constitutional Convention do not indicate that either provision was controversial or debated at all. The "no test" language appeared in the earliest-proposed drafts that were submitted to committees by the Delegates without objection or dissent, as was the final language. The "oath" reference when it first appeared was amended to "oath or affirmation," again without debate or dissent. The significance of the change was not discussed, but commentators have surmised that it was made in deference to the Quakers whose religion prohibited oaths. Likewise, it would allow a person without belief in God to avoid taking an oath.

One delegate to the Convention, Edmund Randolph, in fact pointed to these items when he debated ratification of the Constitution in the Virginia Convention considering it in 1788 as sufficient proof to him that freedom of religion was guaranteed by the Constitution, though it did not expressly say as much. Since these were the only items that related to religion, he reasoned, this confirmed that the new national government had no powers over religion at all. In addition, if a person of any sect could hold office, then no one sect could control Congress and suppress the others, particularly in view of the numerous sects existing in the United States.

The Framers felt comfortable that since they did not give any powers to the national government over religion, that religious freedom was thereby guaranteed. Madison in addition argued in essays that were later collected into the Federalist Papers that the sheer multiplicity of religious groups in the U.S. would always guarantee that none could establish itself as the National Church and that no one group could be oppressed. He too, was initially of the mind that nothing further was needed in the Constitution to guarantee religious freedom. He was later forced by circumstances and by others, particularly by Thomas Jefferson and John Adams who were both in Europe as ambassadors and were not at the Convention, either to change his mind or at least his tactics, as he became the leading advocate for amendments to the Constitution to guarantee basic rights, including freedom of religion.

As the draft of the Constitution was made public, the absence of a religious test for an office-holder as well as the absence of an obeisance to the Almighty did not sit well with some. During the debate over ratification of the Constitution there was criticism about the document's failure to acknowledge, as almost all other such documents had done, that all powers among men came from God. More significantly, the prohibition against a religious test made some fearful that non-Christians and atheists could become office-holders.

Oliver Ellsworth, a delegate from Connecticut to the 1787 Convention, wrote an essay to counter these objections. The "no religious test" provision, he argued, as not hostile to religion but on the contrary:

> *"the sole purpose and effect of it is to exclude persecution and to secure to you the important right of religious liberty. We are almost the only people in the world who have a full enjoyment of this important right of human nature."*

He further observed that in the rest of the world, nations by law had established one religion—leading to the persecution of those who differed. He reminded his readers that no sooner were "popery" abolished in England that the Church of England was set up in its stead and "*severe penalties were inflicted upon all who dissented from the established church.*" When Charles I had power and the Presbyterians had the upper hand, all dissenters were punished. When Charles II and the Church of England were restored, "*the Presbyterians and other dissenters were laid under legal penalties and incapacities*" —and this included disqualification from office by a religious test.

Ellsworth also pointed out that it would be "*the last degree absurd in the United States*" to have a religious test because there were so many denominations.

> "*If it were in favor either Congregationalists, Presbyterians, Episcopalians, Baptists, or Quakers, it would incapacitate more than three-fourths of the American citizens for any public office and thus degrade them from the rank of freeman.*"

Finally, he told his readers that the issue of a religious test in any event really came down to a basic principle:

> "*The business of a civil government is to protect the citizen in his rights, to defend the community from hostile powers, and to promote the general welfare. Civil government has no business to meddle with the private opinions of the people.*"

The First Amendment

James Madison, as noted, also thought that the multiplicity of denominations and sects in the country was sufficient in itself as a defense against oppression by any one group or the government. Much of the reluctance shown by even supporters of the Constitution to ratify it , however, was due to the absence of a Bill of Rights, something which most states themselves had for their own governments—the setting forth of fundamental rights in the framework of the new government so that no Congress could infringe upon those rights. Madison had argued that since the Constitution created a government of limited and specific powers, and since it was not given any powers with respect to religion, the individual had nothing to fear about the federal protection of their rights that resulted by default. An argument, however much he may have believed, remained unconvincing to many and in itself it threatened ratification. Thus toward the end of the ratification process and to induce the last few essential approvals, Madison and the other leading Federalists, as supporters of the Constitution were called, promised that once the Constitution had been approved, they would amend it to provide for the protection of individual rights, and that they would add a Bill of Rights.

True to his word, after the ninth state ratified the Constitution and the new government was formed, Madison, who was elected to the first House of Representatives after having been denied a seat in the Senate by the anti-Federalists led by Patrick Henry, promptly introduced a package of amendments that came to be known as the Bill of Rights. His language was based on clauses already existing in a number of state Constitutions and was further refined and strengthened by the House and Senate committees. The final language on the Freedom of Religion was coupled with other basic freedoms and emerged as the First Amendment:

> *"Congress shall make no law respecting an establishment of religion, or prohibiting the free exercise thereof; or abridging the freedom of speech, or of the press;*

or the right of the people peaceably to assemble, and to
petition the Government for a redress of grievances."
U.S. CONST. amend. XIV

These concepts did not suddenly spring up from nowhere. Nor were they imitations of foreign examples where they had been successful—no such examples existed. Nor were they created by farsighted academics who had deduced from history what would be best for America. Instead they germinated and grew from the soil of America into unique American fruits—thereafter admired and sought to be planted in soil around the world, with varying degrees of success.

Justice Rutledge emphasized this fact in one of his dissenting decisions:

> *"No provision of the Constitution is more closely tied or given content by its generating history than the religious clause of the First Amendment. It is at once the refined product and the terse summation of that history. The history includes not only Madison's authorship and the proceedings before the First Congress, but also the long and intensive struggle for religious freedom in America."*
> Everson v. Board of Education, 330 U.S. 1, 33 (1947).

The Justices in various opinions over the years described the evils to democracy that the First Amendment's religion clause had intended to avoid: embroiling the government in divisive disputes of religious sects; the creation of partisan political parties based on religious differences; the division of citizens between those who were favored and those who were not— insiders and outsiders; the pursuit by groups for increased government funding, with the dominant group obtaining the

41

dominant benefits with consequent resentment and anger by the others who paid taxes equally.

The U.S. Supreme Court in its 1947 *Everson* decision found that providing bus transportation for parochial school pupils was not a prohibited expenditure for religion. But in 1948 it rejected as a violation of the First Amendment, the practice of releasing children in public schools for a period of time for religious education in the school conducted by visiting clergy (McCollum v. Board of Education, 333 U.S. 203 (1948)). Justice Frankfurter in a separate concurring opinion explained that keeping religion out of the public schools was essential for preserving the community from the dangerous strife engendered by religious groups.

> *"Designed to serve as perhaps the most powerful agency for promoting cohesion among a heterogeneous democratic people, the public school must keep scrupulously free from entanglement in the strife of sects.* **The preservation of the community from divisive conflicts, of Government from irreconcilable pressures by religious groups,** *of religion from censorship and coercion, however subtly exercised, requires strict confinement of the State to instruction other than religious, leaving to the individual's church and home indoctrination in the faith of his choice"*
> McCollum at 216 - 17, emphasis added.

"Separation means separation, not something less. . . ." the Justice noted later in his opinion, emphasizing the continued vitality of Thomas Jefferson's metaphor of a wall of separation between church and state (id. at 231).

The principle of freedom of conscience has had such a dominant place in American political life that even in the midst of World

42

War II the Court would not allow the government to compel its citizens to salute the U. S. flag.

> "*To sustain the compulsory flag salute we are required to say that a Bill of Right which guards the individual's right to speak his own mind, left it open to public authorities to compel him to utter what is not in his mind*"
> West Virginia State Board of Education v. Barnette, 319 U.S. 624, 634 (1943).

No American citizen could be forced "*to profess any statement of belief or to engage in any ceremony of assent to one . . .* "(id). The First Amendment's "religion" clause was not confined to traditional religious concepts, but related to the entire breadth of individual liberty and conscience.

The Court has found that the required recitation of a prayer, though studiously non-denominational, in a public school infringed individual liberty (Engel v. Vitale, 370 U.S. 421 (1962)). Such liberty was intended by the First Amendment to be put beyond majorities, elections, the ballot box or the government. When a public authority requires a prayer of any kind, it is indirectly coercing all to conform. Even a moment of silence in public schools "for meditation or voluntary prayer" has been found to be the establishment of religion in violation of the First Amendment (Wallace v. Jaffree, 472 U.S. 38 (1985)). The right to speak, the Court stated in that decision, is complementary to the right to refrain from speaking. So also, the right of an individual to select a religious faith also embraces the right to select none at all.

One of the concerns running through many of the Court's decisions on religion is that any government support of religion would generate partisan groups which, in seeking to gain additional government funding for their own groups, would create the type of bitter divisiveness in public discourse that was irreconcilable.

> *"Ordinary political debate and division, however vigorous or even partisan, are normal and healthy manifestations of our democratic system of government, but political division along religious lines was one of the principal evils against which the First Amendment was intended to protect. . . . The potential divisiveness of such conflict is a threat to the normal political process. . . ."*
> Lemon v. Kurtzman, 403 U.S. 602, 622 (1971).

In Kurtzman the Court held that financial aid to church-related schools in the form of reimbursement for the costs of teachers salaries, text books and the like was in   violation of the First Amendment.

The Justices have sharply differed on the application of the First Amendment's religion clauses to particular fact situations, such as religious displays on government property, but they have been remarkably uniform in their understanding of the core principles underlying that Amendment, with the "Establishment Clause" erecting a wall of separation between church and state and the "Free Exercise Clause" providing for freedom of conscience against every form of coercion or restriction, except for a clear and present danger to public order.

This then, is the core American value of the Freedom of Religion.

Freedom of Religion: Israel

People are allowed to practice a religious faith of their choice in Israel without any government prohibitions. At first glance there certainly seems to be some freedom of religion in Israel, at least

44

to the extent that a person may or may not worship, as he or she pleases. Though there are nine or ten "recognized" religions in Israel, with the Government identifying those organized religions, which are allowed by law to set up marriage and divorce tribunals and handle the religious affairs of their congregations, it appears that even the religions, which are not recognized can at least build places of worship. For those religions which are not officially recognized, it is not clear what the consequences have been, but they do not appear to have faced any significant difficulties, at least none that have entered the mainstream press.

In most cursory reviews, therefore, this would be the beginning and the end of the question, with a conclusion that there is "freedom of religion" in Israel.

But as we have seen above, "freedom of religion" encompasses a great deal more than merely being allowed to attend the mosque, church or synagogue of one's choice, like children free to play, but only within the confines of the sandbox. The subject is exponentially more complex than this one-dimensional view. For Israel's citizens and residents, Jews and Arabs alike, the subject also involves the question of whether one is free *from* religion, intrusions into one's daily life caused by government enforcement of religious dictates. We are obligated therefore to examine the whole universe of this freedom to be able to compare it to the American values described above and to determine whether such American values bear any resemblance to the Israeli ones, as in AIPAC's claim that we "share common core values."

Religion – An integral part of government

What we find is that the government in Israel funds religious activities with the taxes from all of its citizens and residents, including paying the salaries, pensions, etc. of innumerable rabbis throughout Israel, as well as the salaries of ministers and imams, provided they pass muster with the Shin Bet. But that the funding is wildly disproportionate in favor of the Jewish religion and even there, it discriminates in favor of the orthodox and ultra-orthodox streams or sects, so as to generate animosity, resentment and bitterly fierce struggles between groups for the dominant position.

Political parties are created on religious lines, then splintered into even smaller religious factions, with religious leaders for each faction operating from the privacy of their sanctuaries, making the decisions by fiat on how their party's adherents, voters, Ministers or Members of the Knesset, should act or vote on political issues. Cabinet Ministers are engulfed in such questions as which religious laws and interpretations allow which meat products to enter the country. Many government officials first visit their religious "masters" for instructions before they determine a policy or vote on an issue. Many communities are segregated along religious lines of one sort or another and the rules for each community are strictly enforced, whether it is "women to the back of the bus" or no leaven bread to be sold in the stores and on which days.

Students of a certain religious stream, the Haredi, are exempted from military service for religious reasons, then funded in their separate religious schools to study religion to the exclusion of anything commercially or civically useful, into their thirties and forties, supported by more special subsidies and welfare while

46

they marry and then raise children who attend the same government-subsidized religious schools, all the while voting blindly as a block in elections, learning to hate outsiders and shedding only contempt upon the civil government and its officials—ready at an instant to band together into fanatical, riotous, death-defying demonstrations in opposition to one thing or another which their rabbis, who have absolute control over their beliefs and behavior, may oppose for one reason or another.

Favoritism becomes so pronounced and pervasive for the dominant group in every aspect of life, from housing to education, transportation, employment and travel, that its benefits must be carefully and jealously guarded against possible misapplication by the non-favorites—so all citizens and residents over 16 years of age in the entire country of Israel are required to carry IDs which by presence or absence of their year of birth according to the Hebrew calendar immediately identifies them as belonging to the dominant group or not—just in case there were any questions.

The "Status Quo Agreement"

There is at least one thing on this subject that is indeed common to both Israel and the U.S.—the die was cast in the very beginning. Bernard Avishai in his 2008 book, *The Hebrew Republic*, describes how David Ben-Gurion in the Constitutional Assembly and then, in the first Knesset decided against a written constitution primarily to avoid a debate over the role religion would play in the new nation. He made a fateful decision which ultimately determined that religion would play a large role in government, and vice versa. He made a deal with the religious parties at the time, which were orthodox, to leave things as they

47

were under the British Mandate for the time being in what came to be known as the Status Quo Agreement. In effect this set in stone the Israeli model of an established church. Religion was not important to Ben-Gurion, as opposed to Zionism, and the orthodox establishment, which played only a minor role in the creation of the Jewish state, was politically weak and of minor significance, but was just substantial enough to give him the ability to govern without any competitors in his government.

To further guarantee their political support against his opponents, he agreed to not only exempt their ultra-orthodox students from military service, but that the government would allow them to have a separate school system financed by it and, in addition, the government would find a way to support them during their studies. That grant of special privilege to the Haredi enabled the ultra-orthodox establishment and its population to blossom and grow to the powerhouse it is today. As Avishai notes: "It just never occurred to him [Ben-Gurion] that these Orthodox rabbis could eventually constitute a danger." That danger was on full display on July 17, 2010 when Chief Sephardic Rabbi Shlomo Amar threatened to bring down Netanyahu's government if a conversion Bill he favored was not enacted.

From the beginning religion and government was intertwined. Judaism in effect became the state religion; the Orthodox Chief Rabbinate was given legal control of all things Jewish, including marriage, divorce and burial. Jews in Israel had no choice but to follow the precepts of the Chief Rabbinate, that is if they wished to participate in Jewish social customs and practices. In 1953, the Knesset enacted the Rabbinical Courts Jurisdiction Law which set up a nationwide system of government-financed orthodox

Rabbinical Courts to handle the religious matters of Jews. As a concomitant, there would be no provision in law for a civil marriage. If a Jew did not want to be married by an orthodox rabbi, or could not get married in Israel at all because he or she was marrying someone not considered Jewish according to Hebrew law, Halacha, then they had to go to Cyprus or some other foreign country to get married. Israel's law, however, did recognize and validate such overseas marriages. The Jewish Religious Services Law was passed by the Knesset to set up a Minister of Religious Affairs in the government. Then there was the Festival of *Matzot* (Prohibition of Leaven) Law to fix the rules for the type of bread that could or could not be sold on particular festival days. That law also enabled enforcement by creating positions of inspectors, and levying related penalties for non-compliance by both Jews and non-Jews. Other laws were enacted prohibiting the import of pork or other non-Kosher foods and providing for observance of the Sabbath.

Religious political parties -- daily consultation with the rabbi

Political parties were established to promote the interests of particular streams of Judaism. In the first Knesset, the religious parties held 16 of the 120 seats. That number fluctuated over the years and touched a high of 27 in 1999, and today, it is at 19. Though they never formed the largest group, they have wielded a disproportionate influence because of their frequent "king maker" role—their votes putting one or the other of the larger parties on top. As a consequence they have been rewarded with a similar disproportionate part of the budget for their religious constituencies. In the present 32nd Government formed by Benjamin Netanyahu in March of 2009, he accepted into his coalition the three religious parties. Of his 74 Knesset vote majority (61 votes required to form a majority in the 120 seat legislature), the religious parties constituted 19 (Shas: 11; United Torah Judaism: 5; The New National Religious party, also called The Jewish Home: 3).

The largest of the three religious parties is Shas which is described in the Knesset website as a Sephardic-Haredi party. Sephardi are the Jews originating primarily from Middle Eastern countries, dating back to the expulsion of Jews from the Iberian Peninsula. Rabbi Shlomo Amar as Chief Sephardi Rabbi often speaks for the party and Rabbi Ovadia Yosef is its spiritual leader.

Shas had eleven candidates elected to the Knesset in 2009 and Netanyahu appointed four of them to his cabinet, including the Minister of Internal Affairs, Eliyahu Yishai, who is also one of four Deputy Prime Ministers; the Minister of Housing and Construction, Ariel Atias; the Minister of Religious Services, Yakov Margi; a Minister Without Portfolio, Meshulam Nahari; and a deputy Minister of Finance, Yizhak Cohen.

Shas' top demands in the various governments have been primarily financial - the increased funding for its haredi yeshivas and greater allowances for haredi children and men-students. As a member of Shas' Council of Torah Sages, Rabbi Shimon Baadani, was quoted as saying:

> *"For us these elections are in favor of the yeshivas, the ultra-Orthodox junior schools, the mikvahs [ritual baths] -- so how can we be indifferent? Our job in the Knesset is to stop the destruction among the people of Israel, and therefore we allow ourselves to enter this 'golden calf.' Otherwise, what do we have to do with the legislative body? The Torah of Israel is our law."*

Shas' spiritual leader, Rabbi Yosef, however, has expressed a boarder agenda. It is to Rabbi Yosef that each of the Shas Ministers report each day for instructions as to the performance of their duties. At his August 28, 2010 weekly sermon at a synagogue near his Jerusalem home, he was quoted by both *Haaretz* and the *Jerusalem Post* as wishing death on Palestinian Authority President Mahmoud Abbas and all the Palestinians.

> *"Abu Mazen [Abbas] and all these evil people should perish from this world. . . . God should strike them with a plague, them and these Palestinians."*

Shas also insists that Jerusalem remain always united under Israeli rule.

The United Torah Judaism is also an ultra-orthodox or Haredi party, but this one is Ashkenazi, which comprises those Jews who have descended from the Jews of Western and Northern Europe. UTJ has two branches, one is Hasidic and the other is non-Hasidic. It also is primarily interested in the financing of its institutions, child allowances and maintaining Israel's sovereignty over Jerusalem. In addition, it emphasizes the expansion of Israeli settlements in the West Bank. Its spiritual leaders are two men, one who is 100-years-old and the other in his nineties, Rabbis Yosef Shalom Eliashiv and Aharon Shteinman.

Like the other ultra orthodox parties, being educated is not a requirement for high office. Netanyahu appointed the head of the Agudat Israel branch of the UTJ faction, Yaakov Litzman, who was born in Germany and grew up in Boro Park, Brooklyn, as his Deputy Minister of Health. Litzman's biography on the Knesset website states that he has had only a high school

51

education plus "yeshiva studies." But it is not as if an ultra orthodox government minister makes any decision on his own, as the piece on Litzman in *Wikipedia* notes, "he consults the Gerre Rebbe on a daily basis."

Finally, there is the New National Religious party, which is orthodox but not ultra-orthodox and is referred to as a religious Zionist party. Likewise it supports the same right-wing and nationalist policies that the other religious parties maintain.

Since they have been part and parcel of numerous governments, the religious parties have necessarily participated in purely civil issues as well, and consistently have maintained right-wing positions on them.

"Who is a Jew?"

The consequences of this mixing of church and state are evident in every aspect of daily life in Israel. I will take one issue as an example—the heated debate currently consuming the government over what appears to be the religious question of "Who is a Jew?"

To American ears this sounds at first little silly, but in Israel the bitter religious and political battles over the question are far from academic. At times the dispute even threatens to bring down a government.

The significance of the question: "Who is a Jew?" relates both to the material benefits of being Jewish in Israel as well as to a person's religious practices. The material benefits of being Jewish are substantial as many laws favor Jews and the society, including landlords, sellers of property, school administrators, hotel keepers, etc., also favor Jews. In addition, for immigrants to

52

Israel, the material benefits begin with something called the "absorption basket."

The websites of the Israeli Ministry of Foreign Affairs and that of the Ministry of Immigrant Absorption at the time of this writing describe in detail, what they caution as applies generally and could be modified in particular cases, the "absorption basket" for immigrants:

> *"The Law of Return states that every Jew, his/her spouse, his children and grandchildren and their spouses are entitled to immigrate to Israel . . . ."*

A Jew immigrating to Israel is called an "olim," and the process is called "aliyah." The benefits of the immigration package begin upon arrival at the airport and extend for different periods of time, some for three or five years, depending on the service being offered. The assistance covers the whole gamut of a person's needs for integration into society: financial, social, educational, cultural, occupational, and religious. Olims receive temporary living expenses and rental payments; guidance in finding housing and subsidized mortgages when a house is found; training and employment placement services; Hebrew classes; tuition assistance for minors; wage subsidies in many cases for up to six months; etc. In addition, the Jewish Agency and the private organization that the government partly funds, Nefesh B'Nefesh (incidentally, a charitable tax-exempt organization in the U.S.) also pays the air fare for the olim from his/her country of origin to Israel.

Between 1989 and 2004, according to Israel's Ministry of Immigrant Absorption, there were, in round numbers, about 1,200,000 immigrants to Israel, with approximately 960,000 of that number, or 82%, coming from areas of the collapsed Soviet Union. Of the rest, Western Europe accounted for 46,500; North America, 42,000: Latin America, 33,000; Africa, 63,000 with 56,000 of those being Ethiopians; and Asia, 13,000.

During the mass Soviet migration the standards for entry under the Law of Return were broad and flexible, with almost anyone claiming to be Jewish being admitted. They became citizens and received the "absorption basket" benefits. Likewise, though with more of a struggle, the same process occurred for most of the immigrants from Ethiopia.

But there also appear to be many thousands of Ethiopians, and perhaps people from other countries, who were allowed into Israel but were for some reason not admitted under the Law of Return. They therefore, are not citizens and do not receive the benefits of the "absorption basket." These people are perhaps the most desperate and are waiting with increasing frustration and anger for their conversion and entry into Israeli society.

Yet another category of residents are people who did not immigrate to Israel to settle but nevertheless are in Israel legally, one way or another. These are not Jews under either the Law of Return or according to Halacha. Most in this category are the approximately 300,000 foreign workers who entered on work visas, primarily from Thailand, China, the Philippines, and other South Asian nations. Some of them may have become illegal residents, having stayed beyond expiration of their visas but still working for employers taking advantage of the workers' even more vulnerable status.

Finally, there is another group of residents which is rarely mentioned in the papers or by the government, and perhaps constitutes the most desperate one. It consists of the people from lower Africa who have apparently been moving north through the Egyptian borders into Israel seeking work and a more prosperous life. Estimates of the number of these Africans that appear in the newspapers is about 155,000. Though they have been for the most part under the radar, they too have now been determined as yet another "existential threat" to Israel. To fight this newly-discovered threat, Israel has brought in the "usual suspects" of defensive weapons. The government has authorized and funded yet another wall, this one along 240 km (150 miles) of the Israeli/Egyptian border, to the quiet annoyance of the Egyptians. Netanyahu, at a July, 2010 Cabinet meeting, in pressing for faster construction of the wall, which apparently is under the jurisdiction of the Defense Minister, Ehud Barak, is quoted as saying that these infiltrators threatened the democratic and Jewish nature of the state.

Incidentally, the presence of 155,000 black "infiltrators" in the State of Israel makes one wonder about the rationale for the wall the Israelis built between Israel and the West Bank. It was supposedly to keep out the suicide bombers, and not just another tactic to take more land from the Palestinians. If 155,000 people from Africa could slip across Israel's borders, then thousands and thousands of less identifiable Semitic Arabs could easily have infiltrated as well, if they so wished—Wall or no Wall.

The Soviet immigrants and religion

The issue of "who is a Jew" became particularly relevant as a result of the mass Soviet and to a lesser extent, Ethiopian migration into Israel. Newspapers now refer to 350,000 Israelis from the former Soviet Union who have not been recognized as Jews according to Hebrew law, Halacha. This would suggest that of the 963,000 people from the Soviet Union who emigrated to Israel between 1989 and 2004, close to two-thirds qualified as Jews not only for the Law of Return (his or her mother was verifiably Jewish), but also according to Hebrew law. This figure may not be entirely accurate as a portion of those making up the two-thirds may have again moved from Israel to Europe or the Americas. Figures on this double migration are not available.

In any event the newspapers and politicians refer to 350,000 Jewish citizens who are not Jews in the eyes of the Chief Rabbinate and therefore cannot practice their professed religion—at least as far as marriage, divorce and burial are concerned. How many of these 350,000 give any thought or care about this religious impediment is difficult to determine from the newspapers. Many seemed to have joined much of the native secular Jewish population in just ignoring the orthodox establishment, going overseas, for example, to get married in such places as Cyprus (recognized by Israel), and not having a problem with being buried outside the fences of Jewish cemeteries. Whether it was because of these Jews who were not real or full Jews, or some other force, the politicians notwithstanding took up the matter of conversion and made it a national "make or break" question.

The conversion debate

The debate on conversion, and the underlying question of "Who is a Jew?" reached fever pitch around July, 2010. The Russian immigrants, most notably under the leadership of Avigdor Lieberman, presently Israel's Foreign Minister, and his political party, Israel Beiteinu (Israel Our Home), would like to ease the rules for conversion for themselves. The Chief Rabbinate, on the other hand, and the ultra-orthodox political parties, including

Shas under the leadership of Eli Yishai who is the current Interior Minister, and the United Torah Judaism, want to maintain the strict conversion rules, if not, make them stricter. All the Jewish parties, however, agree that whatever the new rules may be, they must exclude any possibility that the approximately 300,000 foreign workers from Thailand, China, the Philippines, and other countries who were brought in to replace the cheap labor force of Palestinians from Gaza and the West Bank after the latter had been locked out at the commencement of the Intifada, could find any way to convert to Judaism, become citizens and obtain the valuable "absorption basket" benefits.

This group has become particularly embarrassing to a Government which is trying to maintain a *Jewish* state. Now they have become a problem. Hundreds of children have been born to these foreign workers while they were in Israel. But by law once a female migrant worker, though originally "legal," becomes pregnant, she becomes "illegal," as does her child. So there are Cabinet meetings about what to do with these natural born residents: are they citizens, legal residents or illegal residents? Do we accept them because they are children, grew up here, speak Hebrew and behave like Israelis, or do we throw them out? The Cabinet meets and sets up committees to consider the issue. The committees studies and studies, then comes out with a recommendation that 400 of the children be deported with their families. The Cabinet accepts the recommendation and those children and their families are to get out within 21 days. Eli Wiesel, apparently living on some other planet, laments that the great and compassionate Jewish people could not possibly be throwing these children out into the street.

The additional estimated 155,000 illegal migrants from Africa that have sneaked across the Egyptian border into Israel have not even been part of the public discussion on conversion, perhaps because it is just too scary for the Israelis even to imagine that this wave of Africans would become part of the conversion question. At any rate this particular illegal group raises only questions of security, border guards, police and deportation in Israeli minds.

Avigdor Lieberman's Israel Beiteinu and the religious parties have made common cause on issues that unite them, primarily along the lines of right-wing nationalism, resistance to international pressures, hostility to Israel's Arab citizens and the aggressive development of settlements in the Occupied Territories. However, as the party representing the Russian-speaking Israelis is secular, uninterested in religious issues and even hostile to those religious rules which interfere with the lifestyles of its supporters, they would have to do a delicate dance with the religious parties also in Netanyahu's coalition in crafting a conversion law that would both ease conversion for the Russians but also at the same time maintain ultra-orthodox control over religion in Israel.

Notation of religion on everyone's ID card

There has been a separate but related battle on another front. It appears that the immigrants during the mass migration of Russians were entered into the Population Registry as Jews and likewise on their IDs. The Central Registry keeps detailed personal information about the citizens and residents of Israel, including religion, ethnicity and other characteristics. The ID cards which residents over 16 have to carry contains an abbreviated list of these characteristics, including the person's religion and ethnicity. The listing of individuals as Jews in both, the Population Registry and the ID cards also became entangled in the conversion debate.

The Chief Rabbinate, having come under the influence of the Haredi or the ultra-orthodox during the 80s and 90s, became stricter and stricter in allowing conversions or in recognizing them, whether performed by Orthodox, Reform or Conservative rabbis. People did develop mechanisms to avoid the increasing restrictions, but the Rabbinate fought back. Cases were brought to court that wound up in the Supreme Court. There came a time when the Haredi-controlled Rabbinate insisted on such greater adherence to an increasing number of Torah requirements or commandments, the 613 *Mitzvot* that the conversion process came to a virtual halt.

Successive governments have tried to resolve what people now considered to be a crisis. Ariel Sharon as Prime Minister, set up a special agency in his office specifically to handle conversions and get the process going again. He appointed a friend from one of the settlements in the West Bank, a religious Zionist Orthodox rabbi, Haim Druckman, as head of the agency. Druckman set up conversion tribunals or courts throughout the country staffed by orthodox rabbis, but these orthodox rabbis were religious Zionists, as distinguished from the ultra-orthodox or Haredi that controlled the Chief Rabbinate. They ran education programs, of at least one year's duration for each course, and then granted the prospects official government certificates of conversion.

That expensive and elaborate program, however, also did not settle the matter. The state conversion courts themselves became bogged down for different reasons including disputes about how orthodox or strict the lifestyles of the proposed converts would have to be before conversion could be granted. Rabbis were sent out to observe the daily lives of the prospects, noting what they ate, how they dressed, what they did or did not do on the Sabbath. Also there were never-ending disputes between the rabbis of the conversion courts and the more orthodox rabbis handling other religious matters.

A more significant impediment to Sharon's conversion strategy was the counter-attack by the Chief Rabbinate, now almost entirely controlled by the ultra-orthodox. Local rabbinate councils would not recognize many conversions as valid, not only Druckman's government-issued certificates, but many other conversions as well. The rejections, however, were not done in accordance with any system or guidelines, but on a case-by-case basis, increasing the frustration and confusion of people who thought they had already finished the conversion process.

People who had gone through a conversion, perhaps years earlier, would register to get married, only to be told that they could not marry because they were not Jews—their conversion was considered invalid by the rabbi, for one reason or another. Worse still, some who had already got married years earlier but unfortunately were now trying to apply for a divorce were told that they could not get a divorce, because they were not Jews, their conversions unbeknownst to them were invalid. Then there was the issue of burial. Families arriving with the body of their deceased loved ones were told they could not bury their relative in the Jewish cemetery for his or her conversion had been invalid.

In 2008 the Rabbinate took a bolder step and just simply declared that all of the government conversions, Druckman's and Sharon's government-financed and operated orthodox education and conversion process, were invalid and would not be recognized—an unknown number, perhaps between 10,000 and 30,000 by that time. A personal difficulty for some people had now become truly a national crisis. Confusion and frustration reigned.

During these developments the ultra-orthodox politicians who were in charge of the Interior Ministry and therefore were keepers of the Population Registry and the issuers of ID cards, decided to short-circuit the whole debate about conversion— they would merely not register these questionable converts as Jews or issue an ID identifying the holders as Jewish. Outrage ensued and soon resulted in cases before the Supreme Court. The Supreme Court ruled in 2005 that the Interior Minister was obligated by law to register anyone who reasonably claimed to be a Jew, as Jewish, making no distinction in types or locations of conversions.

The Interior Minister at the time was Eli Yishai, a member of the ultra-orthodox Sephardic party Shas. His response to the Supreme Court order was to ignore it, except it was reported that he did offer, in jest perhaps, to record these Rabbinate-rejected converts on their ID cards as "Jewish by High Court decision" so as to alert local Rabbinical Courts that these were not real Jews and so were not to be allowed to marry, divorce, etc.

So the outraged petitioners went to the Supreme Court again. The Court then ordered Yishai to register the converts as Jewish or be held in contempt. Incidentally, Eli Yishai accurately reflected the Haredi community as even though he was the Chairman of Shas, Interior Minister and one of four Deputy Prime Ministers, he had had only a yeshiva education: Yeshivat

Hanegev and Yeshivat Porat Yosef, studying the Torah and commentaries on it for his entire educational experience. The Ministry ostensibly complied, though similar complaints of the Interior Ministry's refusal to recognize conversions continued unabated. Even its ostensible compliance was not exactly in good faith. The disputed converts were registered in the Central Population Registry as Jewish but the Minister avoided what he considered the distasteful task of giving them identity cards identifying them as Jews when he knew in his heart they were not Jews. So he just eliminated the category of religion from the cards entirely. Now no one would carry an ID card with the word "Jewish" on them. So much for the unbelievers and the lost. But this was not a cause for concern. Policemen, clerks, soldiers, landlords, school administrators, just about anyone, would still be able to tell immediately if one was Jewish or not. This was because while every ID card stated the holder's date of birth in the normal manner, only Jewish holders had their birthdates listed according to the Hebrew calendar. In addition, Arab IDs listed the name of the person's grandfather, while the Jewish IDs did not. The ID card therefore still served its purpose in that respect.

The conversion Bill: MK Rotem

All of this, however, still left unresolved the conversion issue for approximately 350,000 immigrants of the former Soviet Union who had not yet undergone conversion for one reason or another. The thousands of Ethiopians and assorted others were also in the same position. For the former Soviet residents their party, Israel Beiteinu, now part of the Government, proposed to solve the problem with a bill introduced by Israel Beiteinu's MK David Rotem which was the result of two years of negotiations with the coalition party, Shas and their rabbis. This would have to be an extraordinary feat, as the Israel Beiteinu members were thoroughly secular and the Shas, ultra-orthodox, who didn't want the Russians in their country in the first place.

Rotem's bill, which kept changing its form periodically, attacked the stagnation in conversions by authorizing chief rabbis in every municipality to conduct conversion courses and to grant conversions, which only the rabbi granting the conversion could revoke. This initially seemed to please most observers as now there were many more hands to do the work. In addition, applicants now had a tremendous variety of choices, so in theory they could find a rabbi of their choice, with a conversion program suitable to their lifestyle.

However, the other bomb that was dropped immediately was obviously a price required by Shas, probably on top of promises of Israel Beiteinu's support for additional funding, was that the selected municipal rabbis would have to be authorized by the Chief Rabbinate, which would also now have exclusive jurisdiction over conversions. An unbelievable uproar arose over this provision. The ultra-orthodox would now have complete control, a monopoly over conversions. The Reform and Conservative streams, a small number in Israel but representing most of the Jews in the U.S., went up in arms and reacted as if it were the end of the world, at least, their world.

One side said that the multiplicity of rabbis would now enable freer conversions. The other side saw the end of a united world Jewry with the ultra-orthodox Chief Rabbinate calling all the shots. The American-Jewish community screamed the loudest, as 85% of American-Jews are Reform or Conservative, as opposed to the 85 to 90% Orthodox in Israel, and it feared that the government's putting control of the definition of a Jew in the hands of the ultra-orthodox would make them second-class Jews. An unprecedented letter to Israel's Ambassador to the U.S., Michael Oren, was drafted by U.S. Senator Ron Wyden of Oregon and circulated among Jewish senators for their signatures. Papers quoted Senators Frank Lautenberg and Carl Levin as signatories. It was not clear from newspaper accounts if the letter was finalized and sent, but the leaking of its existence and contents had the same effect. Likewise, Jewish members of the House of Representatives spoke out on the subject, all denouncing the bill in the strongest terms. Leading Reform and Conservative rabbis from the U.S. and the heads of the American umbrella organizations that raise great amounts of money for Israel each year, including Jerry Silverman of the Jewish Federation of North America, traveled to Israel to lobby against the bill.

Netanyahu, after a momentary delay, perhaps like a deer staring into a headlight, heeded the call from the Americans and announced that the Bill would not get to the Knesset, but if it did, he would make sure it was defeated. Lieberman, on the other hand, on behalf of the Israel Beiteinu pledged that the Bill would be voted on in the Knesset before that session ended on Wednesday, July 21, and that it would pass. Shas' Eli Yishai, after consultation with his spiritual leader, Rabbi Ovadia Yosef said the absence of a conversion law would pose "an enormous spiritual danger to the Jewish people." For his part, the Sephardic Chief Rabbi Shlomo Amar, after consultation with his Council of Torah Sages, announced said he would advise the Shas Knesset Members to quit the coalition government if the Bill were defeated.

For the purposes of my comparison, the story ends there.

64

I suspect the subject of conversion is actually more complicated than I have described above, and I may not have got all the details correct, and most certainly have missed many of the nuances, but it is enough to know that a deeply religious question was being decided by the civil government, something like King Henry VIII's setting up the Church of England as separate from the Vatican or the Spanish monarchs in the fifteenth century demanding that the Jews and Moors in newly conquered Andalusia either convert to Catholicism or leave.

What we have found in this review is that all the evils which our Framers, with remarkable foresight, sought to prevent with the First Amendment have flourished in Israel. And all the concerns that our Justices sought to avoid in their First Amendment decisions about the malignant effects on government and religion, and religious freedom, of mixing religion and civil government have played out with a vengeance in Israel.

Some may maintain that religious participation in government is natural for Jews, unlike Christians, because of the nature of the Torah which prescribes rules for day-to-day living. Curiously, this is the same contention made by Muslims about the Koran. This may or may not be true, I know next to nothing about the Koran or the Torah. But even if it were, there is still the question of whether it requires such total immersion by religion in the civil government as there is in Israel, and incidentally, in a number of Muslim countries; nor whether it is a workable formula in a pluralistic society. What I do know is that the Popes and kings from Constantine to George III also thought that Christianity required a union of church and state, only to be proved wrong by the great American Experiment.

Again, this inquiry is not to try to determine or demonstrate which is the better system. It is much simpler and depends on no special qualifications to make the comparison, almost just to be able to read newspapers. I cannot fathom why they are the way they are in Israel, or whether they can or should be changed or in what manner, but only that it is simply not anything like it is in the U.S. and that on this issue, religion and government, contrary to the claims of AIPAC, Israel and the U.S. do not share any "common core value."

Notes: pages 204.

4

HOUSING

"Home Sweet Home." "Home is where the heart is." "A man's home is his castle."

A person's home is basic to his or her life, as it is to the society he or she lives in. Likewise, the rights and privileges related to a person's home. Do citizens have the right to live wherever they want? Can they freely move from one place to another—go and come as they please?

In the U.S., the answer is an emphatic: **Yes**.

In Israel the answer is an equally emphatic: **No**.

Israel is a nation segregated by religion, with Jews living in Jewish towns and non-Jews, primarily Muslim and Christian Arabs, living in their own towns. Where there are Arabs and Jews in the same cities, mixed cities, because of the accidents of history or inevitable economic pressures beyond the control of the government or any community, they live apart from each other in their own neighborhoods.

In addition to the segregation, there is a very significant difference between the resources allocated by the government to Jewish areas as opposed to Arab areas, termed "sectors" in the language of the Israelis. Even though the rate of taxation for all citizens and residents is the same, the government spends significantly more money on housing in the Jewish sectors than in the Arab sectors. This pattern is mirrored in every other aspect of community development as well—roads, water, sewers, electricity, schools, hospitals, fire-fighting, etc. New towns are established for Jews, usually with financial incentives, but not for Arabs. Building permits to expand homes are freely granted to Jews, but not to Arabs. Arab towns that may have existed even before the state of Israel or which grew up by necessity after the movement of refugees caused by the war in 1948, are not "recognized" by the Israeli government so they receive no resources whatsoever, are not connected to the electric or water grids—though still taxed.

Segregation and discrimination by ethnicity and religion is the nature of Israeli society.

The American Way

Slavery in the U.S. was followed by many years of segregated living between black and white Americans. Eventually things changed, and there were landmarks along the way.

All three branches of the Federal government as well as the States of the Union each had a hand in the march to equality. Abraham Lincoln's Emancipation Proclamation was followed by Congress enacting and the States ratifying the Thirteenth and Fourteenth Amendments to our Constitution.

Slavery was abolished by the Thirteenth Amendment in 1865:

> *"1. Neither slavery nor involuntary servitude . . . shall exist within the United States, or any place subject to their jurisdiction."*
> *"2. Congress shall have power to enforce this article by appropriate legislation."*

In 1866, Congress passed the Fourteenth Amendment:

> "1. *All persons born or naturalized in the United States, and subject to the jurisdiction thereof, are citizens of the United States and of the State wherein they reside. No State shall make or enforce any law which shall abridge the privileges or immunities of citizens of the United States; nor shall any State deprive any person of life, liberty, or property, without due process of law; nor to deny to any person within its jurisdiction the equal protection of the laws.*
>
> . . . .
>
> "5. *The Congress shall have the power to enforce, by appropriate legislation, the provisions of this article.*"

Members of the Congress, with fresh memories of a bloody Civil War, passed laws to give effect to these constitutional provisions. Among those laws was the Civil Rights Act of 1866 which provided in part:

> "*All citizens of the United States shall have the same right in every State and Territory as is enjoyed by white citizens thereof to inherit, purchase, lease, sell, hold, and convey real and personal property.*"
> (Rev. Stats.§ 1978, later 42 U.S.C. § 1982.)

In 1870 Congress further provided that:

> "*All persons within the jurisdiction of the United States shall have the same right in every State and Territory to make and enforce contracts, to sue, be parties, give evidence, and to the full and equal benefit of all laws and proceedings for the security of persons and property as is enjoyed by white citizens, and shall be subject to like punishment, pains, penalties, taxes, licenses and exactions of every kind, and no other.*"

Jim Crow

The reforming energy of the Abolitionists and Radicals, however, soon gave way to the Jim Crow laws in the South and to neighborhood segregation ordinances in the cities of the North where the blacks had begun to migrate in large numbers from the South. The words of the Thirteenth and Fourteenth Amendments, beyond ending the formal institution of slavery, in many respects remained just words for decades.

But things slowly changed for an assortment of reasons.

In 1917, the U.S. Supreme Court rendered a landmark decision with respect to housing which gave powerful effect to the Fourteenth Amendment and some of the laws passed pursuant to it. The case, *Buchanan v. Warley*, 245 U.S. 60 (1917), involved an ordinance enacted by the City of Louisville, that was typical of laws in many other municipalities. It required segregation of the races in housing. It paid superficial respect to the Fourteenth Amendment's equality provisions by making the ordinance applicable to both whites and blacks equally, but it required segregation for the purpose of keeping the peace. The title of the Louisville law read as follows:

> *"An ordinance to prevent conflict and ill feeling between the white and colored races in the City of Louisville, and to preserve the public peace and promote the general welfare by making reasonable provisions requiring, as far as practicable, the use of separate blocks for residences, places of abode and places of assembly by white and colored people respectively."*

The ordinance forbade African-Americans from moving in or occupying residences on any block where a majority of the houses were occupied by whites; and equally forbade whites from doing the same on blocks that had a majority of black owners.

The ordinance was challenged in court and eventually reached the U.S. Supreme Court. The State in its arguments in support of the law, as reported in the Supreme Court's decision, maintained that the law was intended *"to promote the public peace by preventing racial conflicts; that it tends to maintain racial purity; that it prevents the deterioration of property owned and occupied by white people . . . ."*

Neither the arguments for racial purity nor promoting the peace, the Court in *Buchanan* held, were sufficient to deny the owners of property the rights and attributes guaranteed by the 14th Amendment and subsequent laws. The ordinance was in violation of the 14th Amendment.

State Courts, as required under the American system of Government, thereafter, followed the Supreme Court's ruling in invalidating local zoning ordinances which separated the races by allocating different areas for their residences, however "fairly located and equitably apportioned" (see, for example, decision of the North Carolina Court, *Clinard v. Winston-Salem*, 217 N.C. 119; 6 S.E.2d 867 (1940).

 To get around this prohibition on local government ordinances, proponents of segregation created the device of "restrictive covenants," clauses in deeds which prohibited the sale or lease of the property to a person of a different race. These were private agreements, they argued, protected by the common law "sanctity of contracts" principle, and were not government actions that would be covered by the 14th Amendment and related laws.

71

In 1948, this line of reasoning was shot down by the U.S. Supreme Court in <u>Shelley v. Kramer</u>, 334 U.S. 1 (1948), which held that the *enforcement* of these otherwise private agreements or clauses in *any* court would amount to state action and therefore were covered by the 14th Amendment. Of course, not being able to enforce the covenants in court would make them ineffective and useless. In that decision the Court wrote:

> *"It cannot be doubted that that among the civil rights intended to be protected from discriminatory state action by the Fourteenth Amendment are the rights to acquire, enjoy, own and dispose of property. Equality in the enjoyment of property rights was regarded by the framers of that Amendment as an essential pre-condition to the realization of other basic civil rights and liberties which the Amendment was intended to guarantee."*

The Civil Rights Movement

A slave unless he can come and go . . .

But it took 20 more years and the revolutionary activity of the Civil Rights Movement of the 1960s for the Court to take the next logical step. In *Jones v. Mayer Co.*, 392 U.S. 409 (1968), it ruled that when the Members of Congress and the ratifying States freed the slaves, they intended them to be truly free. But the black man, the Court reasoned, would not be free if a community could prevent him or her from going into it or from buying a house there. So long as *prejudice, custom or practice* could inhibit the exercise of his rights, there could be no freedom. The Court found that the 13th Amendment's Declaration of Freedom and the subsequent Civil Rights Act applied not only to the actions of a government body but to *private or individual actions* as well.

The Court in *Jones* extensively quoted from statements made in Congress by Senator Lyman Trumbull of Illinois, Chairman of the Judiciary Committee, who would later introduce what became known as the Civil Rights Act of 1866. The Senator said he believed that legislation was needed to give effect to the constitutional amendment abolishing slavery because notwithstanding the enactment of that amendment he nevertheless knew:

> *"that the men whose liberties are secured by it are deprived of the privilege to go and come when they please, to buy and sell when they please, to make contracts and enforce contract, I give notice that . . . I shall introduce a bill . . . that will secure to those men every one of these rights: they would not be freemen without them.* **It is idle to say that a man is free who cannot go and come at pleasure,** *who cannot buy and sell, who cannot enforce his rights . . . ."*
> [Emphasis added.]

The day after the Thirteenth Amendment was ratified by the required number of States, Senator Trumbull introduced what he called a *"more sweeping and efficient"* bill than those previously offered. The intent of the bill was to *"break down all discrimination between black men and white men."*

Justice Stewart, writing for the seven member Supreme Court majority in *Jones*, stated:

> *"Just as the Black Codes, enacted after the Civil War [by the Southern States] to restrict the free exercise of those rights, were substitutes for the slave system, so the exclusion of Negroes from white communities became a substitute for the Black Codes. And* **when racial discrimination herds men into ghettos and makes their ability to buy property turn on the color of**

73

their skin, then it too is a relic of slavery . . . . *At the very least, the freedom that Congress is empowered to secure under the Thirteenth Amendment includes the freedom to buy whatever a white man can buy, the right to live wherever a white man can live. If Congress cannot say that being a free man means at least this much, then the Thirteenth Amendment made a promise the Nation cannot keep."*
[Emphasis added.]

Thus, in America **a person is considered a slave if he or she is not free to come and go as he or she pleases**, to live where one wants—without regard to community attitudes or individual prejudices. The court's application of the 13th Amendment and its related laws to individuals and not just public bodies was based on the Amendment itself and the Civil Rights Act of 1866. In America, freedom trumps community opposition; it trumps custom and practice; it trumps society's prejudices.

At the same time as the Supreme Court was thus defining some of the contours of the Constitution, Congress was enacting the momentous Civil Rights Acts of 1964 and 1968—with the Court and the Congress acting in concert with Martin Luther King, Jr. on the Civil Rights Movement.

With respect to housing, Congress decreed in the 1968 Fair Housing Act (FHA), that:

> *"It is the policy of the United States to provide, within the constitutional limitations, for fair housing throughout the United States."*
> (42 U.S.C. 3601)

> *"[I]t shall be unlawful---(a) To refuse to sell or rent . . . or to refuse to negotiate for the sale or rental of, or otherwise make unavailable or deny, a dwelling to any person*

74

because of race, color, religion, sex, familial status or national origin. b) To discriminate against any persons in the terms, conditions, or privileges of sale or rental of a dwelling. . . because of race, color, religion, sex, familial status, or national origin."
(42 U.S.C. 3604)

The FHA's prohibitions on such discrimination apply to any "person," and is defined to include *"one or more individuals, corporations, partnerships, associations, labor organizations, legal representatives, mutual companies, joint-stock companies, trusts, unincorporated organizations, trustees, . . . receivers, and fiduciaries."*
(42 U.S.C. 3602 (d))

It is beyond any debate, therefore, that racial and religious discrimination in housing in the United States, either by the government or by private individuals and groups, is **both** illegal under laws and also against a **fundamental public policy**. This is a core American value, enshrined in its Constitution, its laws and now its customs and practices.

The Israeli Way

The logical place to start an examination of housing in Israel is with the agency that had been tasked with housing Jews in Palestine, the Jewish National Fund (JNF), also known as Keren Kayemeth LeIsrael (KKL). The JNF, a quasi-Israeli government agency, is peculiar to Israel and has no counterpart elsewhere.

Formation of the JNF

According to the website of the U.S. branch (subsidiary? associate?) of the JNF (curiously it has been granted tax-exempt status as a "charity" by the IRS so that contributions to it are tax-deductible, the resulting additional burden of taxes being shared by the rest of U.S. taxpayers). The JNF was formed by the Fifth Zionist Congress in 1901. Theodor Herzl had a dream of establishing a homeland for the world's Jews who had found themselves persecuted in nation after nation over centuries. That dream led to the formation of a Zionist movement to establish a homeland for the Jews of the world.

To that end the World Zionist Organization (WZO) at their Fifth Congress held in Basle in 1901 established an operational unit which they called Keren Kayemeth LeIsrael-Jewish National Fund (KKL-JNF). At its Sixth Congress, the WZO decided on buying land in Erez Israel, or ancient Palestine, for the Jewish homeland (rejecting Herzl's motion to establish the homeland temporarily in Uganda). The KKL-JNF was to be the land-agency for the WZO, acquiring land in Palestine for the settlement of the Jews. Its headquarters moved several times over the next 20 years until it settled in Jerusalem, where it is now.

In 40 countries around the world today there is a legally chartered organization which calls itself the "Jewish National Fund" and each maintains its separate corporate identity under the laws of its respective countries. Each of these national JNFs, however, has as its main goal the raising of money in its own country which is then sent to an organization in Israel, also called the Jewish National Fund, for projects run in Israel by the Israel-JNF. Each of the 40 JNF's, including our tax-exempt entity in the U.S., considers the Israel-JNF, at various times in its literature and statements, as its World Headquarters, primary agent, agent, or partner.

Collision of the Dream with Reality

Over the next century the WZO realized Herzl's dream of establishing a homeland. But the actual execution of this dream on the ground has created something much more complex than a simple homeland for Jews. This has resulted from the fact that the territory chosen for colonization was not vacant—it was already occupied, mostly by Arabs whose families had lived there for generations, some for one to two thousand years. This clash of dream and reality produced what we now call the very complicated "Middle East crisis" that has bedeviled leaders of the world for over 60 years.

After the establishment of the State of Israel in 1948 the rationale for the continued existence of the JNF was re-examined, since Jews from all over the world were free to come and buy their own land under the Law of Return. But for various reasons it was finally decided to keep the JNF in existence as a special group within the State of Israel, a quasi-government agency, entrusted with the continuing task of raising money over the world and settling Jews on land in Palestine. This concept of a "National Institute," nominally separate from the government but with vast holdings of "national" lands and its extraordinary rights and privileges, which is held by no other organization, is not a familiar concept to Americans, so it requires additional reflection to appreciate the role of the JNF in Israel.

The JNF had owned about 500,000 dunams (a dunam is about a quarter of an acre) of land in Palestine in 1948. These were the properties purchased since 1901 with money raised by the JNF in small amounts (the "blue boxes") all over the world. The properties were leased to Jews, with ownership remaining with the JNF. Part of the Zionist philosophy was that land was to be held in perpetuity for the Jewish nation and not to be accumulated by individuals—so property was leased, not sold, for long-term periods, which were automatically renewable, to Jews who agreed to sublease them only to Jews. (This "lease-only" principle had exceptions and is now being modified so that land can more readily be purchased outright, rather than utilizing the fiction of being leased, though for indefinitely renewable periods.)

After the expulsion or flight of most of the Arabs from the area that then became the state of Israel in 1948, the Government expropriated the land of those Arabs, as well as those Arabs who moved out of their towns during the fighting but still remained in what later became Israel. Of that "abandoned land" it sold 2 million dunams to the Jewish National Fund in 1949 and 1953 (some say at bargain prices; others say at market value) to add to the JNF's holdings, so that JNF's total land ownership amounted to about 2,500,000 dunams, or 13% of the land in Israel proper. (The ownership of 2,500,000 dunams of land can be put in perspective by noting that the City of Tel Aviv covers only 52,000 dunams.) That percentage, 13%, has remained constant to this day (though the figure varies from 10% to 14% in the literature of various Israeli organizations).

Since the land transferred to the JNF by Israel in 1949 and 1953 consisted mostly of areas in cities, towns and villages that had been vacated by the Arab natives, these developed areas have become the most populated areas in Israel so that, by the JNF's own estimates, 70% of the Jewish population of Israel today, lives on lands owned by the JNF.

JNF Memorandum and Articles of Association

The organizing document for the entity in Israel called the Karen Kayemeth LeIsrael-The Jewish National Fund (the same as the name used in the U.S.), is its Memorandum and Articles of Association, 1954, (equivalent to our Articles of Incorporation and by-laws). That Memorandum describes its primary objective:

> *"to purchase . . . any lands . . . in the prescribed region [i.e. land under Israeli jurisdiction] . . . for the purpose of settling Jews . . . ."*

The Covenant

In 1961, the State of Israel entered into an agreement with the Israel-JNF called the Covenant, wherein it was agreed that a newly-established State agency, the Israel Land Administration ("ILA"), would *administer* the lands owned by the JNF. The newly-formed government agency, the ILA, would have 22 people on the board of directors, with 10 of those chosen by the JNF. The Covenant provided further that the lands of the JNF to be administered by the ILA would be "subject to the Memorandum and Articles of Association of Karen Kayemeth LeIsrael," i.e., the Covenant. The Memorandum, as noted above, of course provided that the land owned by the KKL-JNF would be distributed only to Jews.

The Adalah Challenge to the JNF

The JNF practice of discrimination against the Arab residents of Israel has been challenged in Israeli courts. In 2004, a civil rights group in Israel, Adalah, The Legal Center for Arab Minority

Rights in Israel, brought a lawsuit against the Israel-JNF and the Israel Land Administration (ILA) to prohibit it from continuing to offer land, houses and apartments only to Jews and not to Arabs. Its argument was essentially based on the contradiction between Israel's Declaration of Independence, promising equality of all its citizens, Arabs and Jews alike, and the practice of the JNF to provide land only for Jews.

The JNF's Legal Argument

The Israel-JNF answered the lawsuit with the argument that it held land not for the benefit of all Israelis, but only for Jews. It did not deny racial discrimination, but maintained that this was its purpose for being, even though it was now a quasi-government organization and in control of vast amounts of land.

In paragraphs 11, 12, 27 and 28 of its Response to the lawsuit (as translated by Adalah on their website: http://www.adalah.org/eng/jnf.php), the attorneys for the JNF spelled this out in simple and direct language:

> [11] *"The Basic Law. . . the Israel Lands Administration Law(1960) . . . and the Covenant signed between the state and the JNF in 1961 . . . recognized the separate and special status of the JNF, as well as the independent, private, and protected status of the JNF lands that are not part of state lands. The three abovementioned laws and the Covenant assign to the ILA the obligation of administering JNF lands in accordance with its [JNF's] directives and Memorandum that establishes their use by Jews. The three laws intended that the separate existence of JNF lands should be preserved, through their special mission as lands of the Jewish people."*

[12] *"Whoever seeks to prevent the allocation of JNF lands solely to Jews must confront the assertions of these laws . . . . What is the purpose [of these laws] if JNF lands will be considered to be the same as all other state lands and will be marketed to any person, in complete opposition to the purpose of the existence of the JNF?"*

[27] *"The JNF will claim that it should not be obliged to allocate lands in its possession to non-Jews. . . .[T]he imposition of an obligation to allocate them to Jews and to non-Jews will not only disrupt and damage the organization's activities and tasks, but will also nullify entirely the special role of the JNF as the owner of an eternal possession of the Jewish people. The imposition of such an obligation would amount to a declaration of the illegality of the JNF. . . ."*

[28] *". . . [T]he JNF will demonstrate that its activities in purchasing land . . . for the benefit of the Jewish people, and in their allocation to Jews is in complete accord with the founding principles of the state of Israel as a Jewish state, and the value of equality, even if it applies to JNF lands, would retreat before this principle. . . ."* (Emphasis added.)

Thus the JNF, without embarrassment or hesitation, in court papers asserted that favoring Jews in the distribution of land in Israel was a superior principle to equality.

The Chairman of the Israel-JNF at the time, Yehiel Leket, in an affidavit presented in the case, confirmed that the Memorandum and Articles of Association for the JNF prohibited it from leasing or selling lands to non-Jews (Affidavit in Hebrew but partly translated in related *Haaretz* Article dated 01/28/05).

81

The Attorney General's Response for the ILA

In response to the suit on behalf of the ILA, the Israeli Attorney-General , Menachem Mazuz, in February of 2005 belatedly, after 60 years of government-housing discrimination against the 20% of its citizens who are Arabs (mostly Muslim, with some Christians and others), surprised everyone by agreeing with the petitioners. He stated that the Israeli government, in the form of the ILA, could not discriminate between Arab and Jewish citizens in the management of land sales and leases.

The Attorney-General was not, however, being original or liberal, as he could have expected where the Supreme Court would be going if it were forced to rule. The Court in 2000, had already found in the case of *Qa'adan v. Israel Land Administration* that the ILA could not discriminate between Jews and Arabs in the leasing or selling of <u>state</u> lands. It was not much of a step to find that state lands and lands owned by JNF were equivalent, as they were in law and in fact in many ways already.

This was a democracy, he declared, and all citizens were equal. This was headline news in Israeli and foreign newspapers.

. . . The A.G.'s Legal Loophole

This was good copy for the international press. But like the *Qa'adan* case it would mean nothing and was more of the Israeli make-believe because in his next breath the Attorney-General noted that while the *Government* and its agencies, like the ILA, were subject to the laws mandating equality of all citizens, *private* groups and individuals, such as the JNF, were under no such restrictions in Israel.

He therefore immediately proposed that the obstacle he had just presented with his opinion could be circumvented by some kind of exchange of lands between the ILA and the JNF. He suggested, for example, that whenever an apartment or piece of land owned by the JNF and administered by the ILA was requested by an Arab and the Arab was otherwise entitled to such under the rules of that particular tender, then the Arab would be given the land. But immediately an equal amount of land owned by the ILA (not clear if in size or value) would be transferred to the JNF. That way the JNF could stay true to its mandate of selling or leasing only to Jews and the government would stay "true" to its value of equality.

The Israeli Supreme Court, as is its wont, was more than happy to immediately accommodate the Attorney-General's attempt to make the lawsuit moot. It agreed to postpone the case until the Government and the JNF could negotiate a satisfactory land swap mechanism and resolve the issues raised by the case.

Five years later the suit is still suspended, and nothing changed on the ground — Arabs can still not get apartments, houses or land in Jewish areas owned by the JNF, which means most of the developed areas of Israel.

As important as Adalah's lawsuit is, however, I must note that even if they had won and the Israeli Supreme Court held that the Government of Israel could not discriminate in leasing or selling JNF land or housing, it would not have changed matters very much, just as the *Qa'adan* case had not changed anything.

This was because such *government* discriminatory practices are only one of the myriad of obstacles faced by Arabs who try to buy or lease land in most of Israel. One of those endless mechanisms reflecting the prejudices or customs of Israeli society, for instance, is the routine finding by the local city or

83

town screening body that the applicant is simply "not suitable" for the community. This is the community prejudice which the U.S. Supreme Court had found illegal in its 1968 ruling, *Jones v. Mayer Co*. but which is intrinsic to Israel.

As Bernard Avishai in *The Hebrew Republic* notes:

> *"So the message to Arabs has remained pretty much what it always was. If you intend to live in the big cities, you're taking your chances on finding a willing landlord. If you intend to live in veteran towns and settlements, you had better be prepared to go to court. If you intend to apply for new housing, in the developments populating Jerusalem, he Negev, or the Galilee, you had better forget about it."*

The Attorney-General's "get around the law" proposal was immediately and enthusiastically embraced by the JNF. The Chairman of the World or Israel-JNF at the time, Yehiel Leket, welcomed the proposed solution to this *"dilemma"* and assured everyone that *"many of these problems can be resolved practically without recourse to the courts, because legal decisions . . . only exacerbate the situation."* Some kind of exchange program, he suggested, could be negotiated with the government so that the JNF, as a private company not obliged to adhere to the principle of equality for all citizens, could continue to lease or sell its properties only to Jews (from the Israel-JNF website, see its Press Releases dated October 13, 2004, March 6, 2005, August 1, 2006 and September 1, 2006 and its Policy Paper explaining its position on the lawsuit: "Jewish People's Land.")

In the United States, the President of the U.S.-JNF at that time, Ronald Lauder, and the Chief Executive Officer, Russell

Robinson, likewise supported finding a solution to this newly-discovered "technical" difficulty along the lines proposed by the Attorney-General of Israel. They issued a "Special Report" to their members to clarify the controversy surrounding "our continued ownership of land in Israel" created by "a recent court action by Arabs. . . ." In the Report they stated:

> "Providing land for Jews in Israel was JNF's main focus long before the State of Israel was created. . ."

> "JNF however is a private organization that owns 13% of Israel's total land. . "

> " JNF is caretaker of the land held in trust for Jewish people everywhere. A legal order that forces a lease of JNF land to a non-Jew would essentially mean that JNF's land has been nationalized. . . ."

To summarize the JNF's position: we have the lawyers for the Israel-JNF and the World Chairman of the JNF in their written response to the lawsuit claiming that to require the JNF to sell or lease land to non-Jews, that is, subjecting the JNF to the principle of equality, "would amount to a declaration of the illegality of the JNF . . . ." In tandem, the leadership of the JNF in the U.S. issued a statement about "our continued ownership" of land in Israel and argued that the imposition of the principle of equality on the JNF would mean that the JNF's land "has been nationalized."

The JNF Bill

A second tack to avoid the conflict exposed by the Adalah lawsuit between the principle of equality, which the Supreme Court felt was somewhere in the laws of Israel though it was not sure exactly where, and the requirement in the JNF's

85

Memorandum and Articles of Association restricting JNF lands to Jews only, was a proposed law called the "JNF Bill." It was quickly and with little debate passed with overwhelming majority by the Israeli Knesset (64 to 16; preliminary approval—but it is still sitting on the shelf). The proposed law would simply mandate that:

> "*Despite whatever is stated in any law, leasing of Jewish National Fund's lands for the purpose of the settlement of Jews on these lands will not be seen as improper discrimination.*"

This approach, however, was considered by many in Israel to be a bit too tacky. It was unnecessarily direct and too easy for the international community to understand. If a solution could be found to maintain the status quo while at the same time ostensibly show respect for the democratic principle of equality, why embarrass the country internationally with another law specifically approving racial discrimination? The problem, they reasoned, was a "technical" issue that could be finessed without resorting to new laws that would be criticized abroad. (See, e.g., editorial in the *Haaretz Daily*: "A racist Jewish state," July 20, 2007.)

Yet one person who was not embarrassed by the heavy-handed "JNF Bill" was the President of the U.S.-JNF at that time, Ronald Lauder. In a statement issued on July 20, 2007, and appearing on the US-JNF website, in support of what even some in the Israeli Press were calling a "racist" law, he said:

> "*We are gratified that the government of Israel, which since 1961 has been entrusted with management of JNF land through the Israel Land Authority (ILA), recognized that*

86

the land purchased by the Jewish people for the Jewish people should remain in the hands of its rightful owners. . . ."

A Jewish-Israeli commentator reflected upon this JNF controversy:

> *"Israeli democracy is careful not to talk about the constitutional status of the Arabs within its borders.* **It has established a devious system of laws and regulations to expropriate from them rights reserved only for Jewish citizens,** *and even for Jewish non- citizens. The real estate laws are an example of this, as are the actions of the Jewish national Fund and the Jewish Agency, which behave as if the state were only for Jews."* (Emphasis added.)

The Negev Project

A prominent example of the favoritism exercised by the Israeli government towards people, who are Jewish over non-Jews with respect to housing, is the current government program to populate the Negev with more Jews.

The Negev is a large desert region in southern Israel. The JNF, in conjunction with the Israeli government and other partners, has targeted the Negev for the establishment of a significant number of exclusively-Jewish communities in what they consider to be the next phase of the development of Israel.

Just as the JNF had been the primary force to populate with Jews the lands emptied of Arabs by the Jewish armies and Government in 1948 and its aftermath, so too now it is gearing up its world operations to play again the main role in populating with Jews the Negev region of Israel, which the government is now trying to empty of its native Bedouin population.

The Negev, before the founding of the State of Israel in 1948, had been occupied primarily by a pastoral-nomadic group of Arabs called the Bedouin. Their herding way of life necessitated large amounts of desert land about which they could move their livestock. The Israeli government decided that it did not want the Bedouin Arabs to use so much land. So from the 1950s, the government has been trying to drive the Bedouin into a small triangle of land near Beersheba in the southern part of the Negev, reducing the land on which the Bedouin are allowed to live to about 10% of what they had originally occupied. Without the expanse of space in the desert that is needed to tend to their livestock, and crowded into a small enclave, these Bedouin have for the most part ceased to be who they were.

Thus, in one move, just by an announcement, the Israeli government "unrecognized" and demolished all the villages and towns established at any time by the Bedouins in the Negev. This was a process which Israel has been carrying out for years at what seems like a random and haphazard pace. The government, in addition, established seven townships near Beersheva, what it calls the "recognized towns," into which it has been trying, with uneven success, to relocate all of the Bedouin. It is planning to create a total of 13 such towns into which it hopes eventually to concentrate all of the Bedouins.

The process of gathering up all of the Bedouin and moving them into the ghetto towns prepared for them by the State of Israel is always described in JNF and Government literature and websites as generous and benevolent efforts to better the lives of the Bedouin. Only if the Bedouin would move into these Israeli-created towns would they have all the conveniences of modern life—schools, running water, hospitals, etc., though these towns

88

right now are little more than shanties. Every time the JNF mentions developing the Negev for Jews, it also notes how its efforts are at the same time benefiting the native Bedouin.

The only problem with these claims of benevolence, however, is that the Bedouin do not see it that way at all. Rather, they see it as an attempt to destroy their way of life and steal their land from them. Many Bedouin have resisted these forced transfers in their own ways. For example, in June of 2010 19 Bedouin were arrested for attacking Jewish National Fund staff and damaging their property. In July of 2010 the Israelis demolished the "unrecognized" Bedouin village of al-Arakib; 45 structures housing 800 people, their water tanks and generators and scattered their cattle. For their part, the JNF and the Government depict those Bedouin who have resisted moving into the separate townships as people who are poor, uneducated, ill and living unhealthy lives—but on too much land. The Israelis refer to the land on which the un-corralled Bedouin live as "the dispersal," implying that the amount of land being used by these people is just too much.

In the 1950's the Israeli Army had simply pushed by brute force many of the Bedouin off their lands into their Beersheba enclave. Today, the times require more sophisticated methods. So the Israeli government is demanding that the Bedouin produce **documentary** proof of their legal ownership in the form of deeds and formal registration in the land records—something the Israeli government knows does not exist. The Ottomans for centuries and the British during their brief Mandate period pretty much stayed out of the desert. Neither kept any detailed ownership records for the Negev—desert land that was seemingly owned in common by various nomadic tribes. Now the Israelis are demanding such non-existent land records to prove ownership. (For general treatment of the issue, see Human Rights Watch Report dated March 30, 2008.)

Surprisingly, there are some Bedouin who have come up with enough paperwork at least to try to fight the evictions and demolitions in Israeli courts with the assistance of human rights organizations. This has somewhat slowed the Israeli plan to "clean up" the Negev. But considering the history of Israeli Supreme Court decisions that have for the most part ultimately sanctioned whatever the Government has done, most observers doubt anything significant will result other than some delay.

The Government's frustration in trying to clear the desert of the Bedouin is evident in an item from the Israeli Ministry of Foreign Affairs' current website (http://www.mmi.gov.il). Unless you are a Bedouin, the article by the ILA about its Negev Project is unintentionally funny. It scolds the Bedouin for not listening to reason; for not seeing the wisdom of just taking the wildly-generous gifts of money, housing, etc. being offered by the State; for not jumping at the unbelievably-generous offers if the Bedouin would just leave the Negev—where in any event they are illegal "squatters" on land owned solely by the State of Israel. Under the caption: "Background" for the ILA's Negev Project, for instance, the ILA sets out the problem as it sees it:

> *"The Bedouin population of the Negev is 155,000, of which 60% lives in seven permanent townships, and the remainder in illegal homes spread over hundreds of thousands of dunams (these scattered Bedouin localities are referred to as the Bedouin 'dispersal')."*
>
> . . . .

90

> *"In recent years, some of the Bedouin residing in the dispersed area have started claiming ownership of land areas   totaling some 600,000 dunams . . . in the Negev -- over 12 times the area of Tel Aviv!"*

In other words, these Natives are just taking up too much land! This is the Indian Removal Project, but playing out in the Negev and not in 1830, but in 2010. Today this type of activity is called "ethnic cleansing" and not looked upon favorably by civilized nations.

On the U.S.-JNF website in 2007, there was a message posted from Ronald S. Lauder, the then President of the U.S.-JNF:

> *"Jewish National Fund has embarked upon a challenge, a long term vision. The   government of Israel has turned its focus to the Negev, and **we are playing a major role**. Alongside the government and together with KKI,* [he sometimes refers to the World or Israel JNF by its other name] *and other partners, our goal is to cultivate the Negev into a hospitable, habitable, profitable environment to improve the quality of life of its current residents* [the Bedouin] *and become home to a new generation of Israel's* [Jewish] *citizens."*

>   . . .

> *"Blueprint Negev allows us to be **21st century pioneers** and to once again be part of a nation under creation. **New suburban communities** are planned; seven are already established. Residents of Sansana, Garouv, Shomria, Givot Bar, Be'er Milka, Kmehin, and Merhav Am, the newly established communities, give testament to these ideals."*

He may not have intended to allude to the 1830's era, but his enthusiasm in being a "*21st century pioneer*" gives him away.

While they SAY that the project is for the benefit both of the present, the Bedouin, as well as the new, the Jewish, residents, ALL of the developing communities he mentions, are for *Jews only*. Some were established by a unit of religious Jewish soldiers called the Nahal; some by other military units, or by the OR Movement. Only Jews primarily can serve in the military so the communities originally established by military units are for Jews only. The nature of the communities established by the OR Movement is explained on its website, http://eng.or1.org.il, There we are told that the OR Movement is in the business of working for an "*increase in the Jewish population*" in the Negev.

> "*The JNF Blueprint Negev and the OR Movement are working together in order to achieve that goal.*"

Bud Levin, the JNF's National Vice President for Campaign at the time, 2007, in a fundraising letter described the goal of "JNF Blueprint Negev" in somewhat less obfuscating language: "*ensuring a firm Jewish majority.*"

> "*JNF has pledged to be a leading partner in **moving 250,000,000 Israelis to the Negev** over the next five years, laying the groundwork to ensure the success of such an endeavor relieving the population pressure of the Tel Aviv corridor and ensuring a **firm Jewish majority** in the area.*"
> (Emphasis added.)

Part of decoding their messages is to remember that whenever the JNF and its allies talk about "Israelis" the mean only Jewish Israelis.

On the present (June 6, 2010) website of the U.S.-JNF, there is again a listing of some of the new communities being developed by the JNF: Zuqim, Sansana, Carmit, Be'er Milka, Giv'ot Bar, Haruv, Marche Am, Neveh and B'nai Netzarim. **Again, they are for *Jews only*.** See also the article in Wikipedia, "Blueprint Negev," as of June 6, 2010, for a description of the JNF's project.

The Galilee Project

The Arab population of Israel is concentrated in northern Israel, with an Arab mass in Galilee, including the city of Nazareth. The government of Israel has wanted to change that since 1948. Grandiose efforts are still continuing. On the current website of the Israeli the Jewish Agency for Israel, there is a question and answer list under the subject: "Galilee: Achievements and Challenges." Question number 6 reads as follows:

> "What is the demographic problem which faces the Northern Galilee?"

The answer provided by the Agency:

> "Majority of Arab population over Jewish population."

To the government of Israel, this is a problem.

The government's solution to this problem is to team up with government-funded private groups and other organizations around the world to bring more Jews to the Galilee area. The Jews from other parts of Israel would be encouraged with housing subsidies and jobs. For the Jews abroad immigrating to Israel, there would be generous financial and other multi-year support from the Ministry of Immigrant Absorption, something called the "Absorption Basket." According to the Ministry's website and that of Israel's Ministry of Foreign Affairs, the basket of benefits includes "pocket money" and bank checks (with enough money deposited by the government initially to meet living expenses for three months) issued to the immigrants at the airport, together with such documents as Identity Cards, citizenship papers; payment for their flight tickets; payment of their rent for 12 months; subsidized mortgage loans; assistance in obtaining jobs, vocational training and the like, and no payment of income taxes for 10 years.

Major partners for the government in this enterprise are such groups as the Jewish National Fund and Nefesh B'Nefesh. Nefesh describes its "Go North" project as follows:

> *"The 'Go North' program is the first ever formal initiative to populate Israel's northern region with English speaking Olim [Jewish immigrants].The program provides Nefesh B'Nefesh Olim who move to Northern Israel with enhanced financial assistance, as well as social and career support to ensure successful professional and social integration in their new communities.*
>
> *The 'Go North" program is expected to be a catalyst for change and expansion of Jewish communities in the Galilee . . . ."*

One of the first major efforts at the Judaization of the Galilee was the establishment in the 1950's of Upper Nazareth or Nazareth Illit. There had been a municipal election in 1954 in which the Communist Party, the only one espousing Arab interests, won a majority. This incited the government to confiscate about 300 acres of land from the city of Nazareth and its residents. The land was on the hill adjacent to old Nazareth and in the path of Nazareth's natural growth. Only Jews were allowed to live there and the Jewish Agency funneled immigrants to the new community. Nazareth Illit served a number of government purposes. In addition to populating the area with more Jews to counteract the numbers of Arabs, it also asserted in a very visible form, the superiority of Jews over Arabs, since it literally overlooked Nazareth.

But then there is the saying about "the best laid plans," etc. Today the "Jewish" town of Nazareth Illit is almost 20% Arab, and growing. Apparently, this was not JNF land but state land, property appropriated by the State of Israel from the Palestinians. The restrictions on lease of the land or apartments were contained in the mortgages and leases. But as the "Jews-only" clauses in the Jewish Agency mortgages obtained for the original occupants have run their course over 50 years, and since Old Nazareth had been deprived of any land for growth, there has been tremendous pressure from the Arab community in old Nazareth for housing. Thus, along those edges of the new town that are most adjacent to the old town there has been an incursion of Arab homeowners who find the well-maintained town very attractive as well. A growing number of Jews, ignoring the pleas of their neighbors, are abandoning Nazareth Illit—preferring to go to cities like Tel Aviv and getting out of this Arab-flavored environment, which included daily loudspeaker-calls to prayer, from early morning into the night.

Ironically, it was in a nearby Galilee town also set up for Jews-only but on JNF land, the town of Karmiel (Carmiel), where the young Arab couple, the Qa'adans, had generated the case discussed above that undressed the JNF. Unlike Nazareth Illit, apparently, the community in Karmiel was still infused with the Judaization ideal and adamantly has refused to lease or sell to any Arab. It also may have taken a more adamant course of action because its land is owned by the Jewish National Fund.

East Jerusalem

An examination of Israeli values with respect to the rights and privileges surrounding housing in East Jerusalem is technically beyond the scope of what I am doing since it is not part of Israel. I will assume that the AIPAC slogans about "shared core values" mean those principles exemplified among Israeli citizens and in Israel itself. East Jerusalem is not part of Israel and its Palestinian residents are not Israeli citizens. Notwithstanding Israel's claim that it has annexed East Jerusalem, the international community, including the U.S., does not recognize that. Numerous UN Security Council and General Assembly resolutions, joined in by the U.S., have repeatedly rejected that attempted annexation, calling the Israeli laws null and void as well as illegal under various international treaties, including treaties to which Israel is a party. Not that such conclusion has had any effect on Israel, or indeed on the U.S.'s continuing support of Israeli activities. In addition, most of the Palestinians in East Jerusalem rejected the offers of citizenship from Israel in 1967 when Israel acquired East Jerusalem by force.

The Palestinian residents of East Jerusalem for the most part, over 95%, refused to acknowledge Israeli sovereignty over their land which they would need to do by taking the required oath towards Israel. Israel therefore created the status of "permanent residents" for them, something akin to the residency granted to foreigners. This status, though a vulnerable one as Israel has been revoking that status for thousands of Jerusalemites in the past as part of its process to Judaize East Jerusalem, nevertheless gives the Palestinians the valuable rights to travel about Jerusalem and Israel and to work there as well.

However, there have been such extraordinary events occurring in East Jerusalem recently, that it deserves a quick look for what it may tell us about the nature and character of the Israeli government and society.

East Jerusalem ended up on the Jordanian side of the armistice line after the 1948 War and was administered by Jordan till the war of 1967 when it was occupied by the Israeli Army. International law and treaties to which Israel is a signatory, including the United Nations Charter and the Geneva Conventions prohibits a conquering nation from transferring its citizens to the land occupied by its armed forces. Nor do these allow the establishment of colonies on such conquered territories. Nevertheless, Israel has transferred over 200,000 of its Jewish citizens to East Jerusalem and established numerous colonies that allow residency only to Jews.

Leaving aside the fact that the U.S. has failed to ever take serious steps to restrain this outlaw-behavior, other than making periodic public complaints that have lacked any follow-up or consequences, for my purposes it is legitimate to ask, whether the values shown by Israel in this matter are shared by the U.S. Would Americans today find it perfectly OK to take over Toronto or Quebec or the Canadian cities along the Great Lakes together with their resources, declare them as part of the U.S. and then, set up communities for whites only? I think not.

Meron Benvenisti, an Israeli political scientist who had been Deputy Mayor of Jerusalem under Teddy Kollek from 1971 to

1978, anticipated that the Jewish colonization of East Jerusalem would be "ugly." In 1984, he correctly anticipated what the future held for Jerusalem:

> *"There will be a small Jewish majority (56 percent), but most of the Jewish population will remain in West Jerusalem, and therefore the countryside will be overwhelmingly Arab (86 percent).*

> *"The massive Israeli housing construction will erase the old demarcation line but will create scores of new demarcation line between homogeneous Jewish and Arab localities, a tribal map of alienated islands. The spread of Jewish localities will expand points of friction and will make alienation more noticeable to increasing numbers of Jews and Arabs. Interaction will be tenuous. . . .*

> *"Encounters in these places will be characterized by the clear hierarchy that prevails where the Jews are dominant and the Arabs subservient. The metropolitan area will, indeed, function as one unit only in the economic sphere. In all other spheres, it will function as a dual system. Jewish and Arab localities in close proximity will be subject to separate and unequal conditions: administrative, political, judicial, economic, ecological, infrastructural, and social.*

> *"Wherever they settle, the Jews carry the Israeli administrative, political, and welfare state system. They build their own high-level physical infrastructure and enjoy the generous subsidies that attracted them to the West Bank. Imbued with nationalistic pathos, they will monopolize the environment.*

> *"The Arabs will remain subject to the norms of the military government, disfranchised and discriminated*

against even when officially annexed to Israel (like the East Jerusalem Palestinian community) . . . . lacking proper physical infrastructure, fragmented and harassed, and powerless to shape their future or to resist further encroachment.

"This hierarchy of superiors and inferiors, a "horse and rider" coexistence, will prevail throughout greater Israel, but its ugly significance will be truly perceived only in the metropolitan patchwork of tribal enclaves."

Before leaving East Jerusalem, there are two items that deserve special mention: Sheikh Jarrah and the Lieberman Lie.

Sheikh Jarrah

In 1967 when Israeli soldiers marched into East Jerusalem, to the joy of Jews worldwide, they were able for the first time since 1948, to pray at the Western Wall. More than ten thousand of the seventy-thousand Palestinians of East Jerusalem had been born in the western or Jewish part of Jerusalem but had fled or been expelled from it during the war in 1948 and its aftermath. In 1956, 28 of those Palestinian refugee families had entered into agreements with the United Nations Relief and Works Agency (UNRWA) and the Jordanian Custodian of Enemy Property whereby they gave up their refugee status and the related benefits in return for land on which they subsequently built homes in an area of East Jerusalem called Sheik Jarrah. This property had belonged to a Jewish organization before 1948 and had been expropriated by Jordan as enemy property. The 28 families were still living there when the Israelis occupied East Jerusalem. By a new Israeli law that

99

property now in turn came under the jurisdiction of the Israeli General Custodian as property formerly belonging to the Jews. The families, however, were allowed to continue living there.

In 1972 a number of Jewish groups went to court armed with some documents from the time of the Ottoman Empire and claimed to have been the owners of that property before 1948. In 2009, they ultimately won their claims against two of the 28 families who were then summarily evicted by fringe-Jewish settlers who were acting as agents for the owners. The evictions were very physical and brutal, with people dragged out of their homes and their furniture thrown in the street—all in front of cameras and reporters, accompanied by extremist Jewish settlers moving their own furniture into the Palestinian homes with the assistance of the police and private security guards.

The evicted families, however, have not gone quietly into the night but have camped out on the street. They have since become the focus of almost daily demonstrations, arguments, and arrests. The Jewish groups and their agents have submitted various plans with the city which anticipates eviction of all of the 28 families, hundreds of Palestinians, and the erection of 200 housing units for Jews.

What has astonished commentators and observers, however, is not so much the turmoil of the evictions and the vicious street battles that have ensued, all too common as the Jewish settlers try to take over Arab Jerusalem, but the nature of the legal proceedings that resulted in the eviction of the four families, and the possible eviction of the remaining Palestinian families. The courts granted possession to the Jewish groups based on pre-1948, indeed, pre-1918, documentation from the period of the

Ottoman Empire. The Jewish litigants claimed that these old documents proved their ownership and thus their right to take possession.

It did not take long for Israelis of all persuasions to realize how dangerous this precedent could be. Even Israeli-Jews who wholeheartedly supported Israel's annexation of East Jerusalem expressed reservations and anxiety about this line of reasoning. Conservative Jewish professors and students from Hebrew University joined Palestinians and international activists in demonstrating against the evictions. It was all too unsettling. Many Israelis seemed to have been taken aback by this gratuitous, self-destructive and mean-spirited series of events—propelling former 1948 refugees back again into the status of refugees.

What all these good people feared perhaps more than anything else was the possible application of the rule that "what's good for the goose is good for the gander." If Jews could reclaim land based on pre-1948 documentation, then what about the millions of descendants of the 1948 Palestinian refugees who held Ottoman or British Mandate documentation in their hands for property in Israel and West Jerusalem, and some who even had the actual keys to their old houses? The "know-nothing" extremist settlers had rocked the boat, unwittingly giving new life to the Arab demands for the Right of Return.

Larry Derfner wrote in the *Jerusalem Post:*

> *"The government is defending the eviction of the two Palestinian families by saying the houses in Sheikh Jarrah, according even to Israeli courts, were owned by Jews before 1948. That's rich. . . . If Israeli*

*justice in 2009 means restoring pre-1948 Jewish property
rights in the Arab east Jerusalem neighborhood of Sheikh
Jarrah, what about pre-1948 Palestinian property rights
in the Jewish west Jerusalem neighborhood of Baka? Some
of those old houses in Baka look pretty 'Oriental' to me. If
we're going to evict the Hanouns and Ghawis to 're-
Judaize' one side of the Green Line, are we going to evict
the Cohens and Levys to 're-Arabize' the other side? Stay
tuned."*

Professor Zeev Sternhell over at the *Haaretz Daily* expressed his
unease at this attack on what he had hoped was the "finality" of
the War of 1948:

> *"The worst of these [illnesses] is the refusal to
> recognize the finality of the situation that was created at
> the end of the War of Independence., . . . [H]ow is it
> possible that state institutions will lend a hand to an act
> that destroys the very land under our feet? . . . .*

> *"The Jews [in the litigation] came to prove a
> principle -- land that was once owned by Jews is required
> to be returned to the hands of Jews. The question is, how
> much longer will it be possible to maintain a situation in
> which the Jews will have the right to demand ownership
> of Jewish property that has been left on the eastern side of
> the Green Line, while Arabs are forbidden to demand
> rights of ownership to their property that has been left on
> the western side of that same line?*

> *"After all, there are Palestinians, among them
> those who live in East Jerusalem, who have title deeds
> to homes in Talbieh, Old Katamon, Baka, and other
> neighborhoods in the western part of the city. If
> Jerusalem is a united city and all its residents, as the
> authorities claim, are equal before the law, on what moral*

basis can they decide that what is permitted to the Jews is forbidden to the Arabs?"

But the professor and his friends need not have worried. Like most people he was reacting to that already-mentioned ingrained principle of Western culture: "what is good for the goose is good for the gander." However, that principle, perhaps it can be called equality, does not apply in Israel. The Israeli government, including the courts, and in fact Israeli society as a whole, has no difficulty in living with inequality. Equality is not a value in Israel, though they nevertheless insist on repeating that it is: IsraelSpeak. Avishai quotes Rafi Cohen-Almagor, the director of democratic studies at Haifa University:

> *"Israelis do not really have a familiarity with the concepts of democracy. They know the mechanism, so when you ask them about democracy they will say something about majority rule, or balance of powers. But these mechanisms are not principles of democracy -- like liberty, fallibility, equality, tolerance. They are merely functions. Israeli kids hardly study principles."*

This inequality and discrimination begins with the laws of Israel. It is estimated that there are at least 30 laws that discriminate in favor of Jews as opposed to non-Jews (see, for example, the study by David A. Kirshbaum for the Israel Law Resource Center, February, 2007).

Relevant to what is going on in Sheikh Jarrah is one of these laws that was passed after the Occupation of 1967 and is called, innocuously enough, the "Legal and Administrative Matters Law of 1970." Pursuant to that law, Jews who owned property in East Jerusalem before 1948 have the right to reclaim that

103

property. However, Arabs who owned property in West Jerusalem before 1948 have no such right under this law, though they are entitled to compensation, which in fact has never been granted—more IsraelSpeak. Great sounding words and promises, but no delivery, nor was any ever intended. Israeli law is a one-way street. But Israelis really do not feel they need laws to dignify or disguise their discrimination. Even without that law, the Israeli courts have invented dozens of fictions and convoluted reasoning that have sanctioned things done by the Israeli government which even laws in Israel, much less those of the international community, would seem not to permit—they use the language and reasoning of IsraelSpeak.

The Lieberman Lie

Then, there is Lieberman. Not the current Israeli Foreign Minister, Avigdor Lieberman, who is a case in himself, but our own Senator Joe Lieberman, "Mr. Israel." When the dispute arose over the construction of 1,600 apartments for Jews in Arab East Jerusalem during Vice-President Biden's visit to Israel in March of 2010, Prime Minister Netanyahu kept saying that there was nothing wrong with having Jews live in Arab neighborhoods, just as Arabs could live in Jewish neighborhoods. Those absurdly false comments of course were met with ridicule in Israel, as every Israeli knows that Arabs cannot live wherever they want in Israel.

There are numerous layers of laws and bureaucracy, as well as customs and practices that prevent non-Jews from living in Jewish housing developments, Jewish towns or Jewish communities. In the immediate case at hand, Netanyahu was saying that Arabs from East Jerusalem could buy homes in Jewish West Jerusalem. This is simply false, and brazenly so.

By law only Israeli *citizens* have the ability to buy or lease property in West Jerusalem—and as everyone knows Palestinians in East Jerusalem are most definitely **not** citizens, they are "residents," having refused to recognize any sovereignty acquired by Israel's armed forces in 1967. All the land in West Jerusalem has been designated as "state property" administered by the Israeli Land Administration—which by law leases or sells *only to Israeli citizens*. But even if there was not that easy and well-defined obstacle, the Israelis could, and have, come up with half a dozen other ways to keep the Arabs out of Jewish neighborhoods in Jerusalem.

On hearing their Prime Minister saying things like that for the consumption of gullible foreigners, the Jewish residents of Gilo and Har Homa, two of the larger Jewish colonies also created in East Jerusalem, could only have giggled. "Imagine," they probably said to each other, "an Arab! Here!" One columnist wrote this about Netanyahu's comments:

> *"By Israel law, Arabs are effectively prohibited not only from building new homes but even from buying old ones in the Jewish parts of the city [Jerusalem]. . . . The system for Jews and Arabs in Jerusalem is not liberty, justice and equality. The system is separate and unequal, and this has been official policy in Israel's capital for 43 years."*

> *Another commentator said:*

> *"[C]ontrary to the spirit of Netanyahu's words, a Jew from Brooklyn is entitled to buy land in the East Jerusalem Arab neighborhood of Sheikh Jarrah, but a*

Palestinian born in Sheikh Jarrah is not entitled to buy an apartment in the Jewish neighborhood of Har Homa."

All of this is common knowledge in Israel, particularly in Jerusalem. Nevertheless, on the floor of the U.S. Senate, Senator Joe Lieberman defended the construction of the apartment units for Jews-only and uttered this argument:

> *"[T]he permits for this housing are in an area of Jerusalem that is today mostly Jewish. The Israeli Government has taken the position, however, since 1967 that anybody ought to be able to buy property and build and live in any section of Jerusalem they choose to regardless of their religion or nationality or anything else. That is a very American concept."*

Everyone in Israel knows that **everything** about Senator Lieberman's statement was either outright false or, at the very least, dishonestly misleading. Mr. Israel, being such an intimate observer of his "family" in Israel, certainly was aware of what he was doing.

The place where these units were being built, Ramat Shlomo, is not just a Jewish neighborhood in Jerusalem, as Lieberman claimed, as if it were another Boro Park in Brooklyn that had grown up naturally over the years as Jews congregated there. Rather it is a 1996 "made to order" colony, plopped down in the middle of Arab East Jerusalem and established specifically only for Jews, and only for ultra-orthodox Jews at that. Among its other oddities, Ramat Shlomo contains a perfect replica of the Boro Park headquarters of the Chabad Lubavitch in Brooklyn, 770 Eastern Parkway, a brick structure, sitting Disney-like among all the Jerusalem stone structures.

106

The "area" of Jerusalem that Senator Lieberman said was "mostly Jewish" is actually a defensively-walled-off enclave, surrounded by Arab neighborhoods, and forcibly carved out of Arab East Jerusalem by government expropriation of land from the Palestinian owners to settle only Jews on it.

This certainly is not an "American concept," and in fact would be repulsive to most Americans.

Senator Lieberman's brazen mendacity and his puppet-like repetition of the Israeli Prime Minister's lies on the U.S. Senate floor, in almost exactly the same language Netanyahu had used, and even dishonestly characterizing them as "an American concept," gives substance to many people's suspicions about the "dual loyalties" of some American-Jews. Why was he so shamelessly lying to the American people? And on the floor of the Senate? He was doing the work of Israel, and not of America.

Notes: Page 214.

5

FREEDOM OF SPEECH

The Media in Israel certainly seems to enjoy the kind of freedom from apparent government interference that would be envied by journalists in most of the rest of the world. Writers and commentators pursue even the highest political leaders for their corruption, as they did relentlessly the Prime Ministers Ariel Sharon and Ehud Olmert, down to President Moshe Katsav and numerous others. Editorials insult members of the inner cabinet by calling them idiots. The country is labeled a Shin Bet (secret police) state and one where fascism was crowding out democracy. Others complain that the nation was more of a theocracy than a democracy. Every day there is robust debate in newspapers, on the radio, TV and on the internet about almost every possible political issue.

Trying to debate Israel in the U.S.

Indeed, in one respect the Israeli Media seems much healthier than even U.S. Media—that is in its ability and willingness to criticize Israeli policies and actions. For example, while the New York Daily News and the New York Post were calling the Gaza Freedom Flotilla of May 2010 "ships of fools" and characterizing the deadly Israeli commando raid on unarmed civilians as "hell on the High seas"—not for the murdered civilians but for the poor Israeli soldiers, newspapers in Israel were lambasting the attack, though not usually on moral grounds, just that it was poorly-planned and executed.

Overall in the U.S. the Israel Lobby and paranoid pro-Israeli groups are forever jumping on anything even obliquely critical of Israel in the Media and pummeling their authors with accusations of anti-Semitism or worse. Not surprisingly as a consequence there is not much of that criticism, or even reporting on the facts, for example, of what is going on in the Occupied Territories, thanks to defensive self-censorship and a pervasive attitude of "it's just not worth the trouble." In addition, the Israel Lobby and, frankly, many of the Jewish owners of media outlets, affirmatively make sure that Israel always gets to look good on just about anything.

Israel: Gag orders and military censorship

In Israel, on the other hand, the public debate on every possible subject at first seems unfettered since the discourse is so robust and often heated.

But then one learns of the existence of two institutions that are rarely discussed—military censorship and the ubiquitous gag orders issued either by the courts or one of the security services.

Military censorship *per se* seems contrary to a free press and is not standard in democracies except in extraordinary circumstances. Court-ordered gag orders are familiar in most democracies, but not the routine issuance at the request of the prosecution or the gag orders issued directly by one of the security services as it appears to happen in Israel. One journalist opined *that "the military censorship's philosophy [is] that Israeli journalists should be official spokesmen for the defense establishment."*

109

The Press in Israel, he wrote, cannot adequately examine the military in any way, its budgets or operation. *"Security in Israel is treated like a religion that must not be doubted."* In Israel any attempt objectively to examine military programs, examinations that are routine in the U.S. press, *"is bound to fail, because the intelligence agencies are protected diligently by the military censorship and the courts, who rush to issue gag orders."*

So the apparent robust debate after all is not the whole picture. There are voids, empty spaces, and unknown areas. Because one does not know what was not disclosed in the media since it was prohibited by a military censor or a gag order, it is difficult to judge just how much the existence of these institutions affects the otherwise apparent freedom. The relative silence, certainly in the form of criticism, that descended over the Israeli Press during the periods when the Israeli armed forces were engaged in Lebanon and in Gaza is understandable, wherever it may come out in the balance of measuring freedom of the press and its quality. But one is forced to ask, what else? What is unknown? It is simply not possible to determine what and how much information has been suppressed from the public as a result of these institutions. Consequently it leaves a cloud over the issue of a free press in Israel.

Further, is the result of these restrictions just that certain topics or events are not reported, or is the effect more pervasive? Are the events, issues, programs, purposes and the rest that are reported so distorted by what is not reported that the overall picture presented by all the debate and bickering is simply false, or at the very least, misleading, as in "Whistled up to London, upon a Tom Fool's errand," a bum steer? Is it the children playing within the sandbox?

Many Israelis would argue that all times in their country are extraordinary times which require extraordinary measures, like military censorship and gag orders. Well, then, they must live with the logical conclusion that there are no ordinary times in Israel, with the normal behavior of a democracy. Here again, I am not making a judgment, only a comparison between Israeli and American societies and whether this is an area where they have "shared core values." Can the performances of a media operating in perpetual extraordinary circumstances and distorted by military censorship and routine gag orders equal that of the U.S. in terms of freedom? An Israeli commentator noted:

> "In the United States, as in most enlightened and democratic countries, there is no military censorship."

Military Censorship

The website of Israel's Ministry of Foreign Affairs begins its explanation of "Military Censorship in Israel" with the statement that:

> "Under British Mandate law all publications had to receive prior clearance from the military censor. Israel neither abolished nor applied this law."

I am not at all sure what this means: *"neither abolished nor applied."* Does it mean that the law in Israel even today is that **all** publications must be submitted to the censor, but for the time being the government is not enforcing **that** law? Who decides whether to apply that law and when? This seems to create some kind of purposeful ambiguity, hardly suited to a society supposedly governed by the rule of law. What law?

111

At any rate the Ministry further explains that:

> "In 1948 an agreement signed between the government, the army and the press determined that censorship would be based on mutual agreement in order to prevent breaches of state security."

Again, I find this extremely peculiar, a deal that had to be signed by the government, the press AND the army? One would think that the government **included** the military, and that it did not have to enter into an official agreement with it, as if the military were an independent sovereign of some sort, separate and apart from the government. As I will show later, however, this is not so far off the mark in view of the pervasive power of the military in Israel.

The Ministry's statement claims that under this tripartite agreement:

> "the censor supplies to the press a limited list of topics pertaining mostly to military and security-related issues, but not to political ones. Any news item related to these topics has to be vetted by the censor. This means, in effect, that only a small fraction of the news for publication -- only matters pertaining to military or security issues -- has to be submitted for scrutiny."

According to the Israel Ministry of Foreign Affairs, therefore, it is the **military censor** which *"supplies to the press"* a list of topics.

It is difficult to see what is "mutual" about that.

The topics, however, the Ministry assures us, are not political, but pertain *"mostly to military and security-related issues."* **Mostly**? So what about the topics not included in "mostly"? Also, I can think of dozens of issues that are both military and political.

112

Taking some examples in our own country: Can the U.S. "win" in Afghanistan? Should we use predators to knock-off people in Pakistan? What about sanctions on Iran? Would all these topics come under the jurisdiction of the Military Censor if we had an agreement like the one in Israel, so that all discussions in our media relating to these and innumerable other topics would have to be first screened by the Pentagon, or some component of the military. Finally, though not really "finally," since the whole concept seems to be a can of worms, what would an Israeli army with a siege mentality, whose soldiers often shoot first and then ask questions, consider to be within the scope of "security issues."

Wikipedia reports on "Censorship in Israel" that the military censor is also empowered to control information about the oil industry and water supply and, those journalists who bypass the censor may be subject to criminal prosecution and jail time. In other reports we learn that the Censor has also prohibited certain articles on the details of prisoner-exchange negotiations between Israel and Hamas concerning Gilad Shalit, the Israeli soldier captured by Hamas.

The Associated Press in a 2006 article, around the time of the Lebanese War, acknowledged that it had agreed,

> *"like other organizations, to abide by the rules of the censor, which is a condition for receiving permission to operate as a media organization in Israel.*

> *"Reporters are expected to censor themselves and not report any of the forbidden material."*

The AP quoted Israel's Chief Military Censor at the time, Col. Sima Vaknin, as saying:

> *"I can . . . publish an order that no material can be published. I can close a newspaper or shut down a station. I can do almost anything."*

Yossi Melman in an article published in *Haaretz* on July 28, 2010, reflected on the role of journalists vis a vis the military censor. In his opinion the military censor expected the journalist to behave as the spokesmen for the military.

> *"The ability of Israeli journalists to investigate and provide information to the public on defense and intelligence establishment organizations is very limited. These limitations run contrary to the purported goal of being a western democracy. . . . [T]he intelligence agencies are protected diligently by the military censorship and the courts, who rush to issue gag orders."*

The BBC's Deputy Bureau Chief in Jerusalem in 2005, Simon Wilson, tested the censorship rules to his regret. Wilson ignored demands from Israel's security services and its military censors to review the tapes of an interview he had had with the nuclear whistleblower, Mordechai Vanunu.

Vanunu had been released from prison in 2004 after serving 18 years in jail for disclosing to the world information which most governments already knew, that Israel possessed nuclear weapons. His release, however, was conditioned on numerous restrictions, primarily as to his freedom to travel and his ability to speak publicly, including a prohibition against giving interviews to foreign journalists. Nevertheless, since his release he has defiantly challenged those restrictions, which has earned him a number of arrests, house searches, property confiscations, indictments, court visits and additional time in jail. It has also earned him the homage of Pentagon Papers champion, Daniel

114

Ellsberg, who referred to him as *"the pre-eminent hero of the nuclear era."*

I happened to be staying at the St. George Cathedral residence in East Jerusalem in 2007 where Vanunu was also a resident. I understood that it would be good manners to respect his privacy and though I did see him at a distance in the garden, I did not approach him. Soon after I left, I noticed an article in the Israeli press that his apartment at St. George had been raided in the middle of the night by the Israeli Security Services, his computers confiscated, etc. His latest act of defiance has resulted in a three-month jail sentence which he began serving in May, 2010.

BBC's Wilson's own defiance resulted in Israel barring him from the country. At first the BBC refused Prime Minister Ariel Sharon's demand for a letter of apology and a promise not to re-offend. But months later it caved in, to the protests of a number of its journalists, and had Wilson sign such a letter.

Gag Orders

As I have noted, by the nature of the subject—censors who keep things out of the public view, and gag orders which prevent information from appearing in the media—public information about these matters is not readily available. However, an event in 2010 brought both issues to the front pages of papers internationally, though only as a result first of disclosures in blogs and various other outlets on the Internet.

Anat Kamm and Uri Blau

A 23-year-old Israeli journalist, Anat Kamm (in some reports, Kam), was arrested in December 2009 and charged with various espionage violations, primarily copying military documents some years earlier while she was a soldier on national service. She had passed the documents on to an Israeli newspaper reporter, Uri Blau, of *Haaretz Daily*, who used some of them to write articles in November of 2008.

His subsequent articles painted a picture of a lawless military mentality, at least on the topic of assassinations. They disclosed that the Israeli military had sent out hit-squads to the West Bank to assassinate people that were on the Security Services' suspected "terrorist" hit-list. The documents, which included the minutes of various meetings within the military apparatus, portrayed a leisurely back and forth discussion and then, approval for the murders, notwithstanding possibly killing innocent bystanders, all the way up at least to the highest commands in the military, the murders at one point being put off during a visit to Israel of some foreign diplomats. Blau's articles noted, however, that the orders were in frank disobedience of a Supreme Court decision requiring such suspects to be arrested if at all possible without jeopardizing the safety of the Israeli soldiers and police. The "suspects" were not simply to be summarily executed, as they were in the two cases disclosed.

The illegal nature of these assassination orders was what made the stealing of the classified documents into a civil rights issue, as one reporter later noted, a "classic whistleblower" case where the motivation was not to hurt the country, but to help it.

After her secret arrest Kamm was placed under secret house detention and the media was ordered not to report anything on this matter. The media of course complied and this event remained unreported for months.

Uri Blau, apparently not knowing about the arrest of Kamm, in January of 2010 traveled out of the country on assignment. While aboard he learned that Israeli Security Services had broken into his home and had confiscated a number of his belongings, including his computer. He was advised by friends to stay out of Israel for the time being because it looked like the Security Services intended to arrest him upon his return to Israel.

None of these events was immediately reported in the Israeli media because the Security Services had asked a judge, herself an aggressive, former-military prosecutor, to issue a gag order on the whole matter. Nevertheless, word of these events eventually began to circulate on Internet blogs (the breakthrough made by Richard Silverstein on his Tikum Olam website: http://www. richardsilverstein.com). Then, papers outside of Israel wrote articles about it. Meanwhile the Israeli press could only obliquely mention that something was afoot according to the foreign press but they themselves could not report on it. The absurdity of it all finally ended when the gag order, in the face of the information being available all over the world and on numerous Internet sites in Israel, was lifted.

The ensuing debate in the media on the arrest and imminent trial of former soldier and now journalist Anat Kamm was vigorous. The Israeli public generally voiced vehement opposition to the investigative activities of Anat Kamm and Uri Blau. One commentator even thought that as far as the Israeli public was concerned, these "traitors" deserved to be executed. Colleagues in other newspapers questioned the wisdom of the *Haaretz Daily* standing behind its reporter, arguing that it deviated "from acceptable journalistic practice." The *Jerusalem Post's* Caroline Glick, in her usual venomous, vitriolic and delusional style,

117

detected in the Kamm affair a worldwide gang of traitors and criminals conspiring to undo Israel:

> "Kamm's treachery is a deeply disturbing comment on the mindset of the radical Left in Israel. But her crimes are even more alarming when we realize that Kamm is not a lone renegade. In her treasonous activities, she enjoys the support of a massive organization.
>
> "By collaborating with Kamm first by publishing her stolen documents and hiring her as a reporter, and finally by covering up her crimes while suborning Blau's perjury, Haaretz has demonstrated that leftist traitors have a powerful sponsor capable of exacting painful revenge on the State of Israel for daring to prosecute them.
>
> "In facilitating and supporting treason, Haaretz itself can depend on a massive network of supporters in Israel and internationally . . . ."

The angry and hostile reaction of the Israeli public as a whole to the whistleblower Kamm stands in stark contrast to the hero's treatment that American society has given to Daniel Ellsberg, who in 1969 also purloined and made public, classified military documents. Forty years later, he is still revered by Americans and a documentary film about his release of the Pentagon Papers has been nominated for an Oscar.

Indeed, in the U.S. at the time Ellsberg defied hiws government, the circumstances were even more perilous than those in Israel when Kamm transferred her documents to Blau. The U.S. was involved in a very nasty war in Vietnam with hundreds of thousands of soldiers still in battle. The war would claim over 58,000 lives and leave 304,000 soldiers with wounds. On the other hand, Kamm's Israel was not in any official war, though it considers itself always at war. And she was exposing the blatantly-illegal actions of the Military, all the way to the top, in continuing to carry out assassinations without even the modicum of restrictions that had been imposed by the Supreme Court. Yet most of Israeli society would have been happy to see Kamm, and maybe even Blau, drawn and quartered.

What's happened to Anat Kamm?

Uri Blau himself has not returned to Israel as of this writing (September 2, 2010), for fear of arrest and years of imprisonment. The trial of Anat Kamm which was supposed to start in April has just dropped out of the Israeli press, as if it never existed. Though it should be a sensational trial, there have been absolutely no reports of what has been going on—witnesses, evidence, arguments, motions— nothing at all. Why has this momentous event—just disappeared? Is it a result of the military censorship and gag orders?

What else is going on?

Again, when there is institutionalized suppression of information, who knows what is or what is not happening in the country? Only hints of what may be going on in Israel and yet not being allowed to be reported sometimes appears in the Press. The Anat Kamm affair was one such spectacular item, highlighting both the military censorship program and the system of gag orders. But then, there must be many more such situations, some we learn about and others, presumably we never know of because the orders have not been lifted. For instance, on the May 12, 2010, Eli Ashkenazi wrote the following in *Haaretz Daily*:

119

> *"The Nazareth District Court has sentenced an Israeli Arab citizen to seven years in prison . . . for assisting and conspiring with the enemy, a gag order lifted on Sunday revealed. . . ."*

So the public suddenly learns for the first time, when all the action was over, that at one point an Israeli citizen had been arrested. Then, that he was charged with certain crimes. Then he was tried and found guilty. All of this was done in secrecy. Now we are told only the result—seven years in jail. The article by Ashkenazi seemed to be based only on the decision of the court that was made public with the lifting of the gag order.

Apparently Assad Ursan, 58, an Arab who had been born in Israel and was a citizen, had left his hometown when he was 18 (which would put us at 1970, a few years after Israel lifted military government over its Arab citizens) and moved to Lebanon and then Algeria, where he joined Fatah, at that time considered a terrorist organization (though now an ally and a "partner" in negotiations with Israel). Ursan, apparently thinking that bygones were bygones returned to Israel to take up his life, only to be arrested at the border.

Why would information about his arrest, and then, his trial, be kept from the public? Security reasons?—someone who had left Israel in 1970 and who voluntarily returned at the age of 58? Some kind of military reason? But the events for which he was convicted went back 30 and 40 years earlier. Or was it just to keep him from being able to wage an effective defense by gathering public support? Why did the security apparatus decide that they did not want a spotlight put on this matter?

What else is going on in Israel that the public is not allowed to know? And why? Again, is this a "shared core value" with the U.S.?

The NGO Bill

While the press was filled with heated debates related to the disclosure of Anat Kamm's arrest and Uri Blau's exile, the Knesset introduced a Bill its critics say would sharply curtail the activities of the many not-for-profit or non-governmental organizations (NGOs) in Israel. NGOs perform a number of services, from providing humanitarian aid to the residents of Gaza to defending the civil rights of Israeli citizens. Israel's right, and it seems its center as well, have been fulminating against the NGOs since the attack on Gaza in December of 2009. For joining the criticism of that operation, which left 1400 Palestinian dead and even the remnants of its infrastructure further pulverized, and for providing evidence to the Goldstone Commission which investigated the Gaza war on behalf of the UN, the NGOs have been paid back by being targeted and harassed by the government and right-wing groups. Adding to the paranoid ubiquity of the term "existential threat," the right has created a new catchphrase to symbolize yet another worldwide attack on Israel: delegitimation. Now its enemies, including the despised NGOs, are trying to delegitimize Israel, supposedly meaning doing something that is just not nice to Israel, though the Webster Collegiate dictionary defines "delegitimation" as "a decline in or loss of prestige or authority."

The Bill, according to Adalah, would shut down any NGO "if there is a reasonable basis to conclude that the organization is providing information to foreign bodies or is involved in lawsuits abroad against senior officials in the government in

121

Israel and/or officers in the Israeli army regarding war crimes."
It thus would make it illegal to report or give evidence on war
crimes. *"A state that outlaws groups that dare to criticize it cannot be
considered a democracy."* was the *Haaretz'* observation.

Another proposed law aimed at the NGOs, as described in the
New York Times, would require NGOs "that received support
from foreign governments to register with Israel's political
parties' registrar, which could change their tax status and
hamper their ability to raise money abroad." This Bill is in a
more advanced stage of being enacted as it easily passed its first
or preliminary vote (others are needed to become final) in the
Knesset by 58 to 11. The two Bills were among a number of
others which the critics claim are aimed at harassing the Arabs
and stifling dissent that have been introduced on a wholesale
basis in the Knesset since the formation of the Netanyahu
government. What Bills get through the entire legislative process
and become laws is still up in the air, though their very
introduction seems to be part of a propaganda war. The NGOs
of course, as well as many commentators in the international
community and the Liberals in Israel, have attacked these Bills as
undemocratic, fascist and racist, all aimed at eliminating dissent.
Because this episode has overlapped the Anat Kamm matter, the
media's health and vigor seemed to be at their best in the
vigorous public discussions that transpired on these matters.

Excluding a Spanish Clown

Meanwhile, Israel's Interior Minister, Avigdor Lieberman, not
wanting to be left out of this sport of riling up Israel's Left and
international onlookers, flexed some of those old muscles that he
had used as a bouncer in the Soviet Union, this time in bouncing
visitors out of Israel and out of the Occupied Territories. In late

April, 2010, Ivan Prado, Spain's most famous clown, arrived at the Ben-Gurion Airport on his way to Ramallah to organize an international clown festival. For six hours he and his companion were questioned by Shin Bet and Interior Ministry people, then, he was put back on a plane out of the country. Shin Bet's statement to the press read in part as follows:

> "We recommended to the Interior Ministry to prevent his entry into Israel after the findings of the security check produced suspicions about him. . . . the man declined to provide complete information to the security people, especially in regard to his links with Palestinian terror organizations."

This IsraelSpeak was greeted with open derision by newspaper commentators:

> "What links? Was the clown considering transferring Spain's vast stockpiles of laughter to hostile elements? Joke bombs to the jihadists? A devastating punch line to Hamas?"

Lieberman's Foreign Ministry instructed its ambassadors around the world to explain that the clown had been denied entry for "security reasons," in the process giving heartburn to its staff in Spain which had to answer the incredulous questions of the Spanish press about why a clown had raised "security" concerns inn Israel.

Excluding Norm Chomsky

A few weeks later 81-year-old M.I.T. linguist and social critic Norm Chomsky was questioned for several hours by agents from the Interior Ministry at the Allenby Bridge border crossing between Jordan and the West Bank. He was on his way to a lecture at Bir Zeit University in the West Bank. He too was refused entry, this time to the Occupied Territories. When first asked about it, the Interior Ministry initially claimed it had nothing to do with it such that border crossing was under the jurisdiction of the Israeli Defense Forces. But the IDF said it did not know anything. Then, finally the Interior Ministry admitted that it had denied entrance to Chomsky. Asked for what reason, the spokesperson stated:

> *"There are a million reasons why someone would be denied entry into Israel [actually, it was the West Bank, occupied territory] . . . Every case stands alone, and every individual who is denied entry is denied for different reasons."*

Even the editors of the *Haaretz Daily* and the *Jerusalem Post*, which had gone head to head over the Kamm/ Blau matter, were joined in their condemnation of this refusal to allow Chomsky to travel to Bir Zeit University. Chomsky's American colleague, Professor Alan Dershowitz of Harvard, who almost never seems to find any Israeli action questionable, nevertheless commented that people should not be kept from giving their opinions, though he could not help offering a gratuitous insult to the Professor, saying that the Chomsky could not in any event do any damage since he was such an ineffective speaker.

An attorney at ACRI was quoted by the *Jerusalem Post* as saying that Chomsky had made headlines, but that every day foreigners as well as Palestinians were denied entry into Israel or the Occupied Territories because of their political beliefs and opinions. In fact back in January headlines were made when Israel detained Jared Malsin, an American who was the chief English editor of the Maan News Agency, based in the West Bank town of Bethlehem, at Ben Gurion Airport when he was returning from a trip. For no reason that was explained, he was refused entry.

The ACRI attorney cited specific examples of visitors denied entry, including human rights advocates, intellectuals, journalists, public officials, students, etc. In addition, it was impossible, he explained, to determine ahead of time what the guidelines were for a visitor's entry into Israel. It was for that reason that ACRI had taken the Interior Ministry to court and had obtained, in December of 2007, a court order which required the Ministry to publish whatever regulations it used in its decisions to allow or deny entry. The judge in that case observed that the Interior Ministry *"for years . . . has been in breach of the law by not publishing the rules and regulations according to which it operates . . . ."* The Ministry simply ignored the court order, according to the ACRI attorney, and continues to do so as the Ministry still has not published anything.

Playing in the Sandbox?

But, wait! Everyone seems to be engrossed in the civil liberties pros and cons of putting a young and idealistic female whistleblower on trial; exiling an inventive and courageous investigative reporter; suppressing such dissent as is represented by NGOs in Israel, denying entry on "security grounds" to clowns and professors. Could there be a more dramatic and authentic display of the health and strength of freedom of speech in Israel?

But is all of this really the whole picture? Is it enough to prove that freedom of speech is alive and well in Israel? Or is it another example of the sandbox principle—let the children play all they want, just so long as they stay within the sandbox?

125

Freedom of speech in democracies includes not only freedom of the Press, it is not just allowing endless talk and debate. It also means such freedoms that could actually result in changes to the society. It means allowing for the expression of opinions in all their forms—in the establishment of cultural institutions, political parties, running in elections, freedom to move about as one pleases, freedom to associate and to assemble, and even in demonstrating in the streets where all else fails.

In addition, and perhaps more significantly, such freedoms are meaningless if they apply only to one segment of society. They must be available not only to the majority, in Israel that would be the Jews, but also to the minority, the Arabs.

Is there true democratic freedom of speech in Israel as we in America know it? Are members of the minority as free as those in the majority? Or is the vaunted Israeli freedom of speech just a limited freedom of the press, akin to allowing children to play all they want, so long as they stay in the sandbox? Let's use a real test. Let's see what kind of freedom exists for Israeli Arab citizens, particularly those who have tried to change the system which they feel has made them less than second-class citizens.

Azmi Bishara: Political leader

As good a person as any to start with, is Azmi Bishara (also spelled Bisharah). Bishara is an intellectual who had taken to politics. The entry on him in *Wikipedia* as of today (August 12, 2010) has three pages listing his books and articles in English, Hebrew, Arabic and German. He went to the Nazareth Baptist School, Hebrew University in Jerusalem and obtained his Ph.D. in philosophy at Humboldt University of Berlin in 1986 while that part of Berlin was still under Communist rule. He thereafter joined the faculty of Bir Zeit University in the West Bank, later becoming the head of its Philosophy and Cultural Studies Department. In 1996 he ran for and was elected to the Knesset. He is a Christian.

The problem with Bishara, however, is that he has never liked Israel the way it is, and has been trying to change it. As the most prominent Israeli-Palestinian intellectual, he has campaigned to change Israel from an ethnic/religious Jewish state to a nation where all its citizens are equal, not only before the law but equal in fact. To the Israeli government this has made him a traitor, disloyal and treasonous. After enduring a number of arrests, questionings, long criminal trials and endless harassment by the security apparatus since entering politics in 1996—and along the way founding a new political party based on the principle of a nation of all its citizens, Bishara, is not a healthy man (according to a 1999 profile in the *Jerusalem Post*: "*He received a kidney transplant in March 1997 at Hudassah-University Hospital in Jerusalem's Ein Kerem and is a spokesmen for the National Association of Dialysis Patients in Israel*"), and chose exile in April of 2007 to avoid what looked like Israel's plans to put him away in prison for a long time:

> "*What is the meaning of me spending the coming 10 years proving my innocence to the Israelis? . . . I am sure that all of the charges would fall but the process that you have to go through is what worries me. . . . I believe that the larger Arab world as a whole is my homeland.*"

His estimate of ten years to prove his innocence was probably based on the fact that the last time similar charges were brought against him, in 2002, it was not until 2006 that they were finally dismissed. The new allegations, however, had added layers and more sophistication, indicating that the Israeli Secret Service was moving along on the learning curve, and the attitude of the government, and the Jewish public, has only become more hostile and extreme. Of course the whole picture as usual was not available to the public since there was one of those ubiquitous gag orders on the proceedings of the prosecutor, and it had been only partially lifted. The charges seemed to revolve around trips abroad, spying for the enemy, Hizbullah, during wartime, and other cloak-and-dagger espionage and treason allegations—what has become the usual stuffing for the secret police.

Bishara is the best person to describe what Arab citizens of Israel have been facing. Soon after his April 22, 2007 resignation from the Knesset and the beginning of his exile, he explained in an article in the *Los Angeles Times* the most recent charges that had been brought against him in Israel and which had caused him to go leave. In that article he also explained why he was such a "problem" to the Israeli government:

> "These trumped-up charges, which I firmly reject and deny, are only the latest in a series of attempts to silence me and others involved in the struggle of the Palestinian Arab citizens of Israel to live in a state of all its citizens, not one that grants rights and privileges to Jews that it denies to non-Jews. . . . .

> "Today we [Palestinians] make up 20% of Israel's population. We do not drink at separate water fountains or sit at the back of the bus. We vote and can serve in the parliament. But we face legal, institutional and informal discrimination in all spheres of life.

"More that 20 Israeli laws explicitly privilege Jews over non-Jews. . . .

"Most of our children attend schools that are separate but unequal. . . .

"During my years in the Knesset, the attorney general indicted me for voicing my political opinions (the charges were dropped), lobbied to have my parliamentary immunity revoked and sought unsuccessfully to disqualify my political party from participating in elections -- all because I believe Israel should be a state for all its citizens and because I have spoken out against Israeli military occupation. Last year, Cabinet member Avigdor Lieberman -- an immigrant from Moldova -- declared that Palestinian citizens of Israel 'have no place here,' that we should 'take our bundles and get lost.' After I met with a leader of the Palestinian Authority from Hamas, Lieberman called for my execution. . . ."

Fighting for equal rights means treason in Israel

To American ears a struggle by 20% of a country's population for equal rights sounds like a pretty routine civil rights agenda, we have been through that ourselves. Equal rights for all citizens —is quite basic for us and we could only wish such a minority and its endeavor "good luck." However, to the Shin Bet and the government of Israel—it is treason. They have said so in so many words, including in criminal indictments. But how, you would ask, in a "democracy" could agitation for equal rights amount to disloyalty and treason?

I will let the Israeli Secret Service, Shin Bet, speak for itself.

But first some background. In 2006 and early 2007, there had been various documents produced by different Israeli-Arab

129

groups relating to what they hoped to see in the future, an Israel where all its citizens were equal. These were "think tank" documents issued for study and debate, and indeed were called "visionary documents" and were widely discussed in the Israeli-Arab press.

Then, in March of 2007, several Hebrew newspapers reported that Yuval Diskin, the head of Shin Bet, the Secret Service, had told the Cabinet that these documents were subversive, since they challenged the Jewish nature of the state, and that the Arab elite was attempting to radicalize the Arab masses. Having Shin Bet unhappy with what you were reporting in your newspaper was not a good thing and it made Arab editors nervous. One of them, Ala Hlehel, therefore, wrote to the Shin Bet and asked it to clarify just what its position was on the Arab documents, since the reports in the newspapers about his concerns were incomplete and confusing. The Shin Bet obliged and wrote a response to Mr. Hlehel. As detailed in an Adalah press release, itself not challenged by the Shin Bet, it did not deny the reports that had circulated in the papers, which was revealing in itself, and stated in part:

> "[T]he Shin Bet is required to thwart the subversive activity of entities seeking to harm the character of the State of Israel as a Jewish and democratic state, even if their activity is conducted through democratic means, and this is by virtue of the principle of a 'self-defending democracy.' There is nothing wrong with composing such documents, or others, which are seen as constitutional or formative, unless they reflect or encourage unacceptable phenomena of political subversion as stated."

Now, try to figure that one out. Try reading it again.

IsraelSpeak at its best—now you see it, and now you don't. *"Democratic"* here and *"democratic"* there, but not *"democratic"* anywhere.

Use any *"democratic means"* you want, after all this is a democratic country, Diskin wrote, but under the *"principle of a 'self-defending democracy'"* they would *"thwart"* (close the paper down? jail the editor?) you if those activities diminished the *"character of the State of Israel as a Jewish"* state.

What the hell is a *"self-defending democracy?"* And what horrors are allowed to a *"self-defending democracy?"* Who decides when to incite the populace and to summon the troops to defend the democracy?

At the very least this certainly sounded ominous and chilling, probably Diskin's intent. Remember that the request made to Shin Bet by the editor was for an official clarification of reports in newspapers that Diskin was somehow unhappy with the Arabs' "visionary documents" and that he had supposedly warned the Cabinet about the radicalization of Israeli-Arabs, prompting some newspapers to write of possible insurrections by the Arab population.

On first reading it may have appeared to the editor that the Secret Service was saying that it would be considered *"wrong"* for the editor to continue to disseminate information about the documents, since the documents constituted *"subversive activity."* Yet, the only subversive activity mentioned in Diskin's letter was harming the *"Jewish and democratic"* character of the state of Israel. Certainly, seeking equality for all citizens, as the "visionary" documents discussed, would not be contrary to any democratic principle, and in fact most people would consider equality to be an essential democratic principle itself. So Diskin

131

must have viewed the "visionary documents," the vision of equality in the future for all the citizens of Israel, as *seeking to harm the character of the State of Israel as a Jewish"* state.

What might have been most alarming to readers of this letter from the Secret Service was the sudden birth of the *"self-defending democracy"* concept, midwifed by the Shin Bet. Where in the dictionary, or political philosophy, much less in law or custom, is there a *"self-defending democracy"*? What does this constitute? Who can make decisions as to what is *"self-defense?"* Is this a carte blanch to the secret services to defend "democracy" as they see it with tools that come into existence from time to time as necessitated by the need for "self-defense?" When a homeowner is surprised in his bedroom by an armed intruder in the middle of the night, self-defense would allow him to shoot the intruder. Are the Arabs intruding onto the land of the Chosen People?

What would constitute "harming" the Jewish character of the state? A female Arab citizen getting pregnant? -- certainly a "democratic means" of doing such. Is this a warning of future Shin Bet abortion camps for Arab women?

This may or may not have occurred to the Arab editor, Mr. Hlehel, who received Shin Bet's reply. But what he did seem to read it to mean was that possibly the continued publication of those "visionary" documents discussing the goal of achieving equality of all citizens of Israel would be considered an *"unacceptable phenomena of political subversion. . . ."*

This only made Mr. Hlehel more nervous and so he turned to the Legal Center for Arab Minority Rights in Israel (Adalah) for help. Presumably thinking that the Shin Bet had gone out of its mind and certainly did not speak for the government, Adalah wrote to Menachem Mazuz, the Attorney General, and asked in effect, "What gives?"

Well, the response was not at all what was expected. The times apparently had changed. As Bishara would later say about a similar matter: "*The rules of the game had changed.*" Mazuz replied that he fully supported Shin Bet's letter and that in fact it had been cleared with him. In addition Mazuz told Adalah that it could rest assured that whatever the Secret Service might do in the future had the full support of the Attorney-General because "*the activities of the GSS are undertaken in coordination and consultation with the relevant parties within the legal apparatus.*"

This is what the minority is living under in Israel—the threat of prison or exile if it seeks equal rights. This minority is the 1.5 million citizens of Israel, 20% of the population, who happen to be Arab (note: we are not talking about the six million Arabs in the Occupied Territories, another story, but those who are "citizens" in Israel proper, itself).

This had been the message of Azmi Bishara. He has now left. It was like exiling Martin Luther King, Jr., in 1963 after his "I have a dream" speech, and **because** he had given that speech.

One down, 1.5 million to go.

Is this one of the "common core values" that Israel and we share? Are we Americans really soul-brothers to a nation that criminalizes a quest for equality?

If such a well-known leader as Azmi Bishara could be indicted essentially for advocating freedom for his people, equal rights, then what lies ahead for others in Israel who do the same? The answer was not long in coming.

Post–Bishara Israel for Arab MKs

Back in 2002, the Arab Association for Human Rights already thought that the state was targeting the Arab leaders who hade been elected to the Knesset. The Association issued a detailed 31 page- report entitled: "Silencing Dissent." In that report they described how physical assaults on the Arab members of the Knesset by the police and other security services had increased, usually at demonstrations where the Arab MKs were participating. Then instead of investigating the police who had assaulted the legislators, the state investigated the legislators. *"[A]t least 25 police or judicial investigations of the Arab MKS have been opened in the course of this parliament. . . ."* This was contrasted with the fact that during this period there were no recorded cases of Jewish members of the Knesset being assaulted by the Security Services nor were there any police investigations of those members, notwithstanding the frequent attendance by some of the far right-wing MKs at wild and unruly racist demonstrations by settlers.

In 2008, after the Bishara affair, Adalah wrote to the Prime Minister and the Attorney-General complaining about the practice of the Shin Bet in summoning workers of the Arab political party Balad that had been founded by Azmi Bishara under the false pretenses of a police investigation and then questioning them about their political activities, beliefs and connections to Mr. Bishara. The activists "were told that they should refrain from having any contact with Dr. Bishara 'for their own good.'" Adalah charged that the investigations by the Secret Services and the manner in which they were conducted were unlawful.

134

Arab legislators have continued to be targeted by the Secret Service and police, as well as the Attorney-General. Their trips to Arab countries, and that means just about anywhere in the Middle East, inevitably result in accusation by their Jewish MK colleagues, and sometimes by the Attorney-General as well, of treason, aiding the enemy (one law makes it a crime to stay overnight in an "enemy" country, a list of which keeps changing and expanding), Fifth Columnists, etc. Their outspoken opposition to the Occupation and to the Wall and to the seize of Gaza causes the same reaction, as if the Arab minority in Israel should look with favor upon the oppression of their relatives on the other side of the Wall. Some of the reactions have been just rhetorical, but others have resulted in more restrictive laws against their ability to travel or join supporting groups; stripping them of their parliamentary immunity, or arrests and indictments.

As Arab legislator Hanin Zuabi was in the rostrum reporting to the Knesset her experiences on a ship with the Gaza Freedom Flotilla trying to break the Gaza blockade when she was physically attacked by other MKs, most notably by Anastassia Michaeli, a member of Avigdor Lieberman's Russian party. *"You have no place in the Knesset of Israel,"* Michaeli shouted at Zuabi as she rushed to the rostrum, *"you are unworthy of carrying an Israeli ID."*

What a spectacle. Russians rushing the Israeli Knesset's rostrum and , with heavy accents, yelling at someone who could trace her ancestors in Palestine back for hundreds of years, telling her that she "did not belong." Some days later the Knesset voted to strip MK Zuabi of a number of her privileges as an MK.

Free speech: demonstrations and protests

But the most prominent role for the Arab legislators has been participation at street demonstrations and protests. It is not surprising that they are more active in the street than in the Knesset where their total lack of power or influence is on display every day. There is plenty of sound and fury in the Knesset, but nothing of value for the Israeli-Arab minority comes out of it. The Arab MKs have been utterly marginalized in the governmental process. One wonders what is the point of their being there at all. They can do nothing in the Knesset to rectify the inequality of funding for the towns, schools, hospitals, etc., serving their people, much less modify in any way the numerous laws that discriminate against Arab citizens. It would seem that they are there only so Israel could tell the world that the Arab minority enjoys full political freedom.

So the Arab MKs are most effective when they join their fellow-citizens in the street, in the most elementary form of citizen participation. They appear at protests against evictions, house demolitions, the Wall, the arrests of their leaders, the killings by Israeli Security Services, the confiscations of Palestinian properties, the construction of Jewish housing in East Jerusalem, etc., often ending in their being beaten, shot with rubber bullets, tear-gassed or deafened with stun grenades and oftentimes arrested.

Muhammad Barakeh

Muhammad Barakeh (Barakei) is the Chairman of the political party, Hadash, and has been a member of the Knesset for a good number of years. During that time he has repeatedly complained to the authorities about the unnecessary use of force by police at demonstrations and unwarranted arrests. All of his charges against the police or security forces, even those backed up with video or audio evidence, have been brushed aside. Instead, he has been targeted with arrests and indictments. The latest was in November of 2009 when he was indicted for **his** having allegedly assaulted the policemen whom he had complained about at protests against the Wall in Bil'in—and over a three year period, 2004 to 2007.

Sheikh Raed Salah

Some observers of the Israeli scene believe that the cleric and political leader Raed Salah is the most visible figure in Israel today fighting for the social, political and cultural survival of the Arab minority. Over the years he has been arrested a number of times, charged with various "terror" related crimes that carried life sentences, if convicted, and in one instance serving two years in prison while awaiting trial, only to be released upon pleading guilty to the equivalent of spitting in the street. Here is his profile.

> *"Born in 1958 in the city of Umm al-Fahm in the Haifa area, Salah was known for his poetry before becoming involved with the Islamic Movement.* [a religious, charitable and local political organization]

> *"Sheikh Salah succeeded in being elected mayor of Umm al-Fahm that year* [1989], *and was re-elected to the position twice during the 1990s.*

> *"A long-time advocate of the right of return for Palestinian refugees, Sheikh Salah has non-violently protested against the Israeli occupation for decades. His primary focus has been on reinforcing and rebuilding destroyed mosques throughout Israel, and more specifically, protecting the al-Aqsa Mosque in Jerusalem's Old City. The Israeli authorities have arrested Sheikh*

137

Salah on numerous occasions for his promotion of Palestinian human rights.

"In 2003, Salah was imprisoned for two years on charges that he had helped fund Hamas-related activities in the occupied Palestinian territories. A travel ban outside of Israel was placed on him following his release.

"Salah was also arrested in 2007 and prohibited from coming within 150 meters of Jerusalem's Old City after he and four other men allegedly scuffled with an Israeli police officer. At the time, he had been protesting against an Israeli renovation project, which he said threatened the al-Aqsa Mosque.

"Salah was arrested another time in 2007 for incitement after he led a group of protesters through the Wadi al-Joz neighborhood in East Jerusalem in protest of the aforementioned renovation work. Last month, the Jerusalem Magistrate's Court acquitted Salah of all charges related to this incident.

"In January 2010, Salah was sentenced to nine months in jail and six months probation for assaulting the Israeli police officer. The ruling earned condemnation from various public figures – including Palestinian Knesset member Jamal Zahalka and Mustafa Barghouti, among others – who argued that Salah's arrest was a signal that Israel was silencing Palestinians' right to protest.

"As a result of his most recent arrest for participating in the Freedom Flotilla, Salah was sentenced to five days of house arrest, and is forbidden from leaving Israel for 45 days."
(Alternative Information Center, 31 May 2010.)

Ameer Makhoul

One individual, Ameer (Amir) Makhoul, who chose not to pursue Israeli-Arab freedom through politics, instead took the course of working for decades in charitable and civil rights organizations. He heads an organization, Ittijah, which serves as the umbrella for a good number of Israeli-Arab NGOs and is a member of various UN and European organizations. (*"Created in 1995 and based in Haifa, Ittijah works to coordinate the activities and strategies of 64 Palestinian organizations . . . through formations seeking institutional and organizational empowerment and local and international campaigns for the protection of Arab organizations."* Ittijah website.) He is a familiar figure in the European human rights world.

In the middle of the night in early May of this year (2010) operatives from the Shin Bet and the police invaded his home in Haifa and arrested him, in the process confiscating his computers and cell phone as well as those of his wife and two daughters. The Press was ordered to keep the arrest secret, and they did, just as they had kept secret the fact that two weeks earlier Makhoul had been banned by the government from traveling abroad.

But by word of mouth the Arab community became aware of it and demonstrations began immediately. Internet blogs in Israel, including that of Richard Silverstein's, immediately picked up the story and openly flouted the gag order. But the mainstream Israeli Press continued to obey the gag order and only reported that there were disturbances and demonstrations in the Arab communities about something. Finally, after the Israeli Press complained in articles to the effect: "everybody knows, but us," the gag order was lifted, at least "partially."

139

Like in the Bishara case, the charges against Makhoul, and Dr. Omar Sayid, a member of the Arab political party Balad whose arrest weeks earlier had also been kept secret, involve espionage and contact with the enemy — what has become the equivalent of Peter Lorre's: *"arrest the usual suspects"* from *Casablanca*. But as one of the most well-known civil rights leaders in Israel, Makoul's arrest, and charges of his being tortured, brought angry objections from human rights groups worldwide.

Amnesty International released this statement, headed: "ISRAEL MUST STOP HARASSMENT OF HUMAN RIGHTS DEFENDER."

> *"Amnesty International has called on the Israeli authorities to end their harassment of a human rights activist . . . .*
>
> *"Ameer Makhoul is a key human rights defender, well-known for his civil society activities on behalf of the Palestinian citizens of Israel' said Phillip Luther, Deputy Director of Amnesty International's Middle /East and North Africa Programme.*
>
> *"His arrest and continued detention smacks of pure harassment, designed to hinder his human rights work. If this is the case, we would regard him as a prisoner of conscience [and] call for his immediate and unconditional release."*

His arrest was noted first in the blogs, then in the international press and finally in Israel. The *Guardia Unlimited* (U.K.):

> *"Amir Makhoul, 52, who runs an Arab rights group, was arrested by police and Shin Bet security agents last week in a pre-dawn raid at his home in Haifa.*

140

Omar Said, 50, a member of Balad, an Arab political party in Israel was arrested last month. Israeli authorities imposed a gag order on the case to prevent reporting of the arrests in Israel. The order, widely flouted by bloggers, was lifted today.

"The Shin Bet said the two men . . . were suspected of 'severe security offences including contacting a Hizbullah agent.'

"The details of the case against them are not yet clear, but the men are not the first to be accused of working with Hizbullah in recent years. In 2007, Azmi Bishara, a prominent Arab MP in Israel, went into exile after police said they suspected him of supplying information to Hizbullah . . . ."

The *Independent* (U.K.) commented on the arrest of this international figure as well:

"The Israeli authorities finally revealed yesterday that they had been holding a prominent Israeli-Arab human rights activist for several days and had accused him of spying for Lebanon's Hizbollah guerrillas."

And in Israel itself its military censor finally allowed the media to report something. The *Haaretz Daily* noted briefly:

"The military censor on Monday lifted a gag order on news that two Israeli Arab political activists were arrested last week on charges of spying and contact with a foreign agent . . . . At around 3:00 A.M. on Thursday, armed security forces raided Makoul's home in Haifa."

141

"Freedom of speech"?. . . Just don't say "boo"

A final word about "freedom of speech" in Israel. After Palestinian families were evicted from their homes in the Sheikh Jarrah neighborhood of East Jerusalem, there have been weekly protests and demonstrations in support of the Palestinian families who have camped-out nearby. Though the demonstrators, including all kinds of people, from young Palestinians to Jewish professors from Hebrew University, were peaceful, they have routinely been met with violent and brutish tactics from the police. One headline in the December 25, 2009 edition of the *Haaretz Daily* read: "War on Protest." The editors wrote:

> *"The war the police and the Israel Defense Forces are openly waging against protests by left-wing and human rights activists has heated up in recent weeks. As a result, concern is growing over Israel's image as a free and democratic country, one that accords equal and tolerant treatment to all its citizens and residents.*

> *"Nonviolent protest in the East Jerusalem neighborhood of Sheikh Jarrah against the expulsion of Palestinians from their homes by extreme right-wingers have met with a violent and disproportionate police response. The IDF has responded with insufferable harshness to protest against the separation fence in the Palestinian villages of Bil'in and Na'alin. . . .*

> *"Major arrest sweeps are also taking place in these two villages, of protest organizers and members of the popular committees. Some of those arrested have been brought before a military court, charged with incitement and sentenced to lengthy prison terms. . . ."*

142

The only thing I question about this editorial is where the editors got the idea that Israel ever had an *"image as a free and democratic country"* and one that *"accords equal and tolerant treatment to all its citizens and residents."* I have to assume the editors were being sarcastic.

Six months later *Haaretz'* editors were even more pessimistic. In an editorial entitled: "Dangerous incitement," they worried about events which reflected:

> *"a trend aimed specifically at silencing Arabs. The trend is surfacing in most of the parties in the Knesset, with the enthusiastic encouragement of most ministers. . . . [T]he flotilla debacle served those people as a pretext to ratchet up the delegitimization of Israel's Arab citizens and brand them as traitors."*

The *Haaretz* editors did not mention, probably out of professional courtesy, another source of dangerous incitement: their colleagues in the Press. Columnist Caroline Glick in the *Jerusalem Post*, for instance, seemed to see the entire 1.5 million Arab community in Israel, and in particular those who were the most educated, as Fifth Columnists and agents for Hizbullah. She urgently urged the government *"to stop talking and start acting."*

> *"They need to move now to break up enemy organizations like Balad and the Islamic Movement* [two Arab political parties], *arrest their leaders and seize their assets. . . .*

> *"So too, the police, with assistance from the IDF if necessary, needs to uncover and seize illegal arms caches. Hostile villages like Kafr Kanna and Umm el-Fahm, and border towns like Deir el-Asad and Majd el-*

143

Kurum [prominent Israeli-Arab communities] *should be rigorously patrolled."*

Bishara, Salah, Makhoul, Barakeh—the most visible and prominent leaders of the Arab minority in Israel, in jail or in exile. The good news for them and the other Arab leaders is that if they had been residents of the Occupied Territories instead of Israel proper itself, they would have long ago been assassinated. Such are the benefits of "freedom of speech" in Israel.

Is this sordid Israeli record on freedom of speech supposed to be one of the "common core values" that AIPAC means?

Notes: Page 219.

6

THE RULE OF LAW

The Rule of Law: what is it?

Everyone has a sense of what the "rule of law" means, but not everyone could explain it. "No man is above the law" is one way some put it. "A nation of laws and not of men" is another way.

We know that it is a good thing for a country to have and that it is essential to a well-ordered society, where people feel that the law is there to protect them and to keep the peace. In America, we *know* we have it. We also know from newspaper reports that places like Sudan right now, do not have it. Likewise we know that when a dictator can change the law by himself at any time, there is no rule of law in such a country.

More nuanced is where a legislative body or parliament can change everything by a simple vote of a majority. They are elected in a democratic way, so we cannot say the legislative body is a dictator. But majorities can change at each election time, or a temporary majority could be created by some forceful event or series of events. There should be fundamental or underlying values or rules that passing majorities should not be able so easily to change. One senses, particularly of majorities quickly formed by some crisis, that some sort of protection or check would be good to have against their actions made in the heat of the moment.

145

In a country subject to the rule of law, people know what the law is; it is also predictable and that everyone is subject to it, individual citizens, government officials and every part of the government. People, businesses, and institutions can plan for the future because they know what the rules of the game are; they know what the law is and what it will probably be tomorrow and next year. The law of course will change with time, as the community changes, but it will do so incrementally and along with the community.

One good explanation of the "rule of law" would be that given by Jose Maria Maravall and Adam Przeworski in their *Democracy and the Rule of Law* (p. 4):

> "[I]n societies that approximate the rule of law, no group becomes so strong as to dominate the others, and law, rather than reflect the interest of a single group, is used by the many.

> "In any institutional equilibrium, actions are predictable, understandable, stable over time, and limited. Hence, individuals can anticipate the consequences of their own behavior: everyone can autonomously plan one's life."

The concept is as old as Ancient Greece, if not older. *Wikipedia* under its article "Rule of Law" quotes Plato:

> "Where the law is subject to some other authority and has none of its own, the collapse of the state, in my view, is not far off; but if law is the master of the government and the government is its slave, then the situation is full or promise and men enjoy all the blessings that the gods shown on a state."

This is from Plato's *Laws*. What we call the Ancient Greeks, those of the time of Plato and Aristotle, had extraordinary experience in the formations of governments and the behavior of different societies. The Ancient Greeks at one point prospered and multiplied. They had spread out over the Mediterranean and set up colonies as far west as Sicily and the coast of Italy (e.g., Neapolis - "New City," now Naples; and Syracuse in Sicily). Over time each of these colonies became cities of different sizes and developed their own governments. So there was much experimentation in government and much for Plato and Aristotle to study. Plato even tried to counsel one ruler to run his city according to predictable laws but failed in the attempt, his pupil becoming a tyrant. He also was concerned about the constant changing of the laws in Athens by democratic majorities which made life difficult to plan. Both Plato and Aristotle wrote much about how the best government would be one subject to laws, and not to the whim of a single ruler or a temporary majority.

Rule of Law in the United States

The "miracle" of the American experiment with governance had much to do with the way the Founders structured the new government so as to ensure the rule of law.

They did not use that term, as the term is a modern one. It also must be remembered, that in addition to their own experiences with the British Monarchy, the history of the English common law, the years under the Confederation and the experiments of the various colonial governments, many of them had read about Ancient Greece and Rome extensively. Echoes of Plato and Aristotle can be found in the writings of the Founders, including in the *Federalist Papers* of James Madison, Alexander Hamilton and John Jay written to support ratification of the Constitution.

One particular *Federalist Paper* often quoted by scholars and courts on the subject of rule of law is *No. 78* written by Alexander Hamilton, considered to be a brilliant lawyer, approaching genius. In *No. 78* Hamilton treated the subject of The Judiciary, including why the appointed judges on the Supreme Court should have life-terms to safeguard their independence from the Executive and the Congress.

Fundamental law

The Constitution, Hamilton wrote, would be fundamental law. The people crafted this fundamental law and the process of both formulation and ultimate approval was intentionally elaborate and involved many steps, including ratification by most of the states. Only the same type of arduous and elaborate procedure would be allowed under the Constitution to amend it, that is, to change fundamental laws and principles governing our society. This was essential in order to avoid the menace of occasional majorities that may come under the influence of "ill humors" "which, though they speedily give place to better information, and more deliberate reflection, have a tendency, in the meantime, to occasion dangerous innovations in the government, and serious oppressions of the minor party in the community."

Then there are the laws passed by Congress to give force and effect to the fundamental laws and principles embodied in the Constitution. How they related to the Constitution would be a vital issue. Hamilton explained how it would be the job of the judiciary to interpret these laws on behalf of the people, and to

148

reconcile conflicts between laws passed by Congress and the Constitution, nullifying those laws which ran counter to the Constitution. The government created by the Founders was to have limited powers. But the only way to guarantee that these limitations be maintained would be through the judiciary.

A fundamental body of law established by the people: The Constitution. A Congress elected by the people to enact laws to give effect to the Constitution. An Executive to carry out those laws. A Judiciary to make sure the laws of Congress stayed within the limits of the Constitution. This was how the Founders envisioned the rule of law would be established in the United States.

In a society with the rule of law, *"everyone can . . . plan one's life."* In the U.S., from the start, according to Maravall and Przeworski, that rule of law has resulted from the existence of a written Constitution combined with judicial review.

Marshall and the Supreme Court

In 1803, Chief Justice John Marshall, in his *Marbury v. Madison* decision, described the written constitution as "the greatest improvement on political institutions" and noted that "in America . . . written Constitutions have been viewed with so much reverence. . . ." He was referring both to the national Constitution as well as to the constitutions of the several colonies or states that were written even before the national one. John Marshall fought in the Revolution along with his father, a close friend of George Washington. He lived through the period after the Revolution where the original states each debated and enacted their own written constitutions. He watched as the structural weaknesses of the Confederation became obvious and as men gathered in Philadelphia to formulate a better document.

Marshall was a member of the Virginia convention elected to consider ratification of the Constitution and joined James Madison and the other Federalists supported of the Constitution going head to head against such luminaries of Patrick Henry who vigorously opposed ratification.

Marshall in writing about the Constitution did not have to research what the Founders had in mind. He had lived with it all and had debated with them and read all the voluminous pro and con papers written during the ratification debated. Not surprisingly, therefore, there is not one footnote in his 1803 *Marbury* decision where he established the American principle of judicial review of Congressional Acts. In that decision he held an act of Congress to be void because it was contrary to the Constitution. Everyone understood, he explained, that the people intended the Constitution to represent fundamental principles which were only seldom to be changed.

> *"That the people have an original right to establish for their future government such principles as, in their opinion, shall most conduce to their own happiness is the basis on which the whole American fabric has been erected. The exercise of this original right is a very great exertion nor can it nor ought it to be frequently repeated. The principles, therefore, so established are deemed fundamental. And as the authority from which they proceed, is supreme, and can seldom act, they are designed to be permanent."*

Likewise it was obvious to everyone, according to Marshall, that laws passed by Congress were of a different nature, and subject to the superior principles of the Constitution. When the Constitution declares that it is the supreme law of the land, it

>"confirms and strengthens the principle, supposed to be essential in all written Constitution, that a law repugnant to the Constitution is void, and that courts, as well as other departments are bound by that instrument."

Marshall felt quite confident to be able to write:

>"Certainly, all those who have framed written Constitutions contemplate them as forming the fundamental and paramount law of the nation and consequently the theory of every such government must be that on an act of the Legislature repugnant to the Constitution is void.

>"This theory is essentially attached to a written Constitution, and is consequently to be considered by this Court as one of the fundamental principles of our society."

Judicial review

Just as confidently the Chief Justice stated what he thought must appear obvious to all:

>"It is emphatically the province and duty of the Judicial Department to say what the law is."

Obvious. Plain and simple. Everyone agrees, as they naturally must. So the bedrock of our system of government was developed.

A primary purpose for having a fundamental document, such as a Constitution, which could not be changed by a vote of Congress but requires an arduous procedure involving ratification of any such changes by the states, is to protect the public against the passions of the moment and to protect minorities of the moment against the majorities of the moment.

Seven years later, with Marshall again writing for the Court, the Supreme Court now found invalid a state law that it held ran counter to the Constitution. In *Fletcher v. Peck* the Chief Justice wrote:

> "Whatever respect might have been felt for the state sovereignties, it is not to be disguised that the Framers of the Constitution viewed, with some apprehension, the violent acts which might grow out of the feelings of the moment; and that the people of the United States, in adopting that instrument have manifested a determination to shield themselves and their property from the effects of those sudden and strong passions to which men are exposed."

Some years later when Alexis De Tocqueville toured the U.S. and reviewed its institutions, he noted that the American judiciary unlike those in other countries, are "invested with immense political power. He attributed this difference in power to:

> "the simple fact that the Americans have acknowledged the right of the judges to found their decisions on the constitution rather than on the laws. In other words, they have left them at liberty not to apply such laws as may appear to them to be unconstitutional."

John Marshall—Revolutionary War soldier and officer; lawyer; member of the Virginia Convention ratifying the Constitution; Secretary of State and then Chief Justice. In these decisions he cited no authorities in his interpretation of the Constitution. The Constitution speaks for itself, he seems to say, and he draws only the most obvious and evident conclusions from its words. Thus

152

he set for the future of America, the principles of fundamental law versus other acts of legislatures as well as establishing the Supreme Court as the arbiter between the people and the government. He felt he knew the minds of the Framers as he had lived with them and had gone through the long process of forming the Union. He, of course, must have been thoroughly familiar with the thoughts of Madison, Hamilton and Jay, his contemporaries, with whom he had discussed all the issues about which they wrote in the *Federalist Papers*. He probably felt that he was as authoritative as any other person at the time on the subject of what the Founders intended.

Marshall was not devising a personal or unique formation, but only explaining what the Founder had done. If he wanted to he could have quoted from Alexander Hamilton's *Federalist 78* on the issues of the judicial review, the role of the Supreme Court and the supremacy of the Constitution. Later that century, the Justices of the Court would indeed resort to Hamilton's and Madison's writings, just as their successors up to this day have done.

The Civil War and loyalty oaths

In *Cummings v. State of Missouri (1867)*, the Supreme Court struck down a loyalty-oath trying to be imposed on the losing Confederate sympathizers by the victorious Union sympathizers in Missouri who had to suffer under their rule during the Civil War.

No circumstances more intense and bitter than a bloody civil war could serve as a better example of what the Framers had warned about when they set up their structure to prevent people inflamed by events from trampling on the rights and properties of others. This was truly an "existential threat" to the nation.

Justice Field, however, writing for the Court, reviewed the history of Bills of Attainder and then the Missouri loyalty-oath. Cummins was a Catholic priest who had preached and taught in the state without having taken the required oath established by the new Missouri legislature which stated, among many other things, that the person taking the oath had never offered any assistance of the Confederates.

> "The clauses [of the oath] in question subvert the presumption of innocence, and alter the rules of evidence, which heretofore, under the universally recognized principles of the common law, have been supposed to be fundamental and unchangeable. They assume that the parties are guilty; they call upon the parties to establish their innocence' and they declare that such innocence can be shown only in one way -- by an inquisition, in the form of an expurgatory oath, into the conscience of the parties."

Justice Field rejected the oath, holding that

> "[U]nder this form of legislation the most flagrant invasion of private rights, in periods of excitement, may be enacted, and individuals, and even whole classes, may be deprived of political and civil rights."

The Justice then quoted, for support of his interpretation of the Constitution, from a legal paper left by Alexander Hamilton and described in a subsequent book by his son. Hamilton in that paper outlined his arguments in opposition to a loyalty-oath that had been proposed in the New York State legislature immediately after the British had been defeated in the Revolution and before the new national Constitution had been put together. Those refusing to take the loyalty-oath would lose their civil rights and property as well. Hamilton, one of the Founders of the federal Constitution years later, had written:

> *"If we examine it [the oath] . . . we must acknowledge, not only that it was an evasion of the treaty, but a subversion of one great principle of social security, to wit: that every man shall be presumed innocent until he is proved guilty . . . . Nothing can be more repugnant to the true genius of the common law than such an inquisition as has been mentioned into the consciences of men . . . ."*

In 1965 Chief Justice Warren in *United States v. Brown*, in holding unconstitutional a law enacted by Congress which made it a crime to serve on the executive board of a labor organization while being a member of the Communist Party, quoted Madison from his *Federalist 51* and Hamilton from his *Federalist 78*. Now the inflamed passions that had taken over a majority of Congress related to the Cold War and McCarthy Anti-Communism. Justice Warren quoted Hamilton about the evils to a democratic society of things like loyalty-oaths.

> *"Nothing is more common than for a free people, in times of heat and violence, to gratify momentary passions by letting into the government principles and precedents which afterwards prove fatal to themselves. Of this kind is the doctrine of disqualification, disenfranchisement, and banishment by acts of the legislature.*

> *"The dangerous consequences of this power are manifest. If the legislature can disenfranchise any number of citizens at pleasure by general descriptions, it may soon confine all the votes to a small number of partisans, and establish an aristocracy or an oligarchy; if it may   banish*

155

at discretion all those whom particular circumstances render obnoxious, without hearing or trial, no man can be safe, nor know when he may be the innocent victim of a prevailing faction. The name of liberty applied to such a government would be a mockery of common sense."

Rule of Law in Israel

Now we examine a system of governance which Hamilton felt would make applying the name of liberty to it "a mockery of common sense."

Israel has no Constitution or Bill of Rights, but it does have "Basic Laws." One of them, "Human Dignity and Liberty," was enacted in 1992. The stated purpose of the law is *"to establish in a Basic Law the values of the State of Israel as a Jewish and democratic state."*

Citizens of any western democracy would recognize these values and even see some that go elegantly beyond their own cherished liberties. The law provides, in mandatory language, that *"there shall be no violation"* of:

> *"the life, body or dignity of any person,"* or *"the property of a person."* (Paragraphs 2 and 3).

Every person is entitled:

> *"to protection of their life, body and dignity,"* with *"no deprivation or restriction of the liberty of a person by imprisonment, arrest, extradition or otherwise."* (Paragraphs 4 and 5).

Every imaginable liberty is covered, and even some that extend beyond the boundaries of those usually expected in a western democracy, though, curiously, the word "equality" never appears.

"All persons have the right to privacy and to intimacy." What new visions of freedom for the human spirit have the Israelis written. Then *"there shall be no entry into the private premises of a person who has not consented." "There shall be no violation of the confidentiality of conversations, or of the writings or records of a person."* (Paragraph 7).

Commentators marvel at such broad protections for "intimacy" and "dignity," some believing that even though the touchy word "religion" is not expressly mentioned, it must be covered in one of these noble values.

Also listed as one of these *"values of the State of Israel as a Jewish and democratic state"* is the following:

> *"6. (a)All persons are free to leave Israel.*
> *(b)Every Israel National has the right of*
> *entry into Israel from abroad."*

The right to come and go as one pleases—one hears echoes of the American Justices laying out American freedoms in landmark civil rights cases. Certainly the freedom to travel would be considered as one of the fundamental values of a free, democratic society. Let's see how it plays out in real life in Israel.

Freedom of travel

Sheikh Raed Salah: The Cleric

We need to take up Sheikh Raed Salah again, because his story, which told us so much about Israel's alleged "freedom of speech," also gives us instructions on its version of the rule of law.

Again, we recall that this 52-year-old, cleric was born in the Israeli-Arab city of Umm al-Fahm, where he was mayor for three terms during the 1990's under the auspices of a party called the Islamic Movement, a local political, religious and social organization. Before going into politics at the local level, he rejected involvement in national politics, he had studied to be a cleric and also wrote poetry that was widely read in the Israeli Arab community. He was known in the Arab community of Israel for his poetry before becoming more known for his civic and political activities. Married and the father of eight children, this cleric concentrated his politics on funding for local charities and agitating for the right of return for Palestinian refugees, the rebuilding of destroyed mosques and the protection of the al-Aqsa Mosque in Jerusalem's Old City.

He organized a number of protests against what he considered Jewish infringements on the Dome of the Rock and the al-Aqsa Mosque. He attended numerous demonstrations over three decades against what he considered Israeli mistreatment of the Arab minority, and was involved in numerous altercations with the police and soldiers at such demonstrations, resulting in numerous arrests for his political activities. He is considered one of the most outstanding spiritual and civic leaders in the Arab-Israel community.

Sheikh Salah was preparing a pilgrimage to Mecca, Saudi Arabia, when he was served with an Order dated February 16, 2002 from Eli Yishai, the Shas Interior Minister at the time (and now). The Order read as follows, according to the version set forth in the subsequent decision rendered by the Supreme Court. The order also appears in English on the website of Salah's attorneys, Adalah:

> *"In accordance with my authority under section
> 6 of the Emergency Regulations (Foreign Travel), -
> 1948, and having reviewed the recommendation of the
> General Security Service [Shin Bet - the secret service]
> reference number M479168/0202, of 15 February 2002,
> and its appendices, I am convinced that there is a
> significant likelihood that the exit of Ra'ed Salah
> Suleiman Mahajni, . . . from Israel would harm the
> security of the state. I forbid his exit from the country for
> a period of six months, from 16 February 2002 to 15
> August 2002. . . . "*

This was an uncomfortable reminder that there is such a thing as "Emergency Regulations" dating back to the British Mandate which are still on the books in Israel and are selectively utilized whenever an authority feels like using them. There had been no warning to Salah that any travel restrictions were being considered and certainly there had been no hearing -- just an order suddenly appearing.

He went to the Adalah lawyers for help. Adalah appeared before a three judge panel of the Supreme Court on June 10, 2002 and asked for an injunction against the Order. They were told first to appeal to the Minister of Interior before asking any relief from the Supreme Court. The appeal was duly made and rejected as expected by the Minister. The Justices then reviewed the written motions and written arguments of Adalah and those of the Interior Ministry. No oral arguments were allowed, no witnesses were questioned and none of the secret information supplied by the Shin Bet in its package which it called "M479168/0202 upon which the Interior Minister had supposedly based his Order, was shared with Adalah. As the Court in its decision noted, *"we studied, in the presence of counsel for the state only, confidential*

159

material that had been presented, and we were provided with explanations regarding the material."

Justice Jacob Turkel's decision

On July 17, 2002 the Supreme Court dismissed Adalah's petition. The decision was written by Justice Jacob Turkel (Tirkel), who incidentally, was appointed by Prime Minister Netanyahu in June of 2010 to head Israel's internal inquiry into the event known as the Gaza Freedom Flotilla which had resulted in the deaths of nine civilians. In the Interior Minister's papers presented to the court the Interior Minister stated that the reason for the order was his fear that Salah would exploit his trip abroad "to meet with hostile persons."

Justice Turkel, in his eight-page opinion, reviewed a number of prior Supreme Court cases touching on the subject. He cited language in one of those cases as to *"the citizen's freedom to move from the country to abroad is a natural, recognized, automatic right in every democratic state -- and our country is one of them . . ."* Further, such right to leave and return to the country is a natural right, *"one of the fundamental human rights."* Any restriction on it *"gravely infringes the individual's rights."* So far so good, sounds just fine.

However, that right, Justice Turkel noted, even as "enshrined" in the Basic Law, which in what way he did not explain, was entitled to more respect than an ordinary law, was nevertheless relative. In addition to it being relative and not absolute, it was subject to "security concerns," including the provisions of the Emergency Regulations of 1948.

> *"The right to leave the country is important and precious, but can be restricted to fulfill the duty -- also important and precious -- to protect state security and*

160

public safety. In this sense, it is comparable to the freedom of speech, where the public interest in security, order, and safety limit it . . . ."

He quoted with approval another Justice in describing the Court's view of the role of state security in these matters:

"Before us is the extremely important question that affects . . . the security of the state, on the one hand, and freedom of movement of the citizen, on the other hand. The question is not which of them is given priority. **Clearly and unquestionably, and it is not necessary to dwell on this point, matters of state security precede everything,** *and even the fear -- the frank and earnest fear -- of harm in these matters is liable to push aside every other consideration, whatever its weight. . . . "*
(Emphasis added.)

The Israeli Supreme Court could not have been clearer. There simply was not even to be a discussion of balancing priorities— state security trumps, *"pushes aside,"* everything else, *"whatever its weight."* A fundamental rule of interpretation for the Court: slavish obeisance to whatever the state labels as "security." No examination; no balancing. Justice Turkel acted accordingly.

Based on the secret evidence provided by Shin Bet, he was satisfied that allowing Salah to *"exit from Israel is liable to gravely endanger state security."* Netanyahu picked a safe person to head the Flotilla inquiry.

A cleric leaving the country to go on a pilgrimage to Mecca, *"is liable to gravely endanger state security"*? There was a *"frank and earnest fear"* that he would *"meet with hostile persons"*? Since almost every Muslim state is listed in one Israeli law or another as an "enemy" state and each of its inhabitants thereby

161

becoming "hostile persons," it was a safe bet that Sheikh Salah, during his pilgrimage to Mecca which was also being made by millions of other Muslims, would meet up with thousands, if not hundreds of thousands, of "hostile persons."

On almost any level of interpretation, this is a pretty shabby treatment of the supposedly "enshrined" basic or fundamental "natural" right of freedom to travel.

What had I read in that Basic Law just quoted above? What I had thought at first was not only noble and elegant, but plain and simple. The law is called "Basic Law: Human Dignity and Liberty," and as noted above it is intended *"to protect human dignity and liberty"* in a *"Jewish and democratic state."* As noted, civil libertarians would be hard put to criticize the generous list of rights protected by this law. But then what happened in the Salah case? Could the Basic Law not be basic at all, or even any real law at all?

I went to the Knesset website which passed the Basic Law to see if it had any ideas on how this "enshrined" right of travel could so easily evaporate. There I received my first clue as to what was going on. The Knesset's website contains a discussion of the Basic Laws. In that discussion it states:

> *"Regarding the question of the superiority of the basic laws over other laws, there are differences of opinion."*

There are "differences of opinion" on the status of "Basic Laws."?

The Israeli Legislature itself does not even know if it's "Basic Laws" are entitled to any superiority over its other laws, all passed by a majority of those voting at a session of the Knesset, as its website states. Perhaps, the website further notes,

162

seemingly thinking out loud, the use of the term: "Basic" might mean something. Not very enlightening, or encouraging, and somewhat slippery, to say the least, for one trying to gain an understanding of what "Basic Laws" mean.

Basic Law on Human Dignity and Liberty and Justice

So I go back to read more carefully the Basic Law on Human Dignity and Liberty and Justice Turkel's decision. Yes, sure enough, it is all there, but unnoticed on a first reading, invisible in the blinding light of all the noble language in the law. I find that both the Basic Law and Justice Turkel's decision are yet two more prime examples of *IsraelSpeak*.

There is more to this "Basic Law" than meets the eye at first. I realize that Justice Turkel was correct in his decision, at least on the point that there is nothing basic or fundamental or important or even meaningful about the right to travel. The law does not mean what it seems at first to say; these are not fundamental rights which no law could infringe, much less a government minister making an unilateral decision based on secret information. Rather they seem to be wishful pronouncements of ideal rights that would exist in an ideal environment, with any diminishment of the ideal environment to be met with a concomitant diminishing of the enumerated rights—with an Interior Minister's vista of the environment being as good as anyone else's. They may be called "fundamental" and "basic" or "enshrined" or "natural" rights, but in the end they are subject to so many caveats and exceptions that they are clearly meaningless.

Paragraph 8 of that Basic Law should have been a warning:

> *"There shall be no violation of rights under this*
> *Basic Law except by a law befitting the values of the State*

163

of Israel, enacted for a proper purpose, and to an extent no greater than is required."

So people in Israel have the right to travel abroad and *"there shall be no violation of that right,"* **except** by a good and proper law, *"befitting the values of the State of Israel."* This to me says very clearly, that the so-called fundamental rights set forth in this "Human Dignity and Liberty" Basic Law, can be modified, limited or eliminated by a any valid law. Presumably any law passed by the Knesset would be a valid law and presumably would be *"befitting the values of the State of Israel,"* otherwise it would not have passed in the first place. So the fundamental, basic rights set forth in this "Basic Law," can be changed at any time by a majority of the Knesset. As the famous early 19th Century French observer, Alexis De Tocqueville noted, where *"the constitution may undergo perpetual changes, it does not in reality exist."*

But as Justice Turkel pointed out in his decision, there is more. Paragraph 10 provides that the Basic Law does not affect the validity of any law already in force when this law was passed. What's more, the Basic Law cannot be varied, suspended or made subject to conditions by emergency regulations EXCEPT under the Emergency Regulations of 1948—which have always remained in effect. It was under Article 6 of those regulations that Interior Minister Eli Yishai issued the order to Salah.

If a fundamental right can be changed by a majority of the Knesset at any time; or can be subject to an order of some Minister who finds this or that, and if anyone mentions "security" so that all further discussion must cease, then of course there is no right at all, much less a fundamental right. In short, there is no rule of law.

The Salah case is merely an example of what transpires in Israel on a routine basis and with respect to all of the so-called Basic Laws.

Later, on April 22, 2010, when perhaps the most outstanding Arab-Israeli civil rights activist and leader, Ameer Makhoul, arrived at the border with Jordan to go on a trip outside the country, a frequent enough exercise for him as his civic organizations were members of international groups that often met abroad, he was handed an order from the Interior Minister, again it is Eli Yishai, dated the day before, forbidding him to leave the country until June 21, 2010.

As usual, it is a surprise, no hearing or explanation, except that the order was based on the 1948 Emergency Regulations and for security reasons. Though his education consisted only of yeshiva studies, Minister Yishai seemed to have a good handle on the 1948 Regulations. As noted above, a few months later Makhoul was hauled out of bed in the middle of the night and brought to jail. Newspapers were prohibited by a gag order, as they had been on the travel order, from reporting the arrest of the most important and outstanding Palestinian leader of the day. For a week or two he was interrogated by the Shin Bet, not allowed contact with any attorneys or the outside world. An "espionage" indictment followed, for contacts with "enemy agents."

For our cleric Sheikh Salah, the most outstanding Palestinian spiritual leader in Israel, as of this writing (August 1, 2010), he has just begun serving a five-month jail term for allegedly attacking a police officer at a demonstration the Sheikh had organized against some controversial construction by the Jewish government at the walls of the al-Aqsa Mosque in Jerusalem in 2007. Salah was accompanied to jail by a good number of

Palestinian Israeli dignitaries, including members of the Knesset, in a sign of solidarity. The Israeli Finance Minister, Yuval Steinitz, however, called for the revocation of the Sheikh's citizenship.

The unpredictability of what the law is in Israel, and therefore one's inability to plan one's life, the essence of the "Rule of Law," is on display in news about Israel almost every day.

Man About Town: Saber Qashor

Amy Teibel of The Associated Press, under a July 19, 2010 headline entitled: "LYING FOR SEX—OLD SIN MEANS JAIL TIME IN ISRAEL," wrote, with apparent astonishment, an article, published in the *Washington Post*, about a "rape" conviction handed down by the Jerusalem District Court:

> *"Lying for sex. It happens all the time."*

> *"Yes a married Palestinian man has been ordered jailed for 18 months for having sex with an Israeli woman after giving her the impression he too was Jewish, as well as single and interested in a relationship."*

Saber Qashor (Kushour), 30, an Arab-Israeli citizen, married and the father of two children, was sentenced to 18 months in jail, after already having been under house-arrest for two years from the date of the incident in 2008, and fined $2,500.00. His life, he said, had been ruined. The Judge who wrote the decision, Zvi Segal, noted that even though the event wasn't "*a classical rape by force*," and the sex was consensual, the consent was obtained by deception. Segal wrote:

> *"If she hadn't thought the accused was a Jewish bachelor interested in a serious romantic relationship, she would not have cooperated. . . .The court is obliged to*

166

protect the public interest from sophisticated, smooth-tongued criminals who can deceive innocent victims at an unbearable price -- the sanctity of their bodies and souls."

Qashor had left a grocery store in Jerusalem in July of 2008 and was about to get aboard his motorcycle when he was approached by a woman in her twenties. She admired his motorcycle and they talked for a few minutes about it. He introduced himself as Dudu and she, as Maya. Apparently Qashor's nickname is Dudu, but it also a common nickname for Jewish men whose first name is David. In pretty short order, within 15 minutes according to the judge's decision, these heretofore total strangers were having sex on the roof or in a stairway of a nearby building. Maya gave him her cell number and he left, promising to call. When he called two weeks later, however, his cell was traced by the police and he was arrested. Maya had gone to the police sometime after the encounter after learning that Dudu was not Jewish and she filed a rape charge. The charge was later modified to "rape by deception."

The "rape" conviction of course was widely ridiculed in the international press and in blogs—if every person who lied to have sex were in jail, people joked, then half the planet would be a jailhouse. The immense amusement expressed in the blogs, of course, was not shared by the real victim of the "rape," Mr. Qashor.

In an interview after his conviction he told a reporter from the British newspaper, *Guardian Unlimited*, that his partner in the casual 15-minute sexual encounter back in 2008 had not showed any interest in his background. He said that the incident had been a disaster for him and his family and he believed that he

167

would not have been charged, arrested or convicted if he had been Jewish. The *Guardian* reporter noted that they had to have the interview close to the doorway of Qashor's house as going any further would set off the alarm on his electronic ankle bracelet which he had been wearing for over two years and was now continuing to do so pending his appeal of the 18 month jail sentence. Mr. Qashor in a photo accompanying the Associated Press interview bore no resemblance to what Judge Segal had called a *"sophisticated, smooth-tongued"* criminal from which he was protecting the *"public interest"*.

Googling Judge Zvi Segal, who wrote the decision in this case for the Jerusalem court, one finds out that he is a Lieutenant-Colonel in the active reserve service and a Judge on the Military Court of Appeals. In 2005 he had been a visiting "scholar" at Columbia Law School in NYC.

As a further insight into this judge, there is a case in 2005 he handled that involved three Jewish Israeli Border Policemen. The three policemen, while on patrol near the Arab village of Abu Ghosh, just outside Jerusalem but still within Israel, picked up two 17-year-old Palestinians. Ostensibly the police wanted to check to see if the boys were from the West Bank and if so whether they had work papers on them which would permit them to be in Israel. Instead they drove the minors to an isolated location and for half an hour beat them with their batons, forced gravel down their throats, poured dairy products and food leftovers on them and made them kiss their boots, before letting them go.

That would have been the end of it, as such abuse of Palestinians suspected of being in Israel without work papers apparently is common. However the boys upon their return to their nearby

168

village, which was indeed in the West Bank, complained to someone connected to the Palestinian Authority. Two weeks later the Palestinian authorities made a formal complaint to the Israeli government.

The three policemen were arrested and charged. After a trial before Judge Zvi Seal the three were convicted in the Jerusalem court, from the testimonies of the boys as well as the policemen. For these crimes, two of the Border Guards were sentenced to ten and eight months in jail respectively, and the third to six months of community service. Why such a light sentence for the half-hour assault with weapons? Judge Zvi Segal's answer to the press was that the policemen had "expressed remorse at their actions."

Eighteen months for an Arab for a few minutes of consensual sex. Eight to ten months for Jewish policemen for assault and battery with weapons. The "rule of law" in Israel.

Mizrahi: The Policeman

In the same month that Saber Qashor was sentenced to 18 months in jail, the newspapers were filled with accounts of a Jewish policeman, Shahar Mizrahi, who had been sentenced in 2009 to 15 months in jail for a different type of crime. The headlines and controversy this month, however, were caused by the fact that the Supreme Court, upon an appeal by the police officer of his conviction, instead of reversing this rare conviction as generally was expected, actually doubled the sentence from 15 months to 30 months.

The resulting uproar, not just as expected from his police comrades, but also included protests from the highest officer of the national police force, Police Commissioner David Cohen, and

169

from a member of the Cabinet, Public Security Minister Yitzhak Aharonovitch. *"Minister Denounces court for doubling sentence of cop . . . "* ran one headline. The Minister and Police Commissioner charged that the decisions would *"seriously impair the motivation of the police officers standing on the front line of the war on criminals."*

Both officials visited the convicted policeman in jail and promised to continue to support him. The Public Security Minister, Yitzhak Aharonovitch, after meeting with the policeman Mizrahi, announced that he would seek a pardon for the officer from President Shimon Peres and that he had already talked to another Cabinet member, Justice Minister Yaakov Neeman, about what he could do to help. This Minister Aharonovitch, a member of Avigdor Lieberman's party, had caused a public stir a year earlier with a widely-quoted comment. It seems that during a meeting in the field with undercover agents, one of the Jewish policemen apologized to the Minister for his appearance as he had just come from the job. The Minister commented: "You look like a real dirty Arab." When the press asked about this, a spokesman for him made it worse by saying that it was all in jest and that he was just "using common slang."

What had police officer Mizrahi done that did not deserve the 15 months in jail, much less the 30 months? He had killed an Arab by shooting him in the head at close range where there was no danger to the policeman himself and where he never felt that his life was in danger.

Back in July of 2006, Shahar Mizrahi was part of a police undercover squad covering the Jewish town of Pardes Hannah. This is a town near Haifa with a population of about 30,000 people. There had been a number of car break-ins and thefts. Mizrahi and his team saw two men apparently breaking into cars and they approached the men. From here the story gets muddled as Mizrahi admittedly changed his story several times from the date of the incident to his appeal three years later, and even on his sentencing during the following year. In any event what the court after trial found was that the Arab victim, Mahmoud Ghanaim, was seated in the driver's seat of a car; that the driver was trying to leave the scene; that policeman Mizrahi smashed the passenger-side window of Ghanaim's car with the butt of his gun and then, shot Ghanaim point-blank in the head, killing him instantly.

The family claimed that Mahmoud was a taxi driver and was in a family-owned car. The police claimed that he was stealing the vehicle and was attempting to flee. The Trial Court and Appeals Court both accepted that part of the police evidence, and the newspapers followed suit. Everybody, except the family, agreed that Ghanaim was a car thief and was trying to flee the scene.

When the killing first occurred it appeared that the matter would evaporate as such incidents usually did, according to attorneys for Arab rights groups. However, the *Haaretz Daily* conducted an investigation, using photos of the scene, and published articles which seriously put the police story in doubt. After those articles were published, the local prosecutor ordered an investigation. The investigation dragged on for some time, to the annoyance of the Ghanaim family and their attorney. The police had already ignored their demands that Mizrahi be taken off active duty during the investigation. However, a year later the prosecutor filed an indictment against Mizrahi for manslaughter.

171

The Ghanaim family and their attorney vigorously objected to the manslaughter indictment, as they charged that it was a deliberate, intentional killing and that Mizrahi should have been charged with the more serious crime of murder. In addition, they renewed their demands that Mizrahi, now having been indicted, be removed from the police force or at least taken off active duty.

Mizrahi initially said that when he identified himself as a police officer Ghanaim had cursed at him, threatened to kill him and attacked him with a screwdriver. Then Mizrahi changed that to the testimony that after he had pulled his weapon out and ordered Ghanaim to stop, that Ghanaim had tried to run him over. These accounts, which he later again changed, were always supported by the police spokesmen's statements to the media, which most of the media dutifully reported verbatim, as if they were the actual facts of what happened. Even the writers for Ghanaim's champion, *Haaretz*, though they had viewed with skepticism so much of what the police had claimed about this case, nevertheless religiously referred to him as the "car thief."

When the case finally got to trial in 2009, the judge, however, simply could not believe that Mizrahi was in fear of his life or had shot Ghanaim in self-defense when all the other evidence indicated that Ghanaim was unarmed, was seated in a car that had just started to roll, that Mizrahi was at the side of the car smashing the window with his gun and had then shot the driver who had posed no threat to the policeman but was just trying to leave. Later Mizrahi actually admitted in court that he never was in fear for his life, but nevertheless he had shot Ghanaim in self-defense.

Not only did the police department not remove Mizrahi or modify his duties after the killing in 2006, something routinely done in the U.S., or even after the indictment, astonishingly it took no action against him after his conviction for manslaughter in June of 2009. This individual who was now a convicted killer simply continued with his usual duties as an armed police officer. On top of that Mizrahi had been allowed to wear his police uniform during the trial and at all his court appearances. He was still on duty and in uniform when he showed up for his sentencing a few months later in September of 2009, as well as after his sentencing and throughout his appeal to July of 2010. There was simply no limit or end to the support from the police establishment for this convicted killer. It is no surprise then that such an arrogant authority would react with anger and indignity when the Supreme Court increased the sentence from 15 months to 30 months, still of course nothing commensurate with the crime. Yet Major General Shimon Cohen, head of the police's northern district, said after the Supreme Court imposed the 30 month sentence:

> *"This is a difficult day for the family* [Mizrahi's family, not Ghanaim's] *and the police. . . . The district command and its officers will continue to accompany and support the officer's family in the future as we are doing today."*

Police Commissioner David Cohen at the same time said he would set up a "task force" to investigate how the police could help Mizrahi, including backing his pardon request to President Peres.

An article in *Haaretz* by Yitzhak Laor on July 27, 2010 entitled: **"You may not!: Israel is gradually relinquishing the rule of law**

173

and becoming a tribe," said that it was difficult to imagine that a Public Security Minister, in a country like Britain, would continue in his job if he had launched a public campaign against a court verdict like Israel's Security Minister was doing now. Ehud Barak's famous comment, Mr. Laor continued, that 'this is the Middle East, this is not Europe' *"has long become a slogan of bogus citizenship in a Western democracy."*

Jaffar Farakh, director of the Musawa Center for Arab Rights in Israel, said that he had followed 45 similar cases of Arabs killed by policemen in the past ten years, with very few indictments and even fewer convictions, and in those few convictions, the punishment was nominal, as it was in this case. Gideon Levy's column on the subject was entitled: **"A sick police force: A police commissioner who criticizes the Supreme Court is a commissioner who damages the rule of law."** The editorial board of *Haaretz* wrote:

> *"The actual responses to the verdicts constitute defiance of the law and an undermining of the rule of law, the sole interpreter of which is the court. In a state that aspired to democratic life in which the rule of law is a critical value, the minister and police chief would now be ending their terms."*

The extraordinary public shock and indignation shown by the police and the security apparatus in this episode perhaps tells us more about what is going on in Israel than the event itself. The words of the police were not being taken as gospel by all! The effrontery of some news media not to simply quote the police's version of events and let it go at that—this is the usual practice, particularly when it involves Arabs. In the eyes of the police, something was strangely out of order here. The credibility of the

174

police was being questioned, something rarely done. And regardless of the facts, one does not treat the police or a policeman like this—particularly in a war against the Arab citizens of Israel.

For readers who are totally unfamiliar with Israel it should not be thought that all murderers are given just 15 or 30 month sentences. The newspapers recently reported that a killer, of three people in cold blood, was given three consecutive life-terms plus twenty years. In another case reported the same week as the Mizrahi case, a 20-year-old individual was given 18 years in prison for the killing of another 20–year-old with a knife in a bar brawl, what we would consider manslaughter. All the actors in those cases, perpetrators and victims, however, were Jewish. By these standards the prison sentence for officer Mizrahi, who was found to have killed intentionally and while there was no threat to his life, should have come down to between that 18 year sentence for the manslaughter death in a heated bar brawl to that life-term for the cold-blooded murder.

I will watch this case and if this book is still in process after Peres gives his answer on the pardon application, I will try to append a note about it.

Hillary Rubin: The Bride

The lack of dependable standards by which a person could plan a life is not just a phenomenon for Arab-Israeli citizens. It afflicts the Jewish citizens of Israel as well. Take, for example, another newspaper story that appeared the same week when the policeman Mizrahi case was in the news.

A 29-year-old lady by the name of Hillary Rubin had made aliyah to Israel from Detroit in 2006. She felt she was fulfilling a dream of her ancestors as *"Zionism runs in my family"* she told a reporter. Her grandfather's uncle was Zionist leader Nahum Sokolow. This year she had applied for a license to get married and unexpectedly ran into a series of difficulties. She was asked to prove her Jewishness and produced some documents from her rabbis in the U.S. They were not sufficient. The Herzliya Rabbinate asked for the birth certificates and marriage certificates of four generators of her ancestors: her mother, grandmother, great-grandmother and great-great-grandmother. Since her grandparents were Holocaust survivors, there would be no documents from them—*"Who has a death certificate from somebody who was gassed to death?"* she asked. Yet the Rabbinical Court insisted that those documents were necessary before they would approve her marriage as a Jew. *"These things are frustrating because my grandparents were persecuted for being Jewish, and here I am being told I'm not exactly Jewish."*

She has decided to fly to Cyprus with her fiancé and get married there, as of course there is no civil marriage in Israel though it recognizes foreign ones. She has given up trying to convince the rabbinate that she is Jewish and she is beginning to wonder if she made the right decision to immigrate to Israel.

The "Supreme Court": U.S. and Israel.

The only similarity between the Supreme Court of the U.S. and that of Israel is in their names, probably intentionally copied. In addition, there appears to have been some brilliant judges on the Israeli Supreme Court as well. But that's it; in every other conceivable way they bear no resemblance.

The U.S. Supreme Court is unquestioned as the interpreter of the law. American society assumes that fact as a fundamental

176

principle, without exception, as do the other departments of government and its officials, from the President on down to the local Justice of the Peace.

In Israel, the Supreme Court is routinely criticized, questioned and ridiculed. Ministers periodically threaten to submit legislation to fundamentally change its structure and jurisdiction. Its judgments are very often ignored by the other departments or circumvented, either by new legislation or simply by contrary actions of government officials. Israeli society does not look to it as the final arbiter in any sense of the word, and segments of that society are bitterly hostile to it. The Supreme Court competes and is even inferior to the clerics in the Rabbinical Courts on issues that may or may not be religious, while it faces suspicion from the clerics when it touches on issues that are tinged with religion because of the entanglement of religion in the government.

In the U.S. the Court's existence and its appellate status is fixed in the fundamental law of the Constitution. The Court can interpret laws of Congress or actions of the states and measure them against the fundamental principles set forth in the Constitution.

The United States Supreme Court

Alexander Hamilton had written in the *Federalist Papers* that the Judiciary was the weakest branch of the government being constructed under the Constitution and posed the least danger to the liberties of the people. This was because the kind of Court which the Founders created would have to rely upon the Executive to carry out any of its rulings, as it had no means of doing so by itself.

The stark difference between U.S. society and Israeli society on the rule of law and the role of the Supreme Court can be illustrated by two instances where the Executive Department exercised its authority, to the extent of calling out military forces, to enforce the orders of the Supreme Court and Federal District Courts following the 1954 desegregation case of *Brown v. Board of Education*.

Dwight D. Eisenhower

In 1957, nine black or African-American children in Little Rock Arkansas attempted to enroll in that city's all-white High School and were turned away. Their parents then obtained a series of Federal District Court Orders directed at school and city officials requiring the admission of the children in accordance with the dictates of *Brown*. The Governor of Arkansas, Orval Faubus then called out the Arkansas National Guard with orders to surround the school and prevent the children from entering it. President Dwight D. Eisenhower and Governor Faubus had some discussions and then a meeting, with the Governor agreeing to abide by the law. He then, recalled the National Guard troops but far from obeying the Court Orders, he arranged to send in his experience street organizers and strike-breakers. These outside agitators arrived at the school each day, armed, and organized mobs to keep the children from going into the school. The local police were helpless in fact against the massive armed mobs. The President knew that this was as serious a challenge to the principles of our government as any in the country's history, and he acted accordingly.

After issuing formal proclamations ordering that the mobs disperse and allow the children entry into the school, and finding those proclamations disobeyed, he then ordered the

Army to send in regular units of the Army to disperse the mob and allow the Court Orders to be enforced. The nine children with the escorts of Federal Marshall and U.S. troops then entered the school and were enrolled. On the night he ordered the Army to go into Little Rock, he spoke to the American people from the White House and explained his actions:

> "Whenever normal agencies prove inadequate to the task and it becomes necessary for the Executive Branch of the Federal Government to use its powers and authority to uphold Federal Courts, the President's responsibility is inescapable.
>
> . . . .
>
> "As you know, the Supreme court of the United States has decided that separate public educational facilities for the races are inherently unequal and therefore compulsory school segregation laws are unconstitutional.
>
> . . . .
>
> ". . . we are a nation in which laws, not men, are supreme. . . .
>
> . . . .
>
> "The very basis of our individual rights and freedoms is the certainty that the President and the Executive Branch of Government will support and insure the carrying out of the decisions of the Federal Courts, even, when necessary with all the means at the President's command.
>
> "Unless the President did so, anarchy would result. There would be no security for any except that which each one of us could provide for himself."

"The interest of the nation in the proper fulfillment of the law's requirements cannot yield to opposition and demonstrations by some few persons."

"Mob rule cannot be allowed to override the decisions of the courts. . . ."

"A foundation of our American way of life is our national respect for law. . . ."

The President considered this a very serious threat to the existence of the Union; he said this to the public and the same serious concerns are reflected in his diaries and the transcripts of his consultations with other government officials.

The Arkansas Governor of course vehemently objected to this intervention. But so did a number of U.S. Senators and Congressmen from the South, including the Chairman of the Senate's Armed Services Committee, Richard B. Russell of Georgia, considered the most powerful and influential Senator in Washington, as well as and another senior member of that Committee, John Stennis of Mississippi. The Senators protested the use of the Military to enforce integration which they claimed was universally opposed by the citizens of the South. The powerful and influential Senator Russell in his telegram to the President, reminded the President that he was the Chairman of the Senate Committee on Armed Services, and as such he was vigorously protesting the *"highhanded and illegal methods"* being employed by the Armed Forces sent to Arkansas by the President, comparing their tactics to those in *"the manual issued the officers of Hitler's storm troopers."*

In a reply to Senator Russell, who never fought in any war, President Eisenhower, who of course had led the Allied troops against Hitler's armies, had this to say in part:

> *"When a State, by seeking to frustrate the orders of a Federal Court, encourages mobs of extremists to flout the orders of a Federal Court, and when a State refuses to utilize its police powers to protect against mobs persons who are peaceably exercising their right under the Constitution as defined in such Court orders, the oath of office of the President requires that he take action to give that protection. Failure to act in such a case would be tantamount to acquiescence in anarchy and the dissolution of the union."*

> *"I must say that I completely fail to comprehend your comparison of our troops to Hitler's storm troopers. In one case military power was used to further the ambitions and purposes of a ruthless dictator; in the other to preserve the institutions of free government."*

In a letter to Congressman Oren Harris of Arkansas who also had sent a telegram to the President demanding the withdrawal of the Federal troops, the President wrote with a definite sense of history:

> *". . . acquiescence in State use of force to block the implementation of Federal court orders, and acquiescence in the use of violence to thwart the Federal judiciary, would be acceding, first, to anarchy, and second, to the reversion of our Federal system to the impotent confederacy of 200 years ago from which our Union sprang."*

181

John F. Kennedy

Uprooting an evil that had grown for hundreds of years was a monumental task, and several years later the President, John Kennedy this time, had to send in Federal troops twice to put down riots and enforce Federal court orders for African-Americans to be allowed into public universities.

Each time the Governors and enforcement officials of the states, Ross Barnett in Mississippi and George Wallace in Alabama, had defied Federal Court orders and personally blocked the students.

There were riots in the Mississippi town where Ole Miss was located, where two individuals were killed, one, a French journalist covering the crisis, who was found behind a university building with a gunshot to his back. Reports stated that 160 soldiers were injured and 28 U.S. Marshalls were wounded by gunfire.

During the course of the first crisis in 1962, President John F. Kennedy sent a telegram to Mississippi Governor Ross Barnett that opened with the words:

> *"To preserve our constitutional system the Federal Government has an overriding responsibility to enforce the orders of the Federal Courts."*

Israeli Supreme Court

In Israel, the Supreme Court has no fundamental law with which it could review the Knesset's legislation and its own existence and jurisdiction can be changed by the Knesset at any time by a majority vote. There is no Constitution and the so-called Basic Laws can likewise be changed by a majority vote of any Knesset session. The Court has made reference in some of its decisions to what it calls the "fundamental principles" expressed in the

Declaration of Independence, and it has made pronouncements along the lines that all authorities should abide by those principles, but then in the next breath it acknowledges that these are more like ideal goals rather than binding rules because the Declaration of Independence is not the law of the land. In addition, like all other institutions in Israel, it feels itself subservient to the Military and quickly and without question accedes to its judgment on any issue which the Military decides to label as "security."

The brilliant judges who have sat on the Israeli Supreme Court have expended their energies and talents to cloak decisions of theirs that have been contrary to international law and the opinions of legal experts and judges the world over with as much legal jargon and twisted reasoning as possible to obfuscate their deviation from the law that is recognized by all other civilized nations.

While every nation in the world, including the United States, from the very beginning in 1967 have pronounced the settlements in the West Bank and Gaza illegal under international treaties signed by Israel and also under the provisions of the UN Charter, the judges of the Israeli Supreme Court have devised rationales that in their minds have justified the settlements—initially for "security" and military purposes, then subsequently finding the amazing intellectual ability to become oblivious to the hundreds of thousands of civilians permanently camping out at these "military" facilities—now large and booming towns with universities, factories, etc., established and supported by the government.

Wholesale assassinations as state policy, truly in imitation of the original Medieval Assassins who also came out of the Middle

East, have found sanction in the Israeli Supreme Court under one theory or other, again skirting the law of civilized nations and bringing things back to an earlier and darker age.

In stark contrast to the situation in the U.S., in Israel when the Supreme Court issues a decision, it seems that it is up to the discretion of the Executive to enforce the decision or not, or even to assist the losing party in getting around the decision.

In one case the Supreme Court rendered a decision which told the Israel Land Administration that Arabs must be allowed to lease or buy state land and apartments and not just Jews as had hereto been done. The response of the ILA was to nullify the effect of the decision by setting up "community councils" with the authority to reject any candidate as unsuitable to the community. Now it is not the government that is discriminating, it is a community council and they are not governed by any laws about equality or discrimination. The Court seems to have a blind spot about the rule that what cannot be done directly, cannot be done indirectly. The Supreme Court's decision was castrated and rendered useless; with no apparent annoyance expressed by members of the Court.

In another case the Supreme Court ordered that all welfare applicants for state benefits at universities be given the same special benefits that were being given to the Haredi or else the benefits to the Haredi were to cease. The special benefits from the Religious Ministry were now in question. These had always been political payoffs by the largest party at any given moment to get the Haredi party Shas to help it form a government. They now seemed to be in jeopardy. The Haredi ran to Netanyahu. Not to worry, he is alleged to have told them, what we can't do one way, we will do another way. Instead of the Haredi special-benefits money coming from the Religious Ministry which the Court for some reason did not like, we will funnel it through another Ministry. Weeks later the Hiddush Organization for Equality and Freedom, a financial accountability group, discovered 30 million shekels tucked away in an obscure section of the new budget for Shas Interior Minister Eli Yishai's department which they charged was to pay for the special benefits to the Haredi.

The Supreme Court has ordered this or that illegal outpost or settlement to be dismantled. A lot of sound and fury ensues. Troops are ostentatiously called out. There are graphic photos of fights between settlers and soldiers. Years go by but the same outposts continue to exist and indeed multiply like rabbits. Order are issued; nothing changes.

The story of route 443

The Israeli Defense Forces, which has jurisdiction over the West Bank and exercises it through a misleadingly named body called the Civil Administration, confiscated some land from a number of villages for "security" reasons. It said it was going to build a road for the Palestinians of these villages, who had not asked for it, so they then could more easily move between their villages. After it opened the road, Route 443, it was used by Palestinians but also more heavily by the Jewish Settlers who now could move more quickly between their workplaces in Jerusalem and their homes in the West Bank settlements—the real reason for construction of the road.

Some time later some settlers where shot on that road. The IDF assumed that Palestinians had shot the settlers, a good assumption, and that it was the shooters had used the road, though the logic of that second assumption missed most

185

observers since the shooters were more likely stationed somewhere off the road. But it was a good enough excuse for the IDF for closing 443 to Palestinians. The entrances to the road from the villages were blocked by the Military with cement structures and piles of garbage. Palestinians were ordered not to travel on that road or face arrest and imprisonment.

A number of years later and after much litigation, the Supreme Court ordered the IDF to allow Palestinians from the villages to use the road as the IDF had originally promised when it took their land. Many months went by and nothing happened. More orders from the court. Finally, the IDF "opens" the road to the Palestinians, but with certain entrances and exits blocked and checkpoints set up in a certain ways and constructed on yet more confiscated village lands, so that use of the portion of the road now allowed to the Palestinian was pointless—the road effectively for the Palestinians started at nowhere and ended at nowhere. The crestfallen villagers went back to the Supreme Court. "This is a sham," they complained. The Court just shrugged. The IDF did open the road as ordered, it said, the rest is just security matters which the IDF knows best how to handle.

One writer noted:

> *"The story of Route 443 exemplifies the way Israel has become a country of manipulators."*

From the record it appears that the Israeli Supreme Court does what the Military and the Government wants it to do, and on those rare occasions when it does not, it is simply ignored or bypassed.

The judges on this type of court are naturally shunned by the international legal community. Not to worry! Billionaires from

186

the U.S. have set up "think tanks," like the Saban this and the Saban that, as well as absurdly named organizations like the oxymoron "Peres Center for Peace." There are well-paid fellowships, boards of directors, comfortable study trips abroad, publication of their writings, etc. Now *they* are in control. *They* are the ones to do the inviting, and prostitutes from all over the world arrive to sit at their conferences, centered in Tel Aviv, Jerusalem and New York, and accept daily stipends and listen to themselves talk.

Notes: Page 230.

7

ASSASSINATION

This short chapter deals with a subject, the state policy of assassination, that cannot be classified as a "core value," but in fairness I feel I must mention it because it is a rare area where the American government seems to be approaching the practices of the Israeli government, so there is some shared value. Admittedly, there is no indication that our American society itself is moving that way, because so far this kind of thinking seems limited to the military people and their intelligence colleagues in the government.

I had thought that with the end of the neo-con influence under former President George Bush that the slide toward the pit of "negotiation by assassination," at the bottom of which sits the state of Israel, would have mercifully ended. But astonishingly, the former constitutional law teacher, Barak Obama, has out-neo-coned the neo-cons on this subject.

The Geneva Conventions and other international treaties prohibit "extrajudicial" killing or assassination except for very limited circumstances. Extrajudicial killing is one without any form of due process—a trial or other judicial inquiry, with the subject entitled to present some form of defense to whatever it is that he or she may have been suspected of. The Israelis prefer to use the term "targeted killing" as they probably think it sounds less odious.

Negotiation by terror and assassination was always the policy of the Jewish fighters in Palestine and then of the Jewish State at its formation. The Jewish fighters during the British Mandate, particularly near its end, used assassination as a terror weapon against both the British Mandate officials and Palestinian leaders. When the time came to begin cleansing the area for the creation of the Jewish State, assassinations were used as terror tactics to chase the Arabs off their land. No one was exempt.

A future Prime Minister of Israel, Yitzhak Shamir, leader of the "Stern Gang," approved the assassination of the UN peacekeeper, Count Folke Bernadotte, which until now remains as the only example of a government actually killing a high official sent by the UN to mediate a dispute. The leader of the soon to be self-declared State of Israel, David Ben-Gurion, ostentatiously denounced the killing of the Count and sent his newly-formed Army into Jerusalem to disband Shamir's group. However, the Swedish government never accepted Ben-Gurion's denial of responsibility. Sweden's stance seemed to be borne out by later events. No one was ever prosecuted for the supposed crime, and the individual, Yehoshua Cohen, who was the actual person who shot both Bernadotte and the French Colonel Andre Serot, another UN Official, in later years showed up as Prime Minister Ben-Gurion's personal bodyguard.

Since then it has been the policy of the Israeli government to kill first and then, ask questions. It is proud of the reputation of its secret police, the "Shin "Bet, as the premier assassin in the world. Shin Bet chiefs brag in public about the "calm" their assassinations have created. Palestinians who begin to show

189

leadership qualities are picked off and eliminated so that one generation after another of possible resistance leaders disappear from the scene. The sensitivities of other countries are ignored as Mossad killers stalk and kill, as they did in February of 2010 in Dubai.

The Anat Kamm case mentioned in the Freedom of Speech chapter involved Ms. Kamm's transfer of classified military documents to *Haaretz* investigative reporter Uri Blau disclosing that the IDF was routinely ignoring even the few feeble restrictions on assassinations which the Israeli Supreme Court had attempted to impose (please try first to arrest the subject if at all possible and if it is absolutely safe and easy to do so before resorting to killing).

The U.S. move toward the Israeli state policy of assassination is at this time extremely limited, but as a first step down a slippery slope, it is huge.

My attention was drawn to the Israeli assassinations by the stories of killings from unmanned drones that began to appear prominently in newspapers reports beginning in about 2000. With no warning a missile, usually American-made, would rain down from the sky and blow up a car or a house. Civilian "collateral" damage was a constant. A blind cleric in a wheelchair along with his attendants was obliterated in one such attack. Then another Palestinian leader was blown to pieces, along with dozens of others in his apartment building, including his wife who was in his bed with him.

During the Bush II years I also noticed some reports about American drones in Pakistan, killing their "target" along with the usual civilian "collateral damage". Now the man whom we had worked for and got elected to bring us "change" from the right-wing militaristic Bush years, unfortunately has wholeheartedly embraced a policy of assassinations by drones that even Bush would have thought twice about.

In a bewildering policy somersault, at least from the apparent promises of the "Yes We Can" campaign, Barak Obama has become the first President of the United States to publicly authorize the assassination of an American citizen, an individual by the name of Anwar Al-Aulaqi, who is supposed to be somewhere in Yemen according to newspaper accounts. Could this be the Obama "legacy?" Reaction to this watershed decision has been subdued. Perhaps, like me, most people were just too stunned and ashamed by this former constitutional law professor's embrace of the Israeli tactic.

Individuals at the UN have raised questions about America's increasing use of drone-killing in Pakistan, but their efforts to acquire more information from the Obama Administration has been rebuffed. Neither the UN nor any other group, however, is making much of an issue of this at the present time.

Only recently has the usual cast of civil rights organizations taken any action to challenge Obama's unique decision to authorize the extrajudicial killing of an American citizen. A suit has been filed by the Center for Constitutional Rights and the American Civil Liberties Union. I cannot imagine that assassination of a U.S. citizen would pass muster in our courts. It is like throwing the Constitution out the window. What of the right to a trial by jury? to the right against punishment without due process? etc. What indeed, about the American way?

So here, finally, we do find some common ground between at least the governments of Israel and the government of the U.S., though I am sure it is not one of the "shared core values" that AIPAC will brag about.

Notes: Page 234.

8

THE OCCUPATION

What can I say that has not been said about this abomination?

It is disgusting, brutal and morally repugnant.

Households slowly but surely being driven from their homes by trickery, terror, impossible bureaucratic complexities, simple force, and anything else the human species could conceive of, including drowning them in raw sewage runoff. Raids in the middle of the night; assassinations; secret imprisonments; indefinite detentions -- the apparatus of an occupation.

And WE sustain it.

History will condemn them for this abomination.

Yet WE sustain them.

No "shared common core values" here, I would hope.

Notes: Page 235.

CONCLUSION

The mantra that AIPAC has succeeded in getting most U.S. Senators and Representatives repeating at every "Israeli" occasion or occurrence, and that has been on the lips of Presidents for decades, is simply false.

There are NO shared values between the U.S. and Israel, much less "shared core values."

We have looked at all the fundamental issues: democracy, freedom of religion, freedom of speech, the rule of law; and in each case we have found that Israeli society and government bear no resemblance to our society or government.

Yet most Americans have the opposite impression. How did this happen?

Simply put, the Israelis are no fools, to say the least, and they have had a hard core of Fifth Columnists in the U.S. who have helped in churning fact into fiction.

The Israeli's technical talents are conspicuous. They have, for example, legitimately accomplished the extraordinary feat of bringing back a dead language, Hebrew. In addition, there was the instinctive sympathy Americans felt for the underdog, in this case the Holocaust survivors, as well as the predisposition of fundamentalist Christians to accept any song and dance resembling the Bible. So it was not too difficult for the Israelis, with their newly invented language, "IsraelSpeak," to turn fact into fiction.

194

Thus they could take someone else's flourishing orchards that had been carefully cultivated for hundreds of years, call them a desert and then declare that they had miraculously brought forth fruit and honey from the desert. Likewise they could terrorize hundreds of thousands of people into leaving their homes, then brand the victims themselves as terrorists. In each area that we have examined we have seen how they were able to erect a veneer of respectability, a Potemkin village, with their new language. But scratch the surface; open the door; and all the ugliness, brutality and lawlessness become evident.

There being no similarity between America and Israel, Americans must look at the repeated requests of Israel for cluster bombs; predator aircraft; the newest fighter jets; money to pay down loans; joint military exercises; the sharing of intelligence; forgiveness of debt, etc., in the same manner as we look at the requests of one of the "istans" that peeled off from the old Soviet Union. We should do what is best for the interests of the U.S., and nothing that conflicts with it.

It will not be easy to disgorge the poisons implanted by AIPAC and the Israel Lobby. The dual loyalists and the Fifth Columnists will see to that. As I was finishing this book there occurred two perfect examples of how the dual loyalists in this country are damaging American interests.

First there is Iran. The army of Israeli propagandists in the U.S. has been pushing for some kind of violence against Iran with the same fervor as they did with Iraq. Iran is now the "demon-of-the-day" and today's "existential threat." Iran, a nation of 70 million, with a culture and history going back continuously for thousands of years, would ordinarily be an ally of the U.S. But because of the deep-pocketed American friends of Israel, a nation of 7 million which goes back just 62 years, Iran is now also on America's enemy list. No stone is left unturned by the Israel Lobby to further its campaign against Iran.

Israeli propagandists plant stories everywhere. Jeffrey Goldberg, an American journalist who served as a volunteer Israeli prison-guard during one of Israel's attacks on Lebanon, wrote an article in the September issue of *Atlantic Monthly*. Goldberg wrote that from his investigation and interviews, he had determined that Israel will attack Iran within a year and will not bother to ask for an American "green light." This is supposed to get comfortable with the idea of a violent assault on Iran: say it often enough and it should become "normal."

Now the fact of the matter is that Israel could not possibly attack Iran without American support. It needs American influence and approval, for instance, to open up air spaces from Israel to Iran. None of the countries in between would allow Israeli planes over its airspace without American approval. Refueling, logistics and restocking all require American material, if not actual involvement. Any counterattack by Iran, who one must assume will be ready for the Israelis, will also require massive American assistance, including our Navy and Air Force. So what is Goldberg talking about when he claims Israel would proceed without an American "green light?" Just like his passionate run-up stories in support of the Iraq invasion, this is another Israeli journalistic plant, ginning up things for war. A dual loyalist following orders from his Israeli handlers.

Here is another example from this month. Another example. On August 3rd Israel's IDF and the regular Lebanon Army exchanged gunfire on their border, killing one Israeli soldier, three Lebanese soldiers and one Lebanese journalist. In the

196

following days, Michael Oren, Israel Ambassador to the U.S., went on television, got space in the *Washington Post* and angrily raised the question of why the U.S. has been sending military aid to the Lebanese Army.

Like clockwork, on August 9th Howard L. Berman, Chairman of the House Foreign Affairs Committee, Nita Lowery, Chairperson of the House appropriations subcommittee on foreign operations, and Edward Cantor, Republican whip, three dual-loyalists in the U.S. Congress, duly followed what seemed like instructions from Oren and either demanded or actually placed "holds" on the military assistance to Lebanon. Such "holds" are usually honored by an Administration and results in freezing the assistance even though the money had already been appropriated by Congress.

The State Department at first kept repeating that it was in the national interests of the U.S. to strengthen the Lebanese Army and that the aid would continue. After a few days of saying the same thing, however, the State Department announced that it was "reviewing" American aid to the Lebanese Army. An Obama Administration pattern: bending, and then bending some more, and finally backtracking in the face of the Israel Lobby.

How could a very vital long-term U.S. interest, such as strengthening the Lebanese Army as a counter-balance to Hezbollah in the volatile Middle East, suddenly become an item for review?

It is the tail wagging the dog.

Is it already too late?

Notes: Page 236.

197

Notes

INTRODUCTION

Pappe, Ilan. The Ethnic Cleansing of Palestine. Oxford: Oneworld Publications, 2006.

Pappe, Ilan. A History of Modern Palestine 2nd ed. Cambridge: Cambridge University Press, 2006.

Davis, Uri. Apartheid Israel: Possibilities for the struggle within. London: Zed Books, 2003.

Benvenisti, Meron. Sacred Landscape: The Buried History of the Holy Land Since 1948. Trans. Maxine Kaufman-Lacusta. Berkeley: University of California Press, 2000.

Farsoun, Samih K., and Aruri, Naseer H. Palestine and the Palestinians: A Social and Political History. 2nd ed. Boulder: Westview Press, 2006.

Segal, Rafi, and Weizman, Eyal, eds. A Civilian Occupation: The Politics of Israeli Architecture. Tel Aviv: Babel Publications, 2003.

Weizman, Eyal. Hollow Land, Israel's Architecture of Occupation. London: Verso, 2007.

"Israeli Declaration of Independence." Wikipedia. 22 June 2010 http://en.wikipedia.org.

"Proclamation of Independence." Knesset. 22 June 2010 http://www.knesset.gov.il.

Mozgovaya, Natasha. "Obama: Jews' outlook on the future should be a lesson to all Americans." Haaretz Daily 28 May 2010. 30 May 2010 http:www.haaretz.com.

"Remarks by the President at Reception in Honor of Jewish American Heritage Month." The White House, Office of the Press Secretary. 27 May 2010 http://www.whitehouse.gov.

Izenberg, Dan. "Army may release all Deir Yassin docs." The Jerusalem Post 5 May 2010 http://www.jpost.com.

Mearsheimer, John J. "The Future of Palestine: Righteous Jews vs. the New Afrikaners." The Palestine Center. 29 April 2010. 30 April 2010 http://www.thejerusalemfund.org/ht/redisplay. Edited Transcript.

Bloomfield, D. "Seeking peace, or just pretending?" The Jerusalem Post 29 April 2010 http://www.jpost.com.

Klein, Elie. "As a Jew, no place but Israel is home." The Haaretz Daily 16 April 2010. 17 April 2010 http:www.haaretz.com.

"Gen. Petraeus Wrong To Blame 'Insufficient Progress' On Arab-Israeli Peace For Hindering U.S. Goals." Anti-Defamation League 10 March, 2010. 30 May 2010 http://www.adl.org/PresRele.

Bronner, Ethan. "As Biden Visits, Israel Unveils Plan for New Settlements." New York Times 9 March 2010. 30 April 2010 http://www.nytimes.com/1020/03/10/world/middleeast.

Petraeus, General David H. "Statement Before the Senate Armed Services Committee." March 16, 2010. United States Senate Committee on Armed Services. Hearings on Defense Authorization Request for fiscal Year 2011 and the Future Years Defense Program. 111th Congress., 1st Sess. http://armed-services.senate.gov.

Landler, Mark and Cooper, Helene. "Obama Speech Signals a U.S. Shift on Middle East." New York Times. 14 April 2010. 15 April 2010 http://www.nytimes.com.

"Letter from Ronald s. Lauder to President Obama." 15 April 2010. World Jewish Congress http://www./worldjewishcongress.org/en/main/showNews/id/9264.

Smith, Ben. "Dems restive over W.H., Israel feud." 16 March, 2010. 17 March 2010 POLITICO http://dyn.politico.com.

Allen, Jonathan. "Cantor to Rahm: Ease up on Israel." 16 March 2010. 17 March 2010 http://dyn.politico.com.

"Obama Calls Israeli Settlement Building in East Jerusalem 'Dangerous.' " Fox News 18 November 2009. 27 April 2010 http://www.foxnews.com/politics/2009/11/18/obama.

Cong. Rec. 21 April 2010: H2772 - 2776.

Cong. Rec. 15 March 2010: S1497 - 1499.

Cordesman, Anthony H. "Israel as a Strategic Liability?" Center For Strategic & International Studies 02 June 1020. 06 June 2010 http://csis.org/publications/israel-strategic-liability.

Cooper, Helene. "What to Do About Israel?" New York Times 06 June 2010 Week In Review 1.

Wilson, Scott. "Obama's agenda, Israel's ambitions often at odds." Washington Post 5 June 2010 http://www.washingtonpost.com/wp-dyn/content/article/2010/06/04/AR2010060404981_pf.

Wilson, Scott and Glenn Kessler. "U.S. urged Israel to use caution and restraint with aid boars heading to Gaza." Washington Post 3 June 2010 http://www.washingtonpost.com.

Booth, Robert. "Israeli attack on Gaza flotilla sparks international outrage." Guardian Unlimited 31 May 2010 http://www.guardian.co.uk.

Booth, Robert and Harriet Sherwood. "Gaza flotilla attack: autopsies reveal intensity of Israeli military force." Guardian Unlimited 04 June 2010 http://www.guardian.co.uk.

"UN urges inquiry into Israel convoy raid." BBC News 1 June 2010 http://news.bbc.co.uk.

Smith, Ben. "We're the only ones who believe them." POLITICO 1 June 2010 http://dyn.politico.com.

Frank, Joshua. "Gaza flotilla raid: Joe Biden asks 'So what's the big deal here?'" Guardian Unlimited 02 June 2010 http://www.guardian.co.uk.

Crowley, Phillip. Daily Press Briefing. U.S. State Department. 06 June 2010 http://www.state.gov.

Kershner, Isabel and Cowell, Alan. "Israel Holds Hundreds Seized During Raid on Flotilla." New York Times 2 June 2010 http://www.nytimes.com.

Cook, Jonathan. "Barefoot Soldiers on the High Seas?" Counterpunch 09 June 2010. 11 June 2010 http://www.counterpunch.org.

Pfeffer, Anshel and Barak Ravid. "Israel awaiting U.S. green light for internal Gaza flotilla probe." Haaretz Daily 08 June 2010 http://www.haaretz.com.

Ravid, Barak and Amos Harel. "Israel, U.S. agree on nature of Gaza flotilla probe." Haaretz Daily 12 June 2010 http://www.haaretz.com.

Editorial. "Neither Commission nor inquiry." Haaretz Daily 15 June 2010
http://haaretz.com.

Traynor, Ian. "EU raised doubts on Gaza raid inquiry but hopes grow of
blockade easing." Guardian Unlimited 15 June 2010 http://guardian.co.uk.

MacFarquhar, Neil. "U.N. Leader Criticizes Israeli Plan for Inquiry." New York
Times 19 June 2010: A5.

Milbank, Dana. "Netanyahu hears no discouraging words from Obama."
Washington Post 07 July 2010 http://www.washingtonpost.com.

Horovitz, David. "Finally, presidential empathy." The Jerusalem Post 09 July
2010 http://www.jpost.com.

Kessler, Glenn. "Netanyahu: 'America is a thing you can move very easily.' "
Washington Post. 16 July 2010 http://voices.washingtonpost.com.

TODAY'S AMERICA, NOT YESTERDAY'S

Ellis, Joseph J. American Creation: Triumphs and Tragedies at the Founding of
the Republic. New York: Knopf, 2007. 127 - 164.

CHAPTER 1.   DEMOCRACY - For those Who are Jewish

Lis, Jonathan. "Knesset panel slams lack of Arabs in government agencies." The
Haaretz Daily 5 May 2010 http:www.haaretz.com.

Glickman, Aviad. "Arab parties disqualified from elections." Ynetnews.com 12
January 2009.

"Israeli legislative election, 2009." Wikipedia. May 24, 2010
http://en.wikipedia.org.

"Elections in Israel - February 2009." Israeli Ministry of Foreign Affairs 24 May
2010 http://www.mfa.il.

"Hadash," "United Arab List," Wikipedia. 24 May 2010 http:en.wikipedia.org.

"Party Profile: United Arab List - Ta'al." The Institute for Middle East
Understanding (IMEU) 24 May 2010 http://imeu.net.

"Mohammad Barakeh," "Hana Sweid," "Dov Khenin," and "Afu Agbaria." Bing
Reference 24 May 2010 http://www.bing.com/reference/semhtml.

Avishai, Bernard. The Hebrew Republic: How Secular Democracy and Global Enterprise Will Bring Israel peace At Last. Orlando: Harcourt, Inc., 2008.

"Bernard Avishai." Wikipedia. May 25, 2010 http://en.wikipedia.org.

"The Official Summation of the Or Commission Report [Intro & Arab Sector]." Kokhavi Publications 22 May 2010 http://www.kokhavivpublications.com/2003/israel.

Rekhess, Eli. "The Arab Minority in Israel." Dorothy and Julius Koppleman Institute on American Jewish-Israeli Relations, American Jewish Committee. April 2008.

"A Status Report -- Equality for Arab Citizens of Israel," "Reflections on October 2000." The Association for Civil Right in Israel 22 May 2010 http://www.acri.org.il.

"Official Commission of Inquiry into the October 2000 Events." The Legal Center for Arab Minority Rights in Israel (Adalah) 25 May 2010 http://www.adalah.org/eng/commission.php

"Israel." Freedom of Religion and Belief: A World Report. Eds. Boyle, Kevin and Juliet Sheen. London: Routledge, 1997. 435 - 450.

U.S. Department of State. 2009 Report on international Religious Freedom. "Israel and the occupied territories. 08 July 2010 http://www.state.gov.

Dicker, Adam. "As tolerance center opens director says Islamic center should be built away from 9-11 site." Jewish Week. 07 August 2010 http://www.thejewishweek.com.

Eldar, Akiva. "Frank Gehry steps down from Museum of Tolerance project." Haaretz Daily. 15 January 2010. 18 May 2010 http://www.haaretz.com.

"Important Facts on the Israeli Supreme Court Ruling in Favor of the Museum of Tolerance Jerusalem." The Simon Wiesenthal Center. 18 May 2010 http://www.wiesenthal.com.

"The Mamilla Cemetery in Jerusalem." Center for Constitutional Rights. 18 May 2010 http://ccrjustice.org.

Khalidi, Asem. "The Mamilla Cemetery; A buried History." Jerusalem Quarterly, Spring, 2009. 18 May 2010. http://www.jerusalemquarterly.org/ViewArticle.aspx?id=297

"Adalah Petitions Supreme Court in Name of Muslim Religious Leaders Demanding Legal Recognition for Muslim Holy Sites in Israel." Adalah 23 November 2004. 08 July 2010 http://www.adalah.org.

"Supreme Court Orders State to Explain Failure to Recognize Muslim Religious Sites as Holy Sites." Adalah. 21 August 2007. 08 July 2010 http://www.adalah.org.

Benvenisti, Meron. Sacred Landscape: The Buried History of the Holy Land since 1948. Berkeley: U of Cal., 2000.

CHAPTER 2. DEMOCRACY – Without Equality

"Historical Background." The Legal Center for Arab Minority Rights in Israel (Adalah) 26 May 2010 http://www.adalah.org.

Kirshbaum, David A. "Israeli Apartheid -- A Basic Legal Perspective." February, 2007. Israel Law Resource Center http://israellawresourcecenter.org/israellaws/essays/israellawsessay.htm 02 July 2010.

Issacharoff, Avi. "Why is Israel torturing the Palestinian residents of Sheikh Sa'ad?" The Haaretz Daily 26 May 2010 http:www.haaretz.com.

Reuters. "Lieberman's party to seek cabinet okay for loyalty oath." The Haaretz Daily 26 May 2010 http://www.haaretz.com.

Lis, Jonathan. "Controversial 'loyalty' oath bill clears first Knesset hurdle." The Haaretz Daily 26 May 2010 http:www.haaretz.com.

"Population." Central Bureau of Statistics (Israel). 27 May 2010. http://www.cbs.gov.il/population.

Cook, Jonathan. Blood and Religion: The Unmasking of the Jewish and Democratic State. London: Pluto Press,2006.

Avishai, Bernard. The Hebrew Republic: How Secular Democracy and Global Enterprise Will Bring Israel peace At Last. Orlando: Harcourt, Inc., 2008.

Davis, Uri. Apartheid Israel: Possibilities for the Struggle Within. London: Zed Books, 2003.

"Israel: Family Reunification Ruling is Discriminatory" (17 May 2006). Human Rights Watch. 17 April 2010 http://www.hrw.org/en/new/2006.

Kohn, Orna. "Initial Comments on the supreme Court's Ruling on the Nationality and Entry into Israel Law". Adalah's Newsletter, Volume 25, May 2006.

"Eleven Justice Panel of Israeli Supreme Court Holds Haring on Citizenship Law Case" (14 March 2010). The Legal Center for Arab Minority rights in Israel (Adalah) 17 April 2010 http:www.adalah.org/eng/pressrelease.

"Separation Barrier" (May 5. 2010). The Israeli Information Center for Human Rights in the Occupied Territories (B'tselem). 28 May 2010 http://www.btselem.org/Separation_Barrier/20100505-Sheikh_Saed_Ruling.asp.

"210 New Immigrants Enjoy 'Instant' Aliyah." Jerusalem Post 17 April 2010 http://www.jpost.com/LandedPages.

Bar'el, Zvi. "Absentee loyalty." Haaretz Daily 30 May 2010 http://www. haaretz.com.

"Reunification Order to be Extended." Jerusalem Post 3 June 2010 ." Jerusalem Post 17 April 2010 http://www.jpost.com/LandedPages.

Keinon, Herb. "Illegals must pledge allegiance to Jewish state to stay." Jerusalem Post. 10 July 2010 http://www.jpost.com.

Weiler-Polak, Dana and Jonathan Lis. "Palestinians may soon have to swear loyalty to 'Jewish' state." Haaretz Daily. 16 July 2010. http://www.haaretz.con.

"Loyalty to the state is enough." Editorial. Haaretz Daily. 18 July 2010. http://www.haaretz.con.

Levy, Gideon. "It's coming to you." Haaretz Daily. 18 July 2010. http://www.haaretz.con.

Ravid, Barak. "Meridor: Loyalty oath will only make Israeli Arabs more extreme." Haaretz Daily. 19 July 2010. http://www.haaretz.con.

Ravid, Barak. "Netanyahu: Any loyalty oath must define Israel as Jewish state with equal rights for all." Haaretz Daily. 26 July 2010. http://www.haaretz.con.

CHAPTER 3. FREEDOM OF RELIGION

Justice Jackson, West Virginia State Board of Education v. Barnette, 319 U.S. 624, 642 (1943). *"If there is any fixed star in our constitutional constellation, it is that no official, high or petty, can prescribe what shall be orthodox in politics, nationalism, religion, or other matters of opinion, or force citizens to confess by word or act their faith therein."*

Butler, Jon. Religion in Colonial America. New York: Oxford, 2000.

Butler, Chris. "The Age of Religious Wars." The Flow of History 2007. 10 July 2010 http://www.flowohistory.com/units/west/13/FC87.

Kreis, Steven. "Europe in the Age of Religious Wars, 1560 - 1715." The History Guide: Lectures on Early Modern European History 04 August 2009. 10 July 2010 Http://www.historyguide.org/earlymod/lecture6c.html.

Hooker, Richard. "The Wars of Religion." World Civilizations. 1996. 10 July 2010 http://www.wsu.edu/~dee/REFORM/WARS.HTM.

Wikipedia. "Book of Common Prayer." 10 July 2010 http://en.wikipedia.org/wiki/Book_of_Common_Prayer.

Tyerman, Christopher. God's War. Cambridge: Belknap, 2006.

Farrand's Records. "The Records of the Federal Convention of 1787." Library of Congress 12 July 2010 http://memory.loc.gov/ammem/amlaw/lwfr.html.

> CCVIII. Edmund Randolph in the Virginia Convention. ttp://memory.loc.gov/cgi-bin/query/D?hlaw:3:./temp/~ammem_d3Wi::.
>
> JOURNAL Monday August 20th. 1787. http://memory.loc.gov/cgi-bin/query/D?hlaw:5:./~ammem_juyC::.
>
> JOURNAL Thursday August 30. 1787. http://memory.loc.gov/cgi-bin/D?hlaw:4:./temp/~ammem_juyC::.

Levy, Leonard W. "The Bill of Rights." The American Founding: Essays on the Formation of the Constitution. Eds. J. Jackson Barlow, Leonard W. Levy and Ken Masugi. New York: Greenwood, 1988. 295 - 327.

Gaustad, Edwin S. "Religion and Ratification." The First Freedom: Religion & the Bill of Rights. Ed. James E. Wood, Jr. Waco: Baylor UP, 1990. 41 - 59.

Anderson, Thornton. Creating the Constitution: The Convention of 1787 and the First Congress. University Park: Penn State UP, 1993.

St. John , Jeffrey. Constitutional Journal: A Correspondent's Report from the Convention of 1787. Ottawa: Jameson, 1987.

Mount, Steve. "Religion in the original Constitution." The U.S. Constitution Online 03 December 2001. 12 July 2010 http://www.usconstitution.net/cite.html.

Madison, James. "Memorial and Remonstrance Against Religious Assessments." [1875] Religious Freedom Page University of Virginia 10 July 2010 http://religiousfreedom.lib.virginia.edu/sacred/madison_m&r_1785.html.

Constitutional Debates on Freedom of Religion: A documentary History Eds. John J. Patrick and Gerald P. Long. Westport: Greenwood, 1999. 29 - 40; 56 - 80.

Alley, Robert S. Without a Prayer: Religious Expression in Public Schools. Amherst: Prometheus, 1996.

Phillips, Jonathan. Holy Warrior: A Modern History of The Crusades. New York: Random House, 2009.

Tyerman, Christopher. God's War: A New History of the Crusades. Cambridge: Belknap Press of Harvard UP, 2006.

Avishai, Bernard. The Hebrew Republic: How Secular Democracy and Global Enterprise Will Bring Israel Peace at Last.. Orlando: Harcourt, 2008.

Garfinkle, Adam. Politics and Society in Modern Israel: Myths and Realities. Armonk: M.E. Sharpe, 2000. 137 - 142.

Murphy, Emma. Israel: Challenge to Identity, Democracy, and the State. London: Routledge, 2002. 38 - 46.

"Categories of eligibility for assistance from the Ministry of Immigrant Absorption." Ministry of Immigrant Absorption, 19 July 2010 httpL//www.moia.gov.il/Moia_en/SupportEntitled/EntitledImmigrants.htm.

Shetreet, Shimon. "Freedom of Religion in Israel." Jewish Virtual Library. 01 July 2010 http://www.jewishvirtuallibrary.org/jsource/Society_&_Culture/freedom.html.

Articles from Wikipedia http://en.wikipedia.org, Accessed 26 March 2010:

"Religion in Israel."

"Orthodox Judaism."

"Haredi Judaism."

"Cabinet of Israel."

"Zionist Legislation." <u>Institute for Zionist Strategies</u>. 30 June 2010
http://www.izs.org.il/eng/default.asp?father_id=205&catid=215.

Orbach, Michael. "Agudah's 'Yes we can' moment." <u>Jewish Star</u> 28 April 2010. 16
July 2010 http://thejewishstar.wordpress.com.

Spira, Yechiel. "Interior Minister Calls for Enforcement of Chametz Law."
<u>Yeshiva World News</u>. 16 March 2010 http://www.theyeshivaworld.,com.

Wallis, David. "Council of Torah Sages: Digital Divide." <u>Jewish Journal</u> 18
January 2001. 16 July 2010 http://www.jewishjournal.com.

"Torah Sages Council and the Disengagement." <u>Israel National News</u> 23 January
2005. 16 July 2010 http://www.israelnationalnews.com.

Essing, David. "Sharon - Ultra-Orthodox Showdown." <u>Israel Cast</u> 03 January
2005. 16 July 2010 http.://www.isracast.com.

Ronen, Gil. "McDonald's fined for Employing Jew on Sabbath." <u>Arutz Sheva</u> 18
March 2010 http:www/israelnationalnews.con.

"Shas: PM Vowed to Reinstate Avreichim's Stipends." Editor. <u>Matzav</u> 02 July
2010. 05 July 2010 http://matzav.com.

Aemathisphd. "Israel: Judaism for Sale?" <u>Daily Kos</u> 04 March 2009. 01 July 2010
http://www.dailykos.com.

Haisell, Grace. "Israeli Religious Establishment Threatens Peace Agreement."
<u>Washington Report on Middle East Affairs</u> April/May 1994. 01 July 2010
http://www.washington-report.org.

Leibovitz, Liel. "School Daze: A haftorah of outcasts and paybacks." <u>Tablet</u> 18
June 2010. 05 July 2010 http://www.tabletmag.com.

"A nation divided." <u>BBC News</u> 04 June 2000. 01 July 2010 http://news.bbc.co.uk.

<u>Ynet News</u> http://www.ynetnews.com:

 Marciano, Ilan. "Rabbi: Vote Shas or go to hell." 10 March 2005. 16 July
2010.

 Marciano, Ilan. "Rabbi Yosef: Vote Shas, reach heaven." 03 January
2006. 16 July 2010.

" 'Abbas is evil, may the Lord strike him' ." <u>Jerusalem Post</u>. Staff. 29 August 2010
http://www.jpost.com.

207

"Shas spiritual leader: Abbas and Palestinians should perish." <u>Haaretz</u> Haaretz Service. 29 August 2010 http://haaretz.com.

Sofer, Roni. "Ministry of Religious Affairs reestablished." 01 June 2008. 30 June 2010.

Nahshoni, Kobi. "Poll: Most Israelis see themselves as Jewish first, Israeli second." 05   August 2008. 22 May 2010.

Kaniuk, Yoram. "Yishai, how dare you?" 21 October 2008. 16 July 2010.

Shtrauchler, Nissan. "Conversion with confusion." 11 August 2009. 16 July 2010.

Melamed, Ariana "Want to convert? do it on your own time." 26 October 2009. 16 July 2010.

Nahshoni, Kobi." 'Fire rabbis who don't recognize military conversion.' " 20 November 2009. 16 July 2010.

Meranda, Amnon. "UTJ member signs for taxation on non-kosher meats." 25 February 2010. 26 March 2010.

Medzini, Ronen. "MK Rotem: Conversion bill ticket to paradise." 03 March 2010. 26 March 2010.

Meranda, Amnon. "Knesset approves 'thin' civil marriage bill." 16 March 2010. 26 March 2010.

Meranda, Amnon. "Knesset approves taxation on non-kosher meat." 17 March 2010. 26 March 2010.

<u>Jerusalem Post</u> http://www.jpost.com:

Selig, Abe. "Gafni bill stumbles in education panel hearing." 13 July 2009. 15 July 2010.

Rettig Gur, Haviv. " 'Don't open front against Diaspora Jews'." 10 March 2010. 15 July 2010.

Hoffman, Gil, Ron Friedman and Rebecca Anna Stoil. "Peres asks leading rabbi to compromise on conversion bill." 11 March 2010. 15 July 2010.

Rettig Gur, Haviv. "US Jewish leaders concerned over conversion bill." 14 March 2010.

Izenberg, Dan. "Can Israel deny Muslim prisoners bread on Pessah?" 19 March 2010. 26   March 2010.

Izenberg, Dan. "Court rejects Muslim prisoner's demand for bread on Pessah." 25 March   2010. 26 March 2010.

Stoil, Rebecca Anna. "Knesset passes civil union bill." 16 March 2010. 26 March 2010.

Izenberg, Dan. "Petitioners: Recognize state-approved conversion." 28 March 2010. 15 July 2010.

Mandel, Jonah. "Ayalon, Rotem to reassure US critics of Conversion Bill." 23 April 2010. 15 July 2010.

"Making the Tal Law work." Editorial. 26 April 2010.

Mandel, Jonah. "Report reveals stagnation in country's conversion mechanism." 18 May 2010. 15 July 2010.

Mandel, Jonah. "New marriage license guidelines." 26 May 2010.

Mandel, Jonah. "Haredim protest, Margi mulls Jaffa dig bones." 09 July 2010.

"Sharansky expresses disappointment over conversion bill." Staff. 12 July 2010.

Mandel, Jonah. "PM: Conversion bill won't pass." 12 July 2010.

Mandel, Jonah. "Rotem revises conversion bill." 12 July 2010.

Shefler, Gil. "US Jews rally against conversion bill." 13 July 2010.

"Alienating the diaspora." Editorial. 13 July 2010.

Stoil, Rebecca Anna and Gill Hoffman. "Analysis: PM under pressure on conversion." 13   July 2010.

Rosner, Shmuel. "Good week for progressive Jews?" 14 July 2010.

Stoil, Rebecca Anna. "Shas attacked on Knesset floor for recent legislation." 15 July 2010.

Eglash, Ruth. "Reform leader: Israelis worried by conversion bill too." 15 July 2010.

209

Krieger, Hilary Leila. "Conversion bill dismays US senators." 15 July 2010.

Stoil, Rebecca Anna and Gill Hoffman. "PM, FM clash over conversion bill." 15 July   2010.

"Gov't approves two-year budget." Staff. 16 July 2010.

"PM: 'Conversion law bad for the Jews'." Staff. 18 July 2010.

Hoffman, Gil. "Politics: The conversion conundrum." 18 July 2010.

Mandel, Jonah and staff. "Conversion bill debate heats up." 18 July 2010.

Mandel, Jonah. "Orthodox leader: Conversion bill good for Jews." 20 July 2010.

Keinon, Herb. " 'Loyalty oath' still being considered.' " 20 July 2010.

Mandel, Jonah. "Conversion bill postponed by 6 months." 22 July 2010.

Horn, Jordana. "US Jews thankful conversion bill delayed." 22 July 2010.

Mandel, Jonah. "Haredim reject conversion bill freeze." 23 July 2010.

Horovitz, David. "Editor's Notes: Unconverted." 23 July 2010.

Friedman, Ron. "400 foreign workers' kids out." 02 August 2010.

Friedman, Matti. "Israel: Controversial conversion bill shelved." Washington Post. 23   July 2010 http://www.washingtonpost.com.

Haaretz Daily http://www.haaretz.com:

Sheleg, Yair. "Falashmura protest conversion funds cut." 27 November 2001. 14 July 2010.

Alon, Gideon and Moshe Reinfeld. "High Court: All converts must be called Jews in ID cards." 21 February 2002. 14 July 2010.

"An interior minister in contempt." Editorial. 07 March 2002. 14 July 2010.

"Shas, UTJ lash out at NRP's deal." Staff. 24 February 2003. 15 July 2010.

Sinai, Ruth. "Yeshiva, college students to get equal benefits." 13 February 2004. 05 July 2010.

Alon, Gideon and Avirama Golan. "UTJ rabbis unlikely to allow MKs to join Shinui in gov't." 15 July 2004. 15 July 2010.

Barkat, Amiram. "Chief rabbi issues new rules on conversion on the sly." 19 October 2004. 14 July 2010.

Shragai, Nadav and Mazal Mualem. "UJT spiritual leaders still undecided on joining government." 04 January 2005. 15 July 2010.

"Justice has been done to conversion." Editorial. 03 April 2005. 14 July 2010.

Alon, Gideon. "Yishai: Most Supreme Court rulings are anti-religious." 07 April 2005. 14 July 2010.

Rosen, Yisrael. "Conversion like a Latvia diploma." 13 April 2005. 14 July 2010.

Yoaz, Yuval. "The slow track." 12 October 2005. 05 July 2010.

Ettinger, Yair. "UTJ rabbis slam apathy among Haredi voters." 09 March 2006. 15 July 2010.

Golan, Avirama. "Ruth would still be a Moabite." 22 May 2007. 14 July 2010.

Ettinger, Yair. "Shas sages council orders party's MKs to back Peres in presidential race." 07 June 2007. 16 July 2010.

Sinai, Ruth. "Labor MK: Put Ethiopian children in secular schools." 05 December 2007. 14 July 2010.

Rotem, Tamar. "Interior Ministry ignoring High Court ruling on conversions." 28 December 2007. 15 July 2010.

Pfeffer, Anshel. "New Conversion process approved by government." 07 February 2008. 14 July 2010.

Shtrasier, Nehemia. "Herzl is turning in his grave." 14 March 2008. 14 July 2010.

Ettinger, Yair. "Professor who headed conversion probe: Check rabbinic court for criminal actions." 07 May 2008. 14 July 2010.

211

Ettinger, Yair. "Fistfight over conversion in Jerusalem." 07 august 2008. 14 July 2010.

Ilan, Shahar. "Cabinet Secretary: Haredim torpedoing state conversion system." 20   November 2008. 14 July 2010.

Ettinger, Yair. "Conversion controversy threatens to thwart Likud coalition cobbling." 16 February 2009. 15 July 2010.

Ettinger, Yair. "UTJ halts coalition talks with Likud on conversion rules." 24 March 2009. 15 July 2010.

Ettinger, Yair. "Chief rabbi: Israeli conversion certificates valid for marriage." 07 December 2009. 14 July 2010. 14 July 2010.

Ettinger, Yair. "New bill would make conversion insufficient for Israeli citizenship." 7 March 2010. 15 July 2010.

Ettinger, Yair. "Conversion bill crisis threatens coalition." 08 March 2010. 15 July 2010.

Ettinger, Yair. "Sephardi chief rabbi feels 'deceived' over amendment to change conversion rules." 09 March 2010. 14 July 2010.

Ettinger, Yair. "Deal sought on conversion law as ultra-orthodox dig in heels." 09 March 2010. 14 July 2010.

Ettinger, Yair and Mazal Mualem. "Gulf remains between parties on proposed Knesset   conversion bill." 10 March 2010. 14 July 2010.

Pfeffer, Anshel. "A mess no ritual bath could cleanse." 12 March 2010. 14 July 2010.

Itzovich, Judy Siegel and Staff. "Elyashiv: Don't budge Barzilai bones." 26 March 2010.

Sofer, Roni. "Cabinet okays relocation of Ashkelon emergency room." 21 March 2010. 26 March 2010.

Ettinger, Yair. "The invisible hand." 26 March 2010.

Ahren, Raphael. "Ayalon to discuss conversion bill with U.S. Jewish leaders." 14 May 2010. 14 July 2010.

Ettinger, Yair, Nir Hasson, Yanir Yagna, Liel Kyzer and Dan Even. "Haredim riot in Jerusalem after bones removed from Barzilai hospital site." 17 May 2010. 28 June 2010.

"The government's test of principle." Editorial. 06 June 2010.

Ettinger, Yair. "Rabbi of jailed parents: Firing squad wouldn't change our minds." 24 June 2010. 28 June 2010.

Lis, Jonathan. "Bill could force Haredi schools to teach math -- or lose funding." 07 July   2010. 10 July 2010.

Mozgovaya, Natasha and Jonathan Lis. "Reform and conservative Jews fuming ahead of Knesset vote on conversions" 11 July 2010. 14 July 2010.

Strenger, Carlo. "Is Israel alienating the Jews of the world?" 12 July 2010. 14 July 2010.

Mozgovaya, Natasha and Jonathan Lis. "Clashes with U.S. Jewry feared over conversion reform." 12 July 2010. 14 July 2010.

Lis, Jonathan and The Associated Press. "Netanyahu: Vote on conversion reform won't be brought to Knesset plenum." 12 July 2010. 14 July 2010.

Mozgovaya, Natasha. "American Jewish leaders say they feel 'betrayed' by Knesset conversion bill." 13 July 2010. 14 July 2010.

Ettinger, Yair. "The conversion bill demystified." 13 July 2010. 14 July 2010.

Lis, Jonathan. "Knesset committee rubber-stamps Haredi authority over conversions." 13 July 2010. 14 July 2010.

Ettinger, Yair. "Reform rabbi: Israel's pluralism threatened by new conversion law." 13 July 2010. 14 July 2010.

Bassok, Moti and Zvi Zrahiya. "Treasury cancels proposal to lower draft exemptions for Haredim to 22." 15 July 2010.

Golan, Avirama. "Irrelevant Jews." 14 July 2010.

Albashan, Yuval. "Just ask Jenny." 17 July 2010.

Ravid, Barak and the Associated Press. "Interior Minister Yishai: Absence of conversion law poses danger to Jewish people." 18 July 2010.

Levinson, Chaim, Barak Ravid and Jonathan Lis. "Netanyahu and Lieberman try to mend differences amid crises over conversion bill." 19 July 2010.

213

Ravid, Barak and Jonathan Lis. "Netanyahu brokers deal to block new legislation on conversions to Judaism." 22 July 2010.

Pfeffer, Anshel. "U.S. Jews should help Israel redraft its immoral citizenship laws." 23   July 2010.

Friedman, Ron. "Send them back where they came from." Jerusalem Post. 07 June 2010 http://www.jpost.com.

Lappin, Yaakov. "Aharonovitch warns of influx of illegal African migrants." Jerusalem Post. 21 July 2010 http://www.jpost.com.

Lis, Jonathan. "Cabinet postpones vote on deporting migrant's children." Jerusalem Post. 26 July 2010 http://www.jpost.com.

Friedman, Ron. "Report: 46% of foreign workers here illegally." Jerusalem Post. 29 July 2010 http://www.jpost.com.

Friedman, Ron. "400 foreign workers' kids out." Jerusalem Post. 02 August 2010 http://www.jpost.com.

Shamir, Shlomo. "Eli Wiesel: Does deporting children reflect the Jewish spirit?" Haaretz Daily. 06 August 2010 http://www.haaretz.com.

CHAPTER 4.   HOUSING

Avishai, Bernard. The Hebrew Republic. Orlando: Harcourt, 2008. 23 - 43.

Kirshbaum, David A. "Israeli Apartheid -- A Basic Legal Perspective." Israel Law Resource Center February, 2007. 02 July 2010. http://israellawresourcecenter.org/israellaws/essays/israellawsessay.htm.

"Ring Suspected of Trading in Stolen Palestinian Land." Haaretz Daily 27 February 2005 http://www.haaretz.com.

"JNF Centennial Celebration." Jewish National Fund 11 June 2010 http://www.jnf.org.

"JNF World Leadership Conference." Jewish National Fund, Press Release 24 February 2004 http://www.jnf.org.

"Annual Report" (18K) 2005. The State of Israel to the SEC.

"Land Sales to Arabs Could Force JNF Changes." Jewish Week 04 February 2005. 02 July 2010 http://www.thejewishweek.com.

Lehn, Walter and Uri Davis. The Jewish National Fund. London: Kegan Paul, 1988.

Levy, Gideon. "Kahane Won" Haaretz Daily 08 February 2009. 02 July 2010 http://www.haaretz.com.

"41% of Israel's Jews favour segregation." Guardian 24 March 2006. 02 July 2010 http://www.guardian.co.uk.

Affidavit of JNF Chairman Y. Leket and article. Haaretz Daily 16 December 2004. 02 July 2010 http://www.haaretz.com.

"In Watershed, Israel Deems Land-use Rules of Zionist Icon 'Discriminatory.'" Forward 04 February, 2005. 02 July 2010 http://www.forward.com.

"JNF, treasury seek formula for continued Jews-only land sales." Haaretz Daily 28 January 2005 http://www.haaretz.com.

"JNF Land Swap Raises Questions." The Jewish Week 07 January 2005.

"High Court delays ruling on JNF land sales to non-Jews." Haaretz Daily 24 September 2007 http://haaretz.com.

Press Releases -- KKL/JNF. a: 10/13/04; b: 03/06/05; c: 08/01/06; d: 09/01/06. http://www/kkl.org.il/KKL/english.

"Jewish People's Land." KKL/JNF 06/16/06 http://www.kkl.org.il/kkl/english.

"Land Issue" JNF Special Report 16 June 2006 http://www.jnf.org.

"A racist Jewish state." Haaretz Daily 20 July 2007 www.haaretz.con.

"JNF Statement on Knesset Bill." JNF Press Release July 20, 2007.

"A Message from Ronald S. Lauder" Jewish National Fund 02 January 2009 http://www.jnf.org.

"Blueprint Negev," Jewish National Fund 06 June 2010 http://www.jnf.org/work-we-do/blueprint-negev.

"A Message from our National Vice President for Campaign." Jewish National Fund 18 December 2004 http://www/jnf.org.

Lappin, Yaakov. "19 Beduin arrested for attacking JNF staff." Jerusalem Post 23 June 2010 http://www.jpost.com.

215

"Supreme Court Adopts Jewish National Fund's Request to Delay Full Hearing."
The Legal Center for Arab Minority Rights in Israel 27 September 2007
http://adalah.org.

Labor, Yitzhak. "Democracy for Jews only." Haaretz Daily 05 June 2007. 03 March
2010 http://www.haaretz.com.

"Achievements & Challenges" Jewish Agency for Israel 06 June 2010
http://www.jewishagency.org/JewishAgency/English/Jewish%2BEducation/CVo
mpelling%2.

"Go North With Nefesh B'Nefesh" Nefesh B'Nefesh 15 March 2010
http://www.nbn.org.il/gonorth/index.htm.

"Working with Bedouin communities." Jewish National Fund 03 April 2009
http://www.jnf.org/work.

White, Ben. "Israel's Negev 'frontier.'" AlJazeera 07 April 2010
http://english.aljazeera.net.

Manski, Rebecca, "A Desert 'Mirage:' The Role of American Money in Negev
Development." October, 2006 Bustan http://www.bustan.org.

"Israel: End Systematic Bias Against Bedouin." Human Rights Watch 30 March
2008.

"Current Israel Land Administration Projects." http://www.mmi.gov.il.

"Absorption Basket -- Sal Klita." Ministry of Immigrant Absorption 06 June 2010
http:www.moia.gov.il/Moia_en/FinancialAssistance/AbsorptionBasket.htm.

Cross, Sam. "US's 'Great Recession' is boon for aliya." Jerusalem Post 10 June
2010. 12 June 2010 http://www.jpost.com.

Israel Ministry of Foreign Affairs 06 June 2010
http://www.mfa.gov.il/MFA/MFAArchive.

Kraft, Dina. "In Galilee, Israeli Arabs finding greener grass in Jewish areas." JTA
03 November 2008 http:www.jta.org.

"Nazareth Illit." Wikipedia 07 June 2010
http//:www.en.wikipedia.org/wiki/Nazareth_ilit.

"Judaization of the Galilee." Wikipedia 07 June 2010
http//:www.en.wikipedia.org/wiki/Judaization_of_the_Galilee.

Kanaaneh, Hatim. "Upper Nazareth." The Arab Association for Human Rights 03 June 2010 http://www.arabhra.org.

Benvenisti, Meron. The West Bank Data Project: A Survey of Israel's Policies. Washington, D.C.: American Enterprise Institute, 1984. http://www.questia.com.

"Meron Benvenisti." Wikipedia 09 June 2010 http://en.wikipedia.org.

"East Jerusalem." Wikipedia 09 June 2010 http://en.wikipedia.org.

Guego, Elodie. " 'Quiet transfer' in East Jerusalem nears completion." Forced Migration Review 26 (August 2006) http://fmreview.org.

Schneider, Howard. "Israel revoked Jerusalem residency of 4,500 Palestinians in 2008." Washington Post 03 December 2009. 08 June 2010.

"Residency Rights: Revocation of Palestinian residency rights in Jerusalem." Jerusalem Center for Social & Economic Rights 23 April 2009. 08 June 2010 http:www.jcser.org.

Halabi, Usama. "The Legal Status of Palestinians in Jerusalem." Palestine-Israel Journal of Politics, Economics and Culture 4.1 (1997) http://www.pij.org.

Ofran, Hagit. "Interim Summary of Barkat's Term -- Threatening the Two-State Solution." Peace Now. 2009. 06 June 2010 http://www.peacenow.org.

Ofran, Hagit. "Eye On the Ground in East Jerusalem." Settlement Watch 25 March 2010. 09 June 2010 http://settlemenwatcheastjerusalem.wordpress.com.

"East Jerusalem -- Facts and Figures." Association for Civil Rights in Israel June 2008. 08 June 2010 http://www.acri.org.il.

Benvenisti, Eyal and Zamir, Eyal. "Private Claims to Property Rights in The Future Israeli-Palestinian Settlement." American Journal of International Law 89 (1995) 295 - 310 09 June 2010 http://www.questia.com.

Hughes, David, Nathan Derejko and Alaa Mahajna. "Dispossession & "Eviction in Jerusalem: The cases and stories of Sheikh Jarrah." Civic Coalition for Defending Palestinians' Rights in Jerusalem December 2009. 06 June 2010 http://www.adalah.org.

Alyan, Nisreen. "Life in the Garbage: A Report on Sanitation Services in East Jerusalem." Association for Civil Rights in Israel 08 July 2009. 06 June 2010 http://www.acri.org.

217

Dische-Becker, Emily. "Bingo! U.S. Donors fund illegal Jewish settlements." Menassat 5 August 2009. 26 March 2010 http://www.menassat.com.

Derfner, Larry. "Rattling the Cage: Sheikh Jarrah really says it all." Jerusalem Post 26 March 2010 http://www.jpost.com.

Hasson, Nir, and Barak Ravid. "UN, U.K. slam Israel's eviction of Arab families from East Jerusalem." Haaretz Daily 02 August 2009. 15 May 2010 http://www.haaretz.com.

Levy, Gideon. "From Sheikh Jarrah to Sheikh Munis." Haaretz Daily 06 August 2009. 15 May 2010 http://www.haaretz.com.

Hasson, Nir. "Israel delaying East Jerusalem demolitions to calm U.S. ire." Haaretz Daily 19 March 2010. 15 May 2010 http://www.haaretz.com.

"A day in the life of Jews in East Jerusalem." Haaretz Daily 21 May 2010 http://www.haaretz.com.

Sternhell, Zeev. "Israeli actions are turning Jerusalem into a settlement." Haaretz Daily 16 April 2010. 09 June 2010 http://www.haaretz.com.

Selig, Abe. "Hebrew U marches to Sheikh Jarrah." Jerusalem Post 26 May 2010 hrrp://www.jpost.com.

Eldar, Akiva. "The Har Homa test." Haaretz Daily 19 March 2010. 10 December 2007. 06 June 2010 http://www.haaretz.com.

Ronen, Gil. "Despite US Pressure, Har Homa Construction Continuing Quietly." Arutz Sheva 06 June 2010 http://www.israelnationalnews.com.

Kreimer, Sarah. "Guess who's coming to dinner." Haaretz Daily 21 August 2009. 15 May 2010 http://www.haaretz.com.

Eldar, Akiva. "Slouching toward Sheikh Jarrah." Haaretz Daily 21 July 2009. 26 March 2010 http://www.haaretz.com.

Hasson, Nir. "Police arrest 14 protesters in Sheikh Jarrah." Haaretz Daily 14 May 2010 http://www.haaretz.com.

"Israeli Supreme Court Upholds Planning authority Decision to Establish Individual Settlements in the Naqab as part of it "Wine Path Plan" Despite Discrimination against Arab Bedouin Unrecognized Villages." Adalah Press Release 28 June 2010 http://www.adalah.org.

218

"Adalah Petitions supreme Court to Cancel Wine Path Plan for Individual Settlements in the Naqab." <u>Adalah</u>. News Update. 13 April 2006 http://www.adalah.org.

"Israel police raze 'illegal' Bedouin village in Negev." <u>BBC News</u> 27 July 2010 http://www.bbc.co.uk.

CHAPTER 5. FREEDOM OF SPEECH

Derfner, Larry. "How much more evidence does anyone need that Israel, of its own accord, isn't about to budge from the West Bank?" <u>Jerusalem Post</u> 29 April 2010 http://www.jpost.com.

Lazaroff, Tovah. "Israel won't honor outpost pledge." <u>Jerusalem Post</u> 28 April 2010 http://www.jpost.com.

Burston, Bradley. " A Special Place in Hell: Rebranding Israel as a state headed for fascism." <u>Haaretz Daily</u> 18 May 2010 http://www.haaretz.com.

Burston, Bradley. "A Special Place in Hell: The Second Gaza War: Israel lost at sea." <u>Haaretz Daily</u> 31 May 2010 http://www.haaretz.com.

Horovitz, David. "The flotilla fiasco." <u>Jerusalem Post</u> 31 May 2010 http://www.jpost.com.

Editorial. "The price of flawed policy." <u>Haaretz Daily</u> 01 June 2010 http://www.haaretz.com.

Levy, Gideon. "Operation Mini Cast Lead." <u>Haaretz Daily</u> 01 June 2010 http://www.haaretz.com.

Sarid, Yossi. "Seven idiots in the cabinet." <u>Haaretz Daily</u> 01 June 2010 http://www.haaretz.com.

"Military Censorship in Israel." <u>Israel Ministry of Foreign Affairs</u> 04 February 2010 http://www.mfa.gov.il.

"AP Reveals Israeli Censorship, Says it Will Abide by Rules." <u>Editor & Publisher</u> 19 July 2006. 04 February 2010 http://www.editorandpublisher.com.

"Censorship in Israel." <u>Wikipedia</u> 04 February 2010 http://en.wikipedia.org.

"Mordechai Vanunu." Wikipedia 18 June 2010 http://en.wikipedia.org.

Segal, Ze'ev. "The case we're forbidden to report on." Haaretz Daily 07 April 2010 http://haaretz.com.

Levy, Gideon. "If it were up to the people, Anat Kamm would be executed." Haaretz Daily 15 April 2010 http://www.haaretz.com.

Staff reporter. "Israeli journalist Anat Kam under secret house arrest since December." Guardian Unlimited 02 April 2010 http://www.guardian.co.uk.

Izenberg, Dan. "Uri Blau to return illegally copied army documents." Jerusalem Post 29 April 2010 http://www.jpost.com.

Glick, Caroline. "The Haaretz spy scandal." Jerusalem Post 16 April 2010 http://www.jpost.com.

"Skewed priorities in the Anat Kamm Affair." Editorial. Jerusalem Post 12 April 2010 http://www.jpost.com.

Silverstein, Richard. "Haaretz Reporter in Self-Imposed Exile Over Top Secret IDF Leaks." Tikun Olam 30 March 2010 http://www.richardsilverstein.com.

Haaretz Service. "Haaretz editor: IDF censor okayed Haaretz articles in Anat Kam case." Haaretz Daily 08 April 2010 http://www.haaretz.com.

Melman, Yossi. "Israel to lift months-long gag order over security case." Haaretz Daily 07 April 2010 http://www.haaretz.com.

Melman, Yossi. "Leaked espionage case shows Israel only targets the weak." Haaretz Daily 08 April 2010 http://www.haaretz.com.

Blau, Uri. "This isn't just a war for my freedom but for Israel's image." Haaretz Daily 09 April 2010 http://www.haaretz.com.

"How the Shin Bet broke its deal with Haaretz." Editorial. Haaretz Daily 09 April 2010 http://www.haaretz.com.

Eldar, Akiva. "In Israel, reality hides under a 'top secret' stamp." Haaretz Daily 09 April 2010 http://www.haaretz.com.

Izenberg, Dan. "Israeli press stymied by gag on affair reported abroad." Jerusalem Post 07 April 2010 http://www.jpost.com.

"Israeli journalist held under secret house arrest." Maslin, Jared (contributor). Ma'an News Agency 02 April 2010 http://www.maannews.net.

"Israel urged to lift gag order." Ma'an News Agency 02 April 2010 http://www.maannews.net.

Malsin, Jared. "Israel's 'crisis of legitimacy.'" Ma'an News Agency 16 April 2010 http://www.maannews.net.

Edelman, Ofra. "Journalists urge Shin Bet: "Don't press charges against Uri Blau." Haaretz Daily 15 April 2010 http://www.haaretz.com.

Fleming, Eileen. "Deju Vu: Vanunu, Kamm and Blau and the Fragility of Freedom." Arabist (blog) 14 April 2010 http:www.arabist.com.

Izenberg, Dan. "State: Gag order lifted after talks with Blau collapsed." Jerusalem Post 09 April 2010 http://www.jpost.com.

Cook, Jonathan. "Did banned media report foretell of Gaza war crimes?" Ma'an News Agency 19 April 2010 http://www.maannews.net.

Cook, Jonathan. "Case exposes dark underbelly of Israel's security state." Middle East Online 14 April 2010 http://www.middle-east-online.com. Reprinted in Jerusalem Fund 19 April 2010 http://www.thejerusalemfund.org.

Eldar, Akiva. "As a democracy, how can Israel censor citizens' right to know?" Haaretz Daily 16 April 2010 http://www.haaretz.com.

Sengupta, Kim. "Journalist on the run from Israel is hiding in Britain." Independent 02 April 2010 http://license.icopyright.net.

"Daniel Ellsberg." Wikipedia. 28 July 20110 http://en.wikipedia.org.

Ellsberg, Michael. " 'The Most Dangerous Man in America' Nominated for an Oscar." Daniel Ellsberg Website. 28 July 2010 http://www.ellsberg.net.

Kershner, Isabel. "Israeli rights Groups View Themselves as Under Siege." New York Times 06 April 2010:A6.

Adalah Statement. "The Proposed Bill to Conceal Information Constitutes an Admission by its Proponents that Israel has Committed War Crimes." Legal Center for Arab Minority Rights in Israel. 29 April 2010 http://www.adalah.org.

Landau, David. "Israel is sliding toward McCarthyism and racism." Haaretz Daily 29 March 2010 http://www.haaretz.com.

McCarthy, Rory. "Rights groups attack Israeli bill to shut down military critics." Guardian Unlimited 29 April 2010 http://www.guardian.co.uk.

"Kadima and McCarthyism." <u>Haaretz Daily</u>. Editorial 04 May 2010 http://www.haaretz.com.

Friedman, Ron. "ACRI: Chomsky one of many stopped." <u>Haaretz Daily</u> 17 May 2010 http://www.haaretz.com.

Harman, Danna and Amira Hass. "After banned by Israel, Chomsky to give Bir Zeit lecture by video from Amman." <u>Haaretz Daily</u> 18 May 2010 http://www.haaretz.com.

"The value of free speech." Editorial. <u>Jerusalem Post</u> 21 May 2010 http://www.jpost.com.

Ravid, Barak. "Shin Bet deports Spain's most famous clown upon arrival in Israel." <u>Haaretz Daily</u> 06 May 2010 http://www.haaretz.com.

Levy, Gideon. "Israel's security measures? Don't make me laugh." <u>Haaretz Daily</u> 09 May 2010 http://www.haaretz.com.

Schneider, Howard and Samuel Sockol. "Israel removes American employed by Palestinian news agency." <u>Washington Post</u> 21 January 2010. 16 April 2010 http://www.washingtonpost.com.

"Military Court convicts West Bank Palestinian activist of incitement." <u>Haaretz</u>. Haaretz Service and AP 24 August 2010 http://www.haaretz.com.

"EU says convicted Bilin man 'human rights defender.' " <u>YNET News</u> 27 August 2010 http://www.ynetnews.com.

Friedman, Matti (AP) "EU slams Israel's verdict on Palestinian activist." <u>Metro News</u> 25 August 2010 http://www.metronews.ca.

Keinon, Herb. "Government slams Aston's 'meddling' ." <u>Jerusalem Post</u> 26 August 2010 http://www.jpost.com.

Pappe, Ilan. <u>The Ethnic Cleansing of Palestine</u>. Oxford: Oneworld Publications, 2006.

Pappe, Ilan. <u>A History of Modern Palestine</u> 2nd ed. Cambridge: Cambridge University Press, 2006.

"Azmi Bishara" <u>Wikipedia</u> 15 May 2010 http://en.wikipedia.org.

"Illegal Interference by the Shin Bet." <u>Legal Center for Arab Minority Rights in Israel</u> (Adalah). Letter to Menachem Mazuz 22 March 2007. 22 June 2010 http://www.adalah.org.

"AG Mazuz in Response to Adalah." <u>Legal Center for Arab Minority Rights in Israel</u> (Adalah). Press Release 22 May 2007. 22 June 2010 http://www.adalah.org.

"Interrogation of National Democratic Assembly (NDA) - Balad Party activists by the General Security Services (GSS)." <u>Legal Center for Arab Minority Rights in Israel (Adalah)</u>. Letter to Ehud Olmert and Menachem Mazuz 10 April 2008. 22 June 2010 http://www.adalah.org.

Bishara, Azmi. "Why Israel is after me." Los Angeles Times 03 May 2007. 22 June 2010 http://www.latimes.com.

Bishara, Azmi. "We Want to Live." <u>Al-Ahram Weekly</u> 13-19 May 2010 http://weekly.ahram.org.eg.

"Israel 99 Elections Primer: Azmi Bishara" <u>Jerusalem Post</u> 1999. 24 June 2010 http://info.jpost.com/1999/Supplements/Elections99/candidates/bishara2shtml.

Cook, Jonathan. "The Shin Bet and the Persecution of Azmi Bishara." Blog. 05 June 2007. 15 May 2010 http://www.jkcook.net.

Cook, Jonathan. <u>Disappearing Palestine</u>. London: Zed Books, 2008, particularly 157 - 166 ("The Persecution of Azmi Bishara").

Abigail Fraser and Avi Shabat. "Between Nationalism and Liberalism: The Political Thought of Azmi Bisharah." <u>The Israeli Palestinians: An Arab Minority in the Jewish State</u>. Ed. Alexander Bligh. London: Frank Case, 2003. 16-33. Questa Media America 07 June 2010 http://www.questia.com.

Frenkel, Sheera Claire and Dan Izenberg. "Balad colleagues rally to Azmi Bishara's defense." <u>Jerusalem Post</u> 23 April 2007. 12 May 2010 http://www.jpost.com.

"Politics: the rise of 'Bish-Arabism: Why all the buzz about Azmi Bishara's sudden absence?" Editorial. <u>Jerusalem Post</u> 18 April 2007. 12 May 2010 http://www.jpost.com.

"Supreme Court Dismisses Criminal Charges Against MK Dr. Azmi Bishara for his Political Speeches." <u>Legal Center for Arab Minority Rights in Israel</u> (Adalah). Press Release. 14 February 2006. 15 June 2010 http://www.adalah.org.

Dakwar, Jamil. "The Case of MK Dr. Azmi Bishara" Statement to the Inter-Parliamentary Union's Committee on the Human Rights of Parliamentarians, 96th Session -- 15 January 2002. <u>Legal Center for Arab Minority Rights in Israel</u> (Adalah). 15 June 2010 http://www.adalah.org.

"Profile: Israel's Arab voice: Israel's top court has overturned a ban on two Arab politicians standing in this month's general election. Who are Azmi Bishara and Ahmed Tibi?" BBC News 9 January 2003. 15 May 2010.

Nahmias, Roee. "MK Bishara warns Syria of Israeli attack." Ynet News 09 September 2006. 15 May 2010 http://www.ynet.co.il.

Nahmias, Roee. "Hizbullah offers Bishara asylum in Beirut." Ynet News 05 March 2007. 15 May 2010 http://www.ynet.co.il.

Barzilai, Gad. "The Case of Azmi Bishara: Political Immunity and Freedom in Israel." Middle East Report Online 09 January 2002. 15 May 2010 http://www.merip.org.

"Police Probe Arab Knesset member." Aljazeera 16 April 2007. 15 May 2010 http://english.aljazeera.net.

Khoury, Jack and Yoav Stern. "Balad chairman Azmi Bishara's resignation from Knesset takes effect." Haaretz Daily 24 April 2007. 23 June 2010 http://haaretz.com.

Nahmias, Roee. "Bishara says cannot serve as MK if persecuted." Ynet News 12 April 2007. 23 June 2010 http://www.ynet.co.il.

Nahmias, Roee. "MK Bishara resigns from Knesset." Ynet News 22 April 2007. 23 June 2010 http://www.ynet.co.il.

Ilan, Shahar. "Search of Bishara's offices criticized." Haaretz Daily 03 May 2007. 27 June 2010 http://www.haaretz.com.

Yiftachel, Oren. "The Shrinking Space of Citizenship: Ethnocratic Politics in Israel." The Struggle for Sovereignty. Eds. Joel Beinin and Rebecca L. Stein. Stanford: Stanford University Press, 2006. 162 - 174.

Farsoun, Samih and Naseer H. Aruri. Palestine and the Palestinian: A Social and Political History. 2nd ed. Boulder: Westview - Perseus, 2006. 169 - 170.

Davis, Uri. Apartheid Israel. London: Zed Books, 2003. 176.

White, Ben. "Israel seeks to silence dissent." Guardian Unlimited 11 May 2010. 26 June 2010 http://www.guardian.co.uk.

Glick, Caroline. "Hizbullah on the homefront." Jerusalem Post 17 May 2010 http://www.jpost.com.

"Dangerous incitement." Editorial. Haaretz Daily 07 June 2010
http://www.haaretz.com.

"War on protest." Editorial. Haaretz Daily 25 December 2009
http://www.haaretz.com.

"Dangerous police." Editorial. Haaretz Daily 18 January 2010
http://www.haaretz.com.

Levy, Gideon. "Israel's tyranny of the majority is dangerous." Haaretz Daily 29
April 2010 http://www.haaretz.com.

Hasson, Nir and Akiva Eldar. "Arrest at home marks new phase of crackdown
on J'lem rallies." Haaretz Daily 28 March 2010. 15 May 2010
http://www.haaretz.com.

Hasson, Nir. "Israeli civil rights leader arrested in East Jerusalem." Haaretz Daily
17 January 2010. 15 May 2010 http://www.haaretz.com.

Hasson, Nir. "Court frees 17 Sheikh Jarrah protesters, says arrest was illegal."
Haaretz Daily 18 January 2010. 15 May 2010 http://www.haaretz.com.

Hasan-Rokem, Galit. "Sheikh Jarrah is no fairy tale." Haaretz Daily 17 December
2009. 15 May 2010 http://www.haaretz.com.

Cook, Jonathan and Alexander Key. "Silencing Dissent: A Report on the
Violation of Political Rights of the Arab Parties in Israel." Muhammad Zeidan,
ed. Arab Association for Human Rights. October 2002. 26 June 2010
http://www.arabhra.org.

"Interrogation of National Democratic Assembly (NDA) - Balad party activists by
the General Security Services (GSS)." Letter. Legal Center for Arab Minority
Rights in Israel (Adalah) 10 April 2008. 15 May 2010 http://www.adalah.org.

Izenberg, Dan. "Lawyer: Hizbullah 'spy' only questioned on his politics."
Jerusalem Post 29 April 2010 http://www.jpost.com.

Stewart, Catrina. "Israel Bows to pressure and admits arrest of rights activist."
Independent (u.k.) 11 May 2010 http://license.icopyright.net.

"Israeli State War Against Ameer Makhoul." Editor. Ittijah 22 June 2010
http://www.ittijah.org.

Khoury, Jack, Amos Harel and Anshel Pfeffer. "Two Israeli Arabs arrested on
suspicion of spying, contact with Hezbollah." Haaretz Daily 10 May 2010
http://www.haaretz.com.

"The GSS is Attempting to Criminalize the Public Political and Social Activity of Arab Citizens." Adalah Statement. Legal Center for Arab Minority Rights in Israel (Adalah) 10 May 2010 http://www.adalah.org.

"Legal Defense Team Meets Ameer Makhoul after Twelve Day Prohibition." News Update. Legal Center for Arab Minority Rights in Israel (Adalah) 18 May 2010 http://www.adalah.org.

"Serious Suspicion of Shabak (GSS) Use of Illegal Methods of Interrogation Against Human Rights Defender Ameer Makhoul." News Update. Legal Center for Arab Minority Rights in Israel (Adalah) 18 May 2010 http://www.adalah.org.

White, Ben. "Israel imposing occupation tactics on its Palestinian citizens." Electronic Intifada 11 May 2010 http://electronicintifada.net.

"Request to Cancel the Travel Ban Issued Against Mr. Ameer Makhoul." Letter. Legal Center for Arab Minority Rights in Israel (Adalah) 25 April 2010. 15 May 2010 http://www.adalah.org.

"Israel detains Haifa man for alleged spying." Ma'an News Agency 11 May 2010 http://www.maannews.net.

Silverstein, Richard. "Shin Bet Removes Gag, Makhoul and Said Accused of Spying.." Tikun Olam 30 March 2010 http://www.richardsilverstein.com.

McCarthy, Rory. "Two Arab citizens of Israel accused of spying for Hezbollah." Guardian Unlimited 10 May 2010 http://www.guardian.co.uk.

Roffe-Ofir, Sharon. "Israeli Arab figures suspected of espionage." Ynet News 11 May 2010 http://www.ynet.co.il.

"Court Rejected Appeal against Prohibition on Meeting with Lawyers for Ameer Makhoul and Extended the Detention of Makhoul and Dr. Omar Saeed." Legal Center for Arab Minority Rights in Israel (Adalah). Press Release. 12 May 2010 http://www.adalah.org.

Roffe-Ofir, Sharon. "Security scandal angers Arab sector." Ynet News 09 May 2010 http://www.ynet.co.il.

"Israel's repression of its Palestinian citizens unites us in struggle." Editorial. Electronic Intifada 06 May 2010 http://electronicintifada.net.

"Latest on Ameer Makhoul, Secret Arrest, Gag Order, and Silence of Israeli Press." Jerusalem Fund 10 May 2010 http://www.thejerusalemfund.org. Reprinted from Richard Silverstein 's Tikun Olam 10 May 2010.

226

"Two weeks after arrest on spying charges, Makhoul allowed access to lawyers." Haaretz Daily 18 May 2010 http://www.haaretz.com.

Abdu, Janan and Issam Makhoul. "Ameer Makoul's arrest is an assault on all Palestinians in Israel." Electronic Intifada 26 May 2010 http://electronicintifada.net. [Ameer's wife and brother.]

Cooke, Jonathan, "The torture of Ameer Makhoul." Counterpunch 28 - 30 May 2010 http://www.counterpunch.org.

Khoury, Jack and Amos Harel. "Israeli Arabs indicted over spying for Hezbollah." Haaretz Daily 28 May 2010 http://www.haaretz.com.

Harel, Amos. "Were confessions of alleged Hezbollah spies extracted illegally?" Haaretz Daily 28 May 2010 http://www.haaretz.com.

Zacharia, Janine. "2 Arab Israeli activists accused of aiding Hezbollah." Washington Post 28 May 2010 http://www.washingtonpost.com.

Roffe-Ofir, Sharon. "Ittijah: Israel always changing list of 'hostile agents." Ynet News 28May 2010 http://www.ynet.co.il.

"Makhoul and Omar Saeed Vehemently Deny Charges against Them." Legal Center for Arab Minority Rights in Israel (Adalah). Press Release. 27 May 2010 http://www.adalah.org.

"24 Arab organizations demand the release of Ameer Makhoul." Petition. Arab Association for Human Rights. 28 June 2010 http://www.arabhra.org.

"Israel Must Stop Harassment of Human Rights Defender." Amnesty International 16 May 2010 http://www.amnesty.org.

"Raed Salah." Wikipedia 27 June 2010 http://en.wilipedia.org.

"Israeli Arabs charged with terror ties." BBC News 24 June 2003. 27 June 2010 http://newsvote.bbc.co.uk.

Prusher, Ilene R. "Israeli Arab's rising voice of opposition." Christian Science Monitor 26 October 2006. 27 June 2010 http://www.csmonitor.com.

Meranda, Ammon, Neta Sela, Lilach Shoval, Roee Nahmias and Efrat Weiss."Chief Rabbi Metzger says Salah's speech anti-Semitic." Ynet News 16 February 2007. 27 June 2010 http://www.ynet.co.il.

227

Nahmias, Roee. "Sheikh Salah: Western Wall belongs to Muslims." ."Chief Rabbi Metzger says Salah's speech anti-Semitic." Ynet News 18 February 2007. 27 June 2010 http://www.ynet.co.il.

Lis, Jonathan, Yoav Stern and Yuval Yoaz. "State Prosecutor orders police to investigate Salah for sedition." Haaretz Daily 22 February 2007. 26 June 2010 http://www.haaretz.com.

Stern, Yoav and Jonathan Lis. "Police arrest head of Islamic Movement's northern branch." Haaretz Daily 23 March 2009. 15 May 2010 http://www.haaretz.com.

Khoury, Jack and Liel Kyzer. "Islamic leader in Israel convicted of assaulting cop." Haaretz Daily 05 November 2009. 26 June 2010 http://www.haaretz.com.

"Salah acquitted in J'lem rioting case." Jerusalem Post Staff. 11 May 2010 http://www.jpost.com.

Roffe-Ofir, Sharon. "Salah: Beware of crazy person among us." Ynet News 15 May 2010 http://www.ynet.co.il.

"Steinitz: Revoke Salah's citizenship." Jerusalem Post Staff.16 May 2010 http://www.jpost.com.

"Background Information on Sheikh Raed Salah, Palestinian Leader Arrested on Freedom Flotilla." Alternative News. 27 June 2010 http://www.alternativenews.org.

"Raed Salah: IDF tried to kill me." Jerusalem Post Staff. 02 June 2010 http://www.jpost.com.

Amayreh, Khaled. "Name in the news: Sheikh Raed Salah." Al-Ahram Weekly 03 - 09 June 2010 http://www.thepeoplesvoice.org.

Stoil, Rebecca Anna. "Arab MKs visit Libya's Gaddafi." Jerusalem Post 11 May 2010 http://www.jpost.com.

Stoil, Rebecca Anna. " 'MKs' Libya trip violates ethics.' " Jerusalem Post 11 May 2010 http://www.jpost.com.

Izenberg, Dan. "Is Libya an enemy country" The law isn't so clear." Jerusalem Post 11 May 2010 http://www.jpost.com.

Lis, Jonathan and Jack Khoury. "Knesset panel recommends revoking Arab MK's privileges." Haaretz Daily 29 April 2010 http://www.haaretz.com.

"Mohammad Barakeh" Wikipedia 07 June 2010 http://en.wikipedia.org.

"Urgent Intervention on Behalf of MK Barakeh Demanding Criminal Investigation into Security Forces Personnel who Assaulted Anti-Wall Demonstrators." Legal Center for Arab Minority Rights in Israel (Adalah). News Update 21 April 2005. 30 April 2010 http://www.adalah.org.

"Hadash MK Barakei indicted for assaulting cops at Bil'in protest." Jerusalem Post Staff.01 November 2009 http://www.jpost.com.

"The Attorney General's Decision to Indict MK Muhammad Barakeh Seeks only to Criminalize his Political Action." Legal Center for Arab Minority Rights in Israel (Adalah). News Update 04 November 2009. 30 April 2010 http://www.adalah.org.

Macintyre, Donald. "Israelis protest over 'fascist' Jerusalem settlements." Independent 23 January 2010 http://license.icopyright.net.

Khoury, Jack. "European group may probe Israel decision to indict Arab MK." Haaretz Daily 09 March 2010. 15 May 2010 http://www.haaretz.com.

Izenberg, Dan. "Barakeh charges indictment against him is political." Jerusalem Post 10 March 2010. 26 June 2010 http://www.jpost.com.

"Political Trial of MK Mohammed Barakeh Opens before Tel Aviv Magistrates' Court." Legal Center for Arab Minority Rights in Israel (Adalah). News Update 11 March 2010. 15 May 2010 http://www.adalah.org.

"Tel Aviv court Rejects Defense Motion." Legal Center for Arab Minority Rights in Israel (Adalah). News Update 21 April 2010. 15 May 2010 http://www.adalah.org.

Livneh, Neri. "The ravishing blonde." Haaretz Daily. 15 July 2010 http://haaretz.com.

Landau, David. "Boycott the Knesset." Haaretz Daily. 16 July 2010 http://haaretz.com.

"Endangering democracy." Editorial. Haaretz Daily. 15 July 2010 http://haaretz.com.

Melman, Yossi. "The Temple of Security." Haaretz Daily. 28 July 2010 http://haaretz.com.

Lis, Jonathan. "Knesset revokes Arab MK Zuabi's privileges over Gaza flotilla." Haaretz Daily. 13 July 2010 http://haaretz.com.

229

CHAPTER 6. THE RULE OF LAW

Basic Law: Human Dignity and Liberty. Israel Law Resource Center 02 July 2010 http://israellawresourcecenter.org.

"Adalah file Petition to Supreme Court: Travel Restriction on Sheikh Ra'ed Salah is Unconstitutional." Press Release. Adalah 03 June 2002. 26 July 2010 http://www.adalah.org.

"Supreme Court Upholds Travel Ban on Sheikh Ra'ed Salah." News Update. Adalah 12 August 2002. 26 July 2010 http:www.adalah.org.

Sheikh Ra'ed Salah v. Minister of the Interior (HCJ 4706/02). Israel Supreme Court Decision dated 17 July 2002 as appears on Adalah website. 26 July 2010 http://www.adalah.org.

"Raed Salah." Wikipedia. 06 27 2010 http://en.wikipedia.org.

D'Amours, Jillian. "Background Information on Sheikh Raed Salah." Alternative News. 07 June 2010. 27 June 2010 http://www.alternativenews.org.

De Tocqueville, Alexis. Democracy in America. New York: Appleton, 1899 (as shown on Questia. http://www.questia.com).

The following articles on Sheikh Salah appeared in The Jerusalem Post http://www.jpost.com.

"Salah acquitted in J'lem rioting case." Staff. 11 May 2010.

"Steinitz: Revoke Salah's citizenship. Staff. 16 May 2010.

Stoil, Rebecca Anna. "Salah begins five-month sentence." 26 July 2010.

The following articles on Sheikh Salah appeared in The Haaretz Daily http://www.haaretz.com.

Lis, Jonathan, Yoav Stern and Yuval Yoaz. "State Prosecutor orders police to investigate   Salah for sedition." 22 February 2007. 15 May 2010.

Stern, Yoav and Jonathan Lis. "Police arrest head of Islamic Movement's northern   branch." 23 March 2009. 15 May 2010.

Khoury, Jack and Liel Kyzer. "Islamic leader in Israel convicted of assaulting cop." 05   Nov.2009. 26 June 2010.

Khoury, Jack and Haaretz Service. "Court acquits Islamic Movement leader of involvement in Temple Mount riots." 11 May 2010.

"Israeli Arabs charged with terror ties. "BBC News. 24 June 2003. 27 June 2010 http://news.bbc.co.uk.

Prusher, Ilene R. "Israeli Arab's rising voice of opposition." Christian Science Monitor. 26 October 2006. 27 June 2010.

Amayreh, Khaled. "Name in the news: Sheikh Raed Salah." Al-Ahram Weekly. 03 - 09 June 2010. 27 June 2010 http://weekly.ahram.org.

The following articles on Sheikh Salah appeared in Ynet News http://www.ynetnews.com.

Meranda, Amnon, Neta Sela, Lilach Shoval, Roee Nahmias and Efrat Weiss. "Chief   Rabbi Metzger says Salah's speech anti-Semitic." 16 February 2007. 27 June 2010.

Nahmias, Roee. "Sheikh Salah: Western Wall belongs to Muslims." 18 February 2007. 27   June 2010.

Roffe-Ofir, Sharon. "Salah: Beware of crazy person among us." 15 May 2010. 22 May   2010.

The following articles on the policeman Shahar Mizrahi's killing of Mahmoud Ghanaim appeared in The Jerusalem Post http://www.jpost.com.

Hartman, Ben. "Police stunned at Supreme Court ruling." 21 July 2010. 27 July 2010.

Lappin, Yaakov. "Police, Court in war of words." 22 July 2010. 27 July 2010.

The following articles on the policeman Shahar Mizrahi's killing of Mahmoud Ghanaim appeared in The Haaretz Daily http://www.haaretz.com.

Stern, Yoav. "Policeman who shot dead Israeli Arab to go on trial for manslaughter." 07   March 2007. 26 July 2010.

Stern, Yoav. "Rights group slams 'light' indictment for officer who killed Israeli Arab."   17 July 2007. 26 July 2010

"Jewish Teen suspected of stabbing Israeli Arab to death." 08 June 2009. 26 July 2010.

231

Stern, Yoav, Yuval Goren and Mazal Mualem. "Public security minister calls cop 'dirty   Arab." 16 June 2009. 26 July 2010.

Stern, Yoav. "Police officer convicted of fatally shooting Israeli Arab." 07 July 2009. 26   July 2010.

Khoury, Jack. "Cop gets 15 months in prison for killing Israeli Arab." 04 September   2009. 26 July 2010.

Edelman, Ofra. "Cop gets 15 mos. for killing Israeli Arab." 04 September 2009. 27 July   2010.

Khoury, Jack and Haaretz Service. "Supreme Court doubles jail terms for police officer   convicted of shooting Israeli Arab." 21 July 2010.

Khoury, Jack, Tomer Zarchin and Liel Kyzer. "Court doubles prison term for policeman   who killed car thief." 22 July 2010. 26 July 2010.

"Minister in clemency plea for policeman who killed car thief." Staff. 22 July 2010. 26   July 2010.

Lis, Jonathan, Tomer Zarchin and Liel Kyzer. "Minister denounces court for doubling sentence of cop who killed car thief." 23 July 2010. 26 July 2010.

Levy, Gideon. "A sick police force: A police commissioner who criticizes the Supreme Court is a commissioner who damages the rule of law." 25 July 2010.

    "Defiance of the law: The public security minister is wrong to query the sentence of a   policeman convicted of killing car thief." 25 July 2010.

    Kyzer, Liel. "Minister meets cop sentenced to 30 months for killing car thief." 26 July   2010.

    Laor, Yitzhak. "You may not! Israel is gradually relinquishing the rule of law and   becoming a tribe." 27 July 2010.

    Edelman, Ofra. "18 years' jail for freed prisoner who murdered soldier." 28 July 2010.

    Ahren, Raphael. "Sokolow's niece 'not Jewish enough' to marry here." 30 July 2010.

Sarid, Yossi. "Any bastard can be a rabbi." Haaretz 28 August 2010 http://www.haaretz.com.

Beveridge, Albert J. The Life of John Marshall: Frontiersman, Soldier, Lawmaker,1755-1788. Vol. 1. Boston: Houghton Mifflin, 1916. 409 - 430. (Questia Media America, Inc. www.questia.com.)

De Tocqueville, Alexis. Democracy in America. Trans. Henry Reeve. Vol. 1. New York: D. Appleton, 1899. 90 - 105. (Questia Media America, Inc. www.questia.com.)

Hamilton, John C. History of the Republic of the United States Vol. 3, p. 34 (1859) as quoted in plaintiff's brief and in decision of Cummings v. Missouri, 71 U.S. 277, 290 - 293, 330 - 331 (1867) and in U.S. v. Brown, 381 U.S. 437, 444 (1965).

Maravall, Jose Maria and Adam Przeworski. Democracy and the Rule of Law. Cambridge, Eng.: Cambridge UP, 2003. 1 -8, 223 - 250. (Questia Media America, Inc. www.questia.com.)

Robarge, David. A Chief Justice's Progress: John Marshall from Revolutionary Virginia to the Supreme Court. Westport: Greenwood, 2000. (Questia Media America, Inc. www.questia.com.)

Stark, Jack. Prohibited Government Acts: A Reference Guide to the United States Constitution. Westport: Praeger, 2002. 53 - 63. (Questia Media America, Inc. www.questia.com.)

Tamanaha, Brian Z. "Rule of Law in the United States." Theories and Implementation of Rule of Law in Twelve Asian Countries, France and the U.S. Ed. Randall Peerenboom. New York: Routledge Curzon, 2004. 56 - 76. (Questia Media America, Inc. www.questia.com.)

Hamilton, Alexander. "Federalist No. 78". Founding Fathers 24 July 2010 http://www/foundingfather.info.

Madison, James. "Federalist Nos. 44 and 51". Founding Fathers 24 July 2010 http://www/foundingfather.info.

Marbury v. Madison, 5 U.S. 137, 176 - 180 (1803). Cornell University Law School http://www.law.cornell.edu.

Fletcher v. Peck, 10 U.S. 87, 137 (1810). Cornell University Law School http://www.law.cornell.edu.

Cummings v. Missouri, 71 U.S. 277, 322 - 332 (1867). Cornell University Law School http://www.law.cornell.edu.

233

W. Va. Bd. of Ed. v. Barnette, 319 U.S. 624 (1943). Cornell University Law School http://www.law.cornell.edu.

U.S. v. Lovett, 328 U.S. 303 (1946). Cornell University Law School http://www.law.cornell.edu.

U.S. v. Brown, 381 U.S. 437, 444 (1965). Cornell University Law School http://www.law.cornell.edu.

"Civil Rights: The Little Rock School Integration Crisis." Dwight D. Eisenhower Presidential Library 04 August 2010 http://www.eisenhower.archives.gov.

"Integrating Ole Miss: Days of Confrontation." John F. Kennedy Presidential Library 04 August 2010 http://www.jfklibrary.org.

"James Meredith." Wikipedia 04 August 2010 http://en.wikipedia.org.

"IDF segregation bypasses High Court ruling." Haaretz Daily. Editorial 11 May 2010 http://www.haaretz.com.

Issacharoff, Avi. "Let's get smart." Haaretz Daily 30 May 2010 http://www.haaretz.com.

Levinson, Chaim. "Palestinians can use route 443, but Israel will seize Palestinian land to 'secure' it." Haaretz Daily 21 March 2010 http://www.haaretz.com.

Kershner, Isabel. "Israel Partly Reopens West Bank road." New York Times 28 May 2010 http://www.nytimes.com.

Sherwood, Harriet. "Israelis and Palestinians share route 443 again amid suspicion and fear." Guardian Unlimited 27 May 2010 http://www.guardian.co.uk.

Mandel, Jonah. "Shas getting payoff for its school system, says NGO." 06 August 2010. Jerusalem Post http://www.jpost.com.

CHAPTER 7. ASSASSINATION

Shane, Scott. "U.S. approves Targeted Killing of Radical Muslin Cleric Tied to Domestic Terror Suspects. New York Times. 07 April 2010. A12.

Scahill, Jeremy. "Kucinich: White House Assassination Policy is Extrajudicial." Nation. 15 April 2010 http://www.thenation.com.

Shane, Scott. "U.S. Decision to Approve Killing of Cleric Causes Unease." New York Times. 13 May 2010 http:www.nytimes.com.

Kelly, Kathy and Josh Brollier. "Drones and Democracy." Counterpunch. 18 May 2010 http://www.counterpunch.org.

Savage, Charlie. "U.N. Official Set to Ask U.S. to End C.I.A. Drone Strikes." New York Times. 27 May 2010 http:www.nytimes.com.

Gerges, Fawaz. "The Truth About Drones." Newsweek. 30 May 2010 http://www.newsweek.com.

Davies, Nick. "Afghanistan war logs: Task Force 373 -- special forces hunting top Taliban." Guardian Unlimited. 25 July 2010 http://www.guardian.co.uk.

Robinson, Eugene. "Wikileaks reveal the obvious dangers of Afghanistan." Washington Post. 27 July 2010 http://www.washingtonpost.com.

Cooper, Helene and Mark Landler. "Targeted Killing is New U.S. Focus in Afghanistan." New York Times. 31 July 2010 http://www.nytimes.com.

Quigley, Bill. "Why We Sued to Represent Anwar Aulaqi." Counterpunch. 03 August 2010 http://www.counterpunch.org.

Hsu, Spencer S. "Civil rights groups sue Treasury over targeting of terror suspects for killing." Washington Post. 03 August 2010 http://www.washingtonpost.com.

"CCR and ACLU get license & file lawsuit to challenge targeted killings outside of armed conflict." Center for Constitutional Rights. Press Release. 30 August 2010 http://www.ccrjustice.org.

"Folke Bernadotte." Wikipedia 09 April 2010 http://en.wikipedia.org.

Macintyre, Donald. "Israel's forgotten hero: The assassination of Count Bernadotte -- and the death of peace." Independent (UK). 09 April 2010. 18 September 2008 http://www.independent.co.uk.

Harel, Amos. "Ex-Shin Bet chief: Israeli assassination policy led to period of calm." Haaretz 31 May 2005. 06 August 2010 http://www.haaretz.com.

CHAPTER 8. THE OCCUPATION

Kristof, Nicholas D. "The Two Sides of a Barbed-Wire Fence." New York Times 01 July 2010 http://www.nytimes.com.

ADDENDUM

Levy, Gideon. "Twilight zone / The invaders." Haaretz 06 August 2010
http://www.haaretz.com.

"Displacing the Bedouin." Haaretz. Editorial. 08 August 2010
http://www.haaretz.com.

"Israeli authorities destroy over 200 tombs in Jerusalem's Ma'man Allah
cemetery." Middle East Monitor 11 August 2010
http://www.midleeastmonitor.org.uk.

Ettinger, Yair. "Interior Ministry demolishes Bedouin homes." Haaretz. Editorial.
12 August 2010 http://www.haaretz.com.

Bannoura, Saed. "Israeli forces desecrate 200 graves in Muslim cemetery; injure
Sheik with bulldozer." International Middle East Media Center. 12 August 2010
http://www.imemc.org.

Bronner, Ethan. "Gravestone Removals Add Fuel to Jerusalem Museum Dispute."
New York Times. 13 August 2010 http://www.nytimes.com.

Khalidi, Asem. "The Mamilla Cemetery; A Buried History." Jerusalem Quarterly
37 (2009): 104 - 109.

Paone, Arthur. "The Gehry-Goldberg Museum of Tolerance in Jerusalem." You
Tube (2007) http:www.youtube.com.

"Petition for Urgent Action on Human Rights Violations by Israel." Mamilla
Campaign 10 February 2010. 19 August 2010 http://mamillacampaign.org.

ADDENDUM TO
THE RULE OF LAW

The Bedouin

As noted above, the Israelis keep trying to clear their southern properties, the Negev, of their Arab citizens so as to make the area more attractive to their Jewish citizens, who, inconveniently, just do not seem very interested in living in "frontier" conditions. At the same time that the government was creating new Jewish towns in the Negev and encouraging Jews to move there with large financial incentives, it was demolishing existing Bedouin villages.

In August of 2010 as part of that ongoing effort the Israel Lands Administration enlisted a large contingent of police and proceeded to bulldoze another Bedouin village, this one called Al-Arakib, leaving hundreds of families homeless.

Basic to the concept of the rule of law is equal treatment and set rules for all, so that every person could plan his or her life. No Bedouin, at least, can make any plans for tomorrow.

What's more, the actions are self-destructive. An *Haaretz* Editorial wondered about the new eternal enemies that Israel had just created:

> *"It's hard to understand why Israel is pushing a significant sector of its citizens toward extremism and crime.*

237

*On the ruins of Al-Arakib a new generation of Bedouin will
sprout that is alienated from the state, enraged and desperate. "*

The Mamilla Cemetery

Eradicating the Dead as well as the Living

After the 1948 war the largest, 33 acres, Muslim cemetery in
Palestine, Mamilla, fell on the Jewish side of the Armistice Line.
Immediately much of the cemetery was cleared of its thousands
of tombstones, turning the land into parks and plots for
buildings in West Jerusalem, without even bothering to remove
the tens of thousands of skeletons beneath the surface. What
remained was a sorry remnant of a cemetery, made more so
over the following decades by the Jewish authorities' refusal to
allow Muslims to maintain the cemetery.

As noted above, around 2005 the Jerusalem municipality granted
a portion of the cemetery that had already been turned into a
parking garage on top of the cemetery to a Los Angeles group,
the Simon Wiesenthal Center, to construct a "Museum of
Tolerance" on the site. A petition against that decision is being
taken to the United Nations by descendants of people buried in
the cemetery, represented by the New York based Center for
Constitutional rights. Now in the middle of August, 2010, some
more bad news for Mamilla.

While workers for religious Muslim groups, having finally
received permission to restore the cemetery, were in the process
of refurbishing some of the graves, Jerusalem police suddenly
arrived in the middle of the night and hundreds of newly
restored tombstones were bulldozed and carted away in
dumpsters. The city claimed that the tombstones were "fakes"

which had been placed on plots that were *not part of the cemetery* in an attempt by the Muslims to expand the cemetery.

Even the *New York Times'* bureau chief seemed puzzled by that claim, and its subsequent confirmation by ever-compliant courts and the Israeli Antiquities Authority.

The Israeli claim was of course absurd. A section in the middle of a thousand year old cemetery suddenly becomes a non-cemetery, now belonging conveniently to the municipality of Jerusalem? But being a correspondent in Israel, he apparently knows better than to say what everyone else is saying. So he just gives us a little clue at the end of his article on the incident, noting in passing:

> *"On both sides of the disputed area there are, however, acknowledged gravesites."*

The cleared land which the Jewish municipal authorities claimed was not a portion of the cemetery was between Muslim burial monuments that no one disputes. I remember the location, having seen it myself back in 2007. You cannot miss it, as its been there for a thousand years. There is a fence in front of the cemetery that says it is a cemetery -- I saw it. Yet plots deep within the cemetery, and right next to a famous Moslem tomb, that of al-Amir Ala' al-Den al-Kabkabi, suddenly is not part of the cemetery, according to the same right-wing Jerusalem municipality that was also busy with demolishing "illegal" Arab homes in East Jerusalem.

Disgusting nonsense upon disgusting nonsense, duly blessed by the municipal judiciary. Perhaps the Jewish managers of

239

Jerusalem think that this is 1948 and they can again just bulldoze sacred ground into oblivion.

No one can predict on any day what is legal and what is not in Israel. Such is the rule of law in Israel.

This is the photo appearing with the *New York Times* article of August 14, 2010 mentioned above. It was taken by *Times* photographer Rina Castelnuovo and shows some of the plots just cleared of headstones by the Jerusalem municipality, right next to the al-Kabkabi tomb.

In my 2007 visit the Mamilla cemetery I saw was a mess and only a fraction of its former 33 acres, about two and a half acres. The place had been in total neglect because the Israelis from 1948 had refused to give the Islamic Endowment (the *Waqf*), permission to maintain it. Of the thousands of tombstones and markers present in 1948, there was only a handful left now.

Apparently sometime in 2010 religious Muslim groups, including the Al-Aqsa Foundation, were allowed to enter the cemetery to fix it up. What I suspect happened was that the Foundation not only up-righted or cemented together tombstones that had broken or fallen, but also created memorial replicas for those graves whose tombstones had disappeared or had totally disintegrated. The Jewish leaders of Jerusalem jumped on this as a pretext to bulldoze everything in that section of the cemetery, new and ancient headstones alike, and cart them all away, probably in preparation for tearing off another Arabic limb of Jerusalem. They called the memorial stones "fakes," were duly backed up by officials from the Antiquities Authority and supported by the press, who called the stones headstones as "phony" (*Jerusalem Post*, August 18, 2010).

The following several photos are from my 2007 visit. My first photo shows the same al-Kabkabi tomb as appears in the August 14th *Times* photo. The second photo indicates a relatively recent attempt by someone to refurbish an old gravesite by adding a replica headstone. The other photos show gravesites in various stages of neglect that the Foundation must have been refurbishing when the police and bulldozers arrived.

241

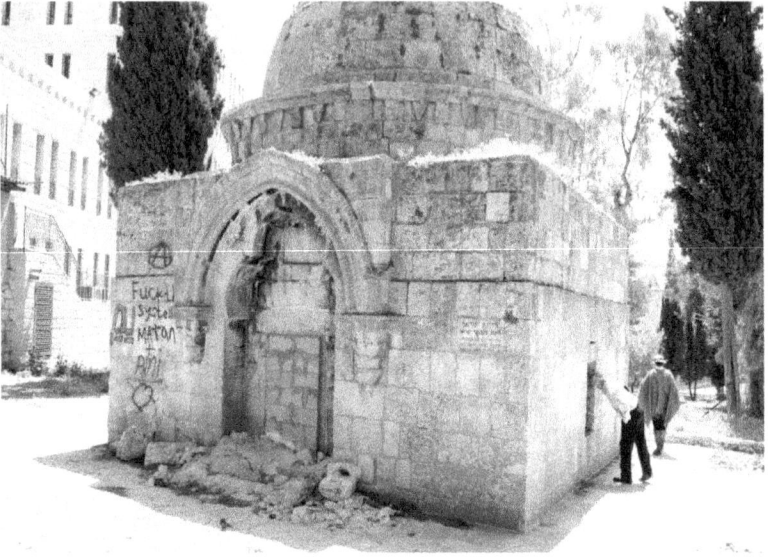

Above. 1) The al-Kabkabi tomb in 2007. Note the vandalism.

Above. 2) Note the modern memorial marker I found in 2007 which had been added to this ancient gravesite. This is probably similar to what the Foundation had been putting up in 2010 on old gravesites. But it was used as an excuse by the municipality to call everything "phony" and to bulldoze both the new plaques as well as the remains of the ancient tombstones.

242

2007 - 3, 4 and 5

2007- 6

2007- 7 and 8

2007 - 9

2007-10 (Above photos by Arthur Paone, Mamilla Cemetery, Jerusalem. May, 2007.)

Finally, below are some photos of the clearing incident taken by members of the Al-Aqsa Foundation who were at the site and which appear in an August 11, 2010 article in *Middle East Monitor*.

2010- 1 and 2 The police arrive together with the Jerusalem "authorities" and their bulldozers.   *Middle East Monitor*

2010-3 *Middle East Monitor*

2010-4 *Middle East Monitor*

2010-5 *Middle East Monitor*

2010-6 *Middle East Monitor*

The purpose of this book is not to judge what is right and what is wrong, but to conduct a comparison of American and Israeli societies to determine if the AIPAC mantra that the U.S. and Israel share "common core values" or that our societies are like "family" is true or not.

The relevant question about this all too typical incident then is whether the administration of any U.S. city shares with Israel whatever that core value might be which would compel it to send police and bulldozers into the Chestnut Street Cemetery in Cincinnati; or the Shalom Memorial Park in Chicago; the New Mt Sinai Cemetery in St. Louis; the Mount Richmond Cemetery in Staten Island; the Touro Synagogue Cemetery in Newport; the Sharon Memorial Park in Massachusetts or the Ahavi Shalom Cemetery in Portland -- and bulldoze hundreds of tombstones and cart them away to the dump. Then when the trustees of those cemeteries complain about it in municipal court, the further question is whether the trustees would be told that the desecration and vandalism were perfectly OK.

If you can imagine that happening in America, then you would have to conclude that America and Israel do indeed share common values.

Notes: Page 236.

Index

250

251

255

256

Y

Z

www.ingramcontent.com/pod-product-compliance
Lightning Source LLC
LaVergne TN
LVHW011217080426
835509LV00005B/180